AF559653

GLOBAL ECONOMIC CRISIS AND IMPACT ON INDIAN ECONOMY

GLOBAL ECONOMIC CRISIS AND IMPACT ON INDIAN ECONOMY

Edited by

ANIL KUMAR THAKUR

and

DEEPTI TANEJA

Published on behalf of
THE INDIAN ECONOMIC ASSOCIATION

DEEP & DEEP PUBLICATIONS PVT. LTD.
F-159, RAJOURI GARDEN, NEW DELHI-110027

GLOBAL ECONOMIC CRISIS AND IMPACT ON INDIAN ECONOMY

ISBN 978-81-8450-357-9

Typeset by S.S. COMPOSERS
3190, Mohindra Park, Shakur Basti, Delhi-110034.

Printed in India at MAYUR ENTERPRISES
WZ Plot No. 3, Gujjar Market, Tihar Village, New Delhi-110018.

Published by DEEP & DEEP PUBLICATIONS PVT. LTD.
F-159, Rajouri Garden, New Delhi-110027.
Phones: 25435369, 25440916
E-mail: ddpbooks@yahoo.co.in • ddpubs@gmail.com
Showroom:
2/13, Ansari Road, Daryaganj, New Delhi-110002 • Telefax: 23245122

Contents

Preface ix

List of Contributors xiii

Anil Kumar Thakur and Deepti Taneja
Introduction xv

1. *Manoj Panda*
Global Economic Crisis and Indian Economy 1

2. *Archna Singh*
Global Economic Crisis:
The Ideas of Keynes Reinstated 13

3. *R. Arunachalam*
Global Financial Crisis and the Indian Economy 28

4. *Amalesh Banerjee*
India's Revival Agenda and Global Economic Crisis 48

5. *S.B. Mishra*
Global Financial Crisis and its Impact on the Indian Economy 56

6. *Ratan Kumar Ghosal and Saikat Bhattacharyya*
Globalization, Global Meltdown and the Indian Economy 78

7. *Dhiraj Kumar Bandyopadhyay*
Global Economic Crisis: A Macroeconomic Explanation of Structuralist Theory and Verification of "Decoupling Hypothesis" on the Indian Economy 94

8. *D.K. Nauriyal and Bimal Sahoo*
Financial Crisis: Indian Economic Growth and External Sector 124

9. *Shri Prakash and Ritisnigdha Panigrahi*
A Study of Interrelation between London and Indian Stock Market and Impact of the Global Slowdown on the Indian Economy 148

10. *Abhishek Kumar*
Global Financial Meltdown and its Impact on the Indian Economy 173

11. *Mahendra Ranawat and Veenu Yadav*
Contagion Effect of Global Financial Crisis on Stock Market in India 187

12. *Rajiv Kumar Bhatt*
Impact of Global Financial Crisis on Indian Economy 201

13. *K.M. Naidu, L.K. Mohan Rao, P.V. Manjushree, and K. Mahesh Naidu*
Global Financial Crisis and its Impact: Need for a Comprehensive and Swift Action 215

14. *Purna Chandra Mishra*
Global Economic Crisis and the Indian Economy 236

15. *Swami Prakash Srivastava*
Global Financial Crisis and Its Impact on the Indian Economy 254

16. *Chandra Kant Singh and Rajesh Kumar*
Global Economic Crisis and the Indian Economy 279

17. *R.K. Shah*
Global Financial Crisis and its Impact on the Nepalese Economy 287

Index 312

Preface

In the late 1990s a group of Asian economies—economies that produced about a quarter of the world's output and were home to two-thirds of a billion people—experienced an economic slump that bore an eerie resemblance to the Great Depression of 1930s. The kind of economic trouble that Asia experienced a decade ago, is precisely the sort of things we thought (we now know that it was wrongly so) that we had learned to prevent. The perception of the common man was that in the bad, old days big, advanced economies with stable governments, like Britain in the 1920s, might have had no answer to prolonged periods of stagflation and deflation; but between John Maynard Keynes and Milton Friedman, we thought that we knew enough to keep that from happening again. Smaller countries, like Australia in 1931, may once have been at the mercy of financial tides, unable to control their economic destiny; but nowadays sophisticated bankers and government officials, not to mention the International Monetary Fund and the World Bank, are supposed to quickly orchestrate rescue packages that contain such crisis before they spread. Governments, like that of the United States in 1930-31, may once have stood by helplessly as national banking system collapsed; but in the modern world, deposit insurance and the readiness of the Federal Reserve to rush cash to threatened institutions are supposed to prevent such scenes. These were, as we know now, the perceptions of the non-thinkers only.

No sensible person thought that the age of economic anxiety was past. In fact they opined that we should have realized a decade ago only that our confidence was misplaced. Japan spent most of the 1990s in an economic trap. Asia went from boom to calamity virtually overnight—and their story reads as if it were taken straight out of the financial history of the 1930s.

People, especially in the developed world, thought, as Nobel Laureate Paul Krugman puts it, "It was as if bacteria that used to cause deadly plagues, but had long been considered conquered by modern medicine, had reemerged in a form resistant to all the standard antibiotics. But it is only a limited number of people who have actually fallen prey to the newly incurable strains." He however had cautioned the world then only, "Even those of us who have so far been lucky would be foolish not to seek new cures, new prophylactic regimens, whatever it takes, lest we turn out to be the next victims." Well, as the events stand now, we were foolish. And the plague was upon us all.

Simply and briefly putting it, the blame for the crisis that originated in the U.S. goes to the 1999 repeal of the Glass-Steagall Act, which then allowed the commercial banks to get into investment banking business and thereby take on more risks. The lending happened to the sub-prime borrowers too, i.e., to the borrowers with not so sound credit worthiness. The key rationale for this lending was the belief that it didn't really matter, form the lender's point of view, whether the borrower could actually make the mortgage payments: as long as the home prices kept rising, troubled borrowers could always either refinance or pay-off their mortgage by selling the house. But, by the late spring of 2006, the weakness of the real estate market started sinking in. House prices began dropping, slowly at first, then with growing speed. By the second quarter of 2007, according to the widely used Case-Shiller home price index, prices were only down about 3 per cent from their peak a year earlier. Over the course of the next year, they fell by more than 15 per cent. As soon as the home prices started falling, houses became hard to sell and default rates began rising. The business houses whose borrowers' base consisted of a large number of sub-prime borrowers began registering a rise in the default rates. The housing bubble had burst and the sub-prime crisis, that became a foundation stone for the currency and the financial crisis, ready to engulf the world due to large scale integration of the world economies, had begun.

For the last few years, and it has not yet ended completely, we are living in a new era of depression economics and John Maynard Keynes, the economist who made sense of the Great Depression, is now more relevant than ever. Keynes concluded his masterwork, *The General Theory of Employment, Interest and Money*, with a famous disquisition on the importance of economic ideas: "Soon or late, it is ideas, not vested interests, which are dangerous for good or evil."

The quintessential economic sentence is supposed to be "There is no free lunch"—it says that there are limited resources, that to have more of one thing you must accept less of another, that there is no gain without pain. Depression economics, however, is the study of situations where there is a free lunch, if we can only figure out how to get our hands on it, because there are unemployed resources that could be put to work. The true scarcity in Keynes's world, and ours, is therefore not of resources, or even of virtue, but of understanding. We will not achieve the understanding we need, unless we are willing to think clearly about our problems. Some people say that our economic problems are structural, but the great economists believe that the only important structural obstacles to world prosperity are the obsolete doctrines that clutter the minds of men. Clarity of the issues and an understanding of the policy menu available to us to get out of the crisis is therefore very important, to have strong and consistent global economic fundamentals and the associated growth rates.

ANIL KUMAR THAKUR
DEEPTI TANEJA

List of Contributors

Abhishek Kumar, Branch Head, Tata AIG, Muzaffarpur, Bihar.

Amalesh Banerjee, Chairman, IBMR 110B, N.S.C. Bose Rode, Regent Park, Kolkata.

Archna Singh, Research Scholar, Department of Economics, University of Allahabad, Allahabad.

Bimal Sahoo, C/o D.K. Nauriyal, IIT Roorkee, Roorkee.

Chandra Kant Singh, Nitishwar Singh College, Samastipur, Dist. Muzaffarpur (Bihar).

D.K. Nauriyal, Professor, Department of Humanities and Social Sciences, Indian Institute of Technology, Roorkee, Uttaranchal.

Deepti Taneja, Assistant Professor, Department of Economics, Delhi College of Arts and Commerce, Delhi University, Delhi.

Dhiraj Kumar Bandyopadhyay, Research Associate in Economics, Centre for Urban Economic Studies, University of Calcutta and Research Coordinator, IDSK, Kolkata.

K. Mahesh Naidu, Research Scholar, College of Commerce, Management and Information Sciences, S.V. University, Tirupati.

K.M. Naidu, UGC Emeritus Fellow in Economics, Sri Venkateswara University, Tirupati, Andhra Pradesh.

L.K. Mohan Rao, Principal, Andhra University College of Arts and Commerce, Visakapatnam, Andhra Pradesh

Mahendra Ranawat, Principal, B.N.P.G Girls' College, Udaipur, Rajasthan.

Manoj Panda, Centre for Economic and Social Studies, Hyderabad

P.V. Manjushree, Associate Professor, GITAM University, Visakhapatnam, Andhra Pradesh.

Purna Chandra Mishra, Lecturer, Department of Economics, Zisaji Presidency Govt. College, Kiphire, Nagaland.

R. Arunachalam, Professor, Department of Economics, University of Madras, Madras.

R.K. Shah, Associate Professor, Department of Economics, M.M. Campus, Nepalgunj, T.U. Nepal.

Rajesh Kumar, Department of L.S.W. Magadh University, Bodh-Gaya.

Rajiv Kumar Bhatt, Reader, Department of Economics, Banaras Hindu University, Varanasi.

Ratan Kumar Ghosal, Professor of Economics, Department of Commerce, University of Calcutta, Calcutta.

Ritisnigdha Panigrahi, Research Associate, BIMTECH, Greater Noida, (U.P.).

S.B. Mishra, Reader in Economics, M.P.C. Autonomous College, Takatpur, Baripada, Mayurbhanj, Orissa.

Saikat Bhattacharyya, Research Scholar, Department of Commerce, University of Calcutta, Calcutta.

Shri Prakash, Dean (Research), BIMTECH, Greater Noida, (U.P.).

Swami Prakash Srivastava, Reader, Department of Economics, Dayalbagh Educational Institute, Agra (U.P.).

Veenu Yadav, Research Scholar of Department of Economics, Mohan Lal Sukhadia University, Udaipur, Rajasthan.

Introduction

This book is a compilation of the papers presented under the theme Global Economic Crisis and Impact on the Indian Economy at the 92nd Annual Conference of the Indian Economic Association held in December 2009 at KIIT University, Bhubaneswar. Prior to the events that came into light in 2007, most economists, to the extent that they thought about the subject at all, regarded the Great Depression of the 1930s as a gratuitous, unnecessary tragedy. Nothing like The Great Depression, they thought, could ever happen again. But on August 9, 2007, French Bank BNP Paribas, suspending withdrawals from three of its funds, marked the beginning of the end of the thought that Depression cannot hit the world again. The great financial crisis of the twenty-first century had begun. As the Nobel Laureate Paul Krugman puts it, though not the return of depression itself, but the depression economics had staged a stunning comeback.

In this backdrop of the global economy going into a slump, the theme of the seminar was aptly chosen, to make clear the notions of what really happened and what could now be done to steer clear of the crisis that had hit us all. We received a number of papers from all parts of the country that have been compiled in this book.

The paper by **Manoj Panda** brings to fore the effects the Indian economy faced due to the global economic crisis and concludes that the impact was faced by the Indian economy in terms of both the GDP loss and a fall in the exports of goods and services.

Archna Singh felt that many parallels can be drawn between the current financial crisis and the Depression of 1929. The main culprit for the present financial crisis was the financial pyramid created through financial innovations, the policy prescription of which was in tandem with the Keynesian doctrine of efficient regulation and government intervention.

R. Arunachalam ex`lained the financial crisis by drawing a parallel with the East Asian Crisis and debated upon the role of IMF in this context. Through various tables and graphs, he showed, in detail, the impacts of the US financial crisis on Indian stock market, industrial sector, trade sector and capital flows.

Amalesh Banerjee was of the opinion that the global recession was the outcome of mismanagement of the complex and irrational financial activities of the capitalist world. Although India was not as seriously affected by this crisis as many other open economies were, but India launched the reforms and revival agenda to once again have a robust economy

S.B. Mishra provided both micro and macro-economic explanations for the genesis of the crisis and established that India had not escaped unscathed in the present crisis because its economy had become more integrated with the rest of the world. A policy regime, with immediate, short-term as well as medium-term measures, to effectively tackle the crisis was also presented.

Ratan Kumar Ghosal and **Saikat Bhattacharyya**, in their paper, tried to investigate the genesis of global crisis and also explored the likely impacts of the same on our economy. They also gave the avenues of disentangling our economy from the evil effects of global crisis.

Dhiraj Kumar Bandyopadhyay's paper tried to link up the present global economic crisis with the predictions in Marx's Capital and also drew parallel to Keynesian framework in providing a solution to the same. It concluded that, as was the Keynesian strategy, the depressive conditions may continue in absence of sufficient demand for liquidity.

Though various regression techniques used in their paper, **D.K. Nauriyal** and **Bimal Sahoo**, established the effect of variables like the export, import, FDI and FII flows along with the lag value of GDP on the present value of GDP. They asserted that the slowdown of the Indian economy is expected to be reversed only with the recovery of the global markets, until which the government can stimulate the domestic demand through fiscal and monetary measures.

Shri Prakash and **Ritisnigdha Panigrahi** showed the models of integration of the Indian economy with the rest of the world. To show the integration, correlations between the Bombay Stock Exchange Prices and the London Stock Exchange Prices were calculated and established that the troughs and peaks of the two markets, by and large, coincided with each other.

Abhishek Kumar studied the impact of the financial crisis on the Indian economy in terms of the impacts on the growth rate, foreign capital flows, foreign trade, real economy and the fiscal sector. According to him, there was a minimal effect on the Indian economy and the credit for this goes to India's approach to financial globalization, i.e., allowing gradual current account convertibility and a more calibrated approach towards full convertibility on the capital account.

Mahendra Ranawat and **Veenu Yadav** highlighted, through advanced econometric models, the effect of the global financial crisis on the stock market in India. They concluded that the 'decoupling theory' is not something that really works because policy responses to a crisis are unlikely to prevent the spread among other countries.

Rajiv Kumar Bhatt focused on the fact that the Indian financial sector emerged without much damage because of the strong regulatory framework in place. He further felt that the new paradigm of growth must entail infrastructure and foodgrain-led growth strategy, which can simultaneously remove both recession and food crisis in India.

K.M. Naidu, L.K. Mohan Rao, P.V. Manjushree and **K. Mahesh Naidu** in their paper blamed six main characters for the present financial crisis that originated in the US and spread to almost all parts of the world. They were Alan Greenspan (the former Chairman of US Federal Reserve), Bill Clinton, George Bush, the banks, the system of fair value accounting and the credit rating agencies. The paper also talked of the effects on the Indian economy, especially in terms of raised fiscal deficit, and chalked out paths to be followed at both the international and national levels to curb this problem.

After analyzing the cause and the impact, especially in terms of employment, of the crisis on the Indian economy, **Purna Chandra Mishra**, in his paper, presented the policy initiatives taken by the Indian government to lift the economy out of recession. Policy stands with respect to certain most affected sectors as well as the policy measures taken by the government were discussed in detail in the paper.

Swami Prakash Srivastava's paper threw light, in detail, on the impacts of the crisis on the abilities of the economies to have high growth trajectories and to achieve the Millennium Development Goals.

Chandra Kant Singh and **Rajesh Kumar** very articulately pointed out the fact that the third world countries were hit more severely than thought of because the recession had led to a squeeze in their living standards. They explained that how, even in periods of boom, the living standards of the people in the third world countries had declined due to deterioration in terms of trade against the primary sector. The way forward, according to them, was therefore, a foodgrain-led growth strategy, sustained through larger government spending.

R.K. Shah studied the impact of the global crisis on the Nepalese economy and concluded that though, being an underdeveloped and less globally integrated economy Nepal was not much affected directly by the crisis, the indirect effects were felt due to a downturn in overseas employment, tourism, exports, foreign aid and investment.

There has been an earnest attempt in this book at bringing together the views of the people with different perceptions and policy recommendations on this vital situation that had plagued the economies the world over. We are grateful to all the contributors for the valuable ideas and opinions presented in their papers. We are also grateful to Mr. G.S. Bhatia, Deep & Deep Publications Pvt. Ltd., for timely publication of the book.

ANIL KUMAR THAKUR
DEEPTI TANEJA

1

Global Economic Crisis and Indian Economy

MANOJ PANDA

Financial crisis is a common feature of market-based economies. Every economy is likely to face it sometime or other. One IMF study counts 113 episodes of financial stress after World War II; 60 of them originated from the banking sector. The current global financial crisis began with the US sub-prime mortgage problem in mid-2007. Since the crisis originated in the heart of the world economy, its contagion effect spread very quickly, first to Europe and then to rest of the world. By end of 2008, it was evident that almost the entire world was affected one way or the other. As events unfolded and the severity of the crisis exceeded the worst earlier apprehensions, it became common in public discussions to compare the current crisis with the Great Depression of the 1930s. Counter measures, which broadly followed Keynesian prescriptions, have been initiated in various countries since late 2008.

Several factors have contributed to the building up of the crisis. The primary structural factor has been the prevalence of large and persistent global macroeconomic imbalances across major economic powers characterized by large heterogeneity. US trade deficit running over two decades reached a peak of 6.1% of gross domestic product (GDP) in 2006. On the other hand, some of the Asian economies had large current account surpluses. US spent more than its income while China invested much less compared to its savings rate which varied between 40%-50% of its GDP.

Conventional view was that US citizens consumed too much and saved very little. A few years ago, an influential section in the US put forth the 'global savings glut' hypothesis and held the view that US consumed too much because rest of the world consumed too little. After all, world income and expenditure balance must be maintained *ex-post*. This approach treats US consumption as a residual and echoes a Johansenian type macro closure. The savings glut hypothesis located the cause for the problems faced by US outside the country and implicitly indicated that the large trade and fiscal deficits in the US was essentially because it was acting as 'consumer of the last resort' and bearing the burden of imbalances caused by foreigners. This obviously is in the tradition of making a virtue of own mistakes.

Many analysts had expressed concern about danger of global imbalances without adequate action at the national or international level. Some authors, however, viewed the imbalances as natural but transitory consequence of globalisation of the financial market. Several others were, however, worried about the emerging global imbalances and its implications. Cline (2005), for example, viewed the US macroeconomic trajectory as unsustainable and advocated coordinated exchange rate realignment by G-20 countries in a manner similar to 1985 'Plaza Agreement'. Eichengreen (2006) reviewed four different perspectives on global imbalances and argued that "uncertainty about whether a disorderly correction is imminent does not justify inaction." He suggested progressively tightening fiscal policy for the US and loosening fiscal policy for China and East Asia to stimulate domestic demand.

It is against this backdrop that the emergence of the US sub-prime crisis became the immediate cause of the global economic crisis. Availability of easy loan at low interest rates led to a housing boom in the US. With soaring property prices, banks were happy to provide sub-prime loans to customers of doubtful repaying capacity assuming that mortgaged property could anyway be sold to recover the loan. The housing bubble burst eventually. The structured financial market spread of the contagion to EU.

Reddy (2009b) characterizes the current crisis as "synchronised extensive excesses" of several factors. Some underlying causes responsible for these developments, apart from the above, are: (a) innovation of new complex products by the financial sector and using them to redistribute wealth in its favour; (b) inadequate regulation and supervision, (c) resulting inability of policy-makers to appreciate the potential externalities of failure of financial sector on the belief of that market would correct itself.

INDIAN GROWTH PROCESS PRIOR TO THE CRISIS

During the last two decades, market-friendly reforms have created a favourable economic environment for integration of the Indian economy with the world economy. The break from the stagnant "Hindu growth rate" of 3.5 per cent witnessed after independence occurred around 1980 when the economy recorded a growth rate of about 5.5 per cent per annum. Further acceleration of the economy to a medium-run growth path of above 8% in recent years could be clearly seen from Figure 1 which depicts the growth rates during 1951-2008 on a 5-year moving average basis.

India's GDP stands at about US $1.2 trillion in nominal terms and about $3.2 trillion in PPP terms. It is not a major player in world trade as judged by its share of 1.2% in world merchandise trade value, though it plays a larger role in service trade with a share of 2.7% of world transactions. But, trade and capital flows have been major driving forces in bringing about structural changes in recent years in the economy. The share of exports of goods and services in GDP increased substantially from 11.7% in 1999-2000 to 22.1% in 2006-07. Imports too rose from 13.6% to 25.1% during the same period. The share of current account transactions in GDP currently at above 45% is comparable to other large countries. Foreign investment which was only $13-15 billion till 2006-07 suddenly rose to $45 billion (a third of which was FDI) in 2007-08. India was getting

FIGURE 1

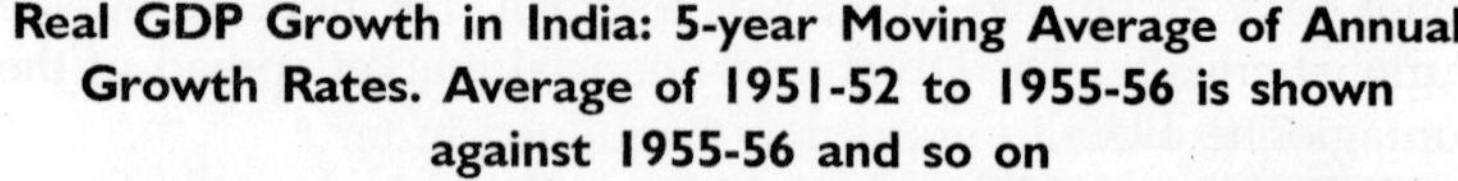

Real GDP Growth in India: 5-year Moving Average of Annual Growth Rates. Average of 1951-52 to 1955-56 is shown against 1955-56 and so on

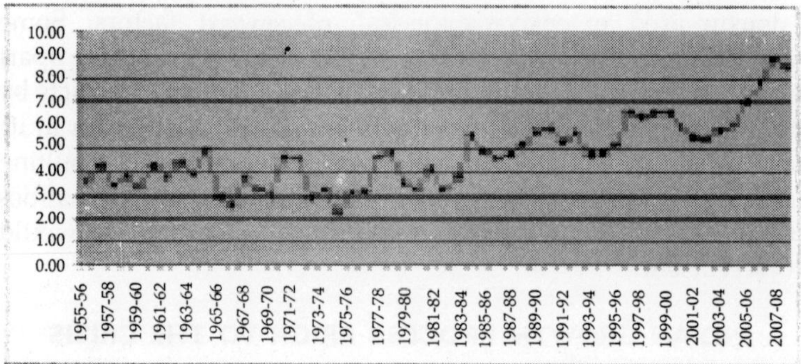

considerably integrated with the global economy in the decade prior to the crisis. With a long-term average GDP growth rate close to 7 per cent per annum (6.8% over a 16-year period 1992-2008), India was seen to be among the fastest growing economies in the world. It recently entered the group of 'lower middle income' countries as per the classification of the World Bank.

The recent high growth phase of 8%-9% during 2003-07 looked to be sustainable in the medium-run given that the economy had withstood several shocks like the East Asian crisis, border tension, the Iraq war, oil price fluctuations and major droughts without major disruptions. Policy-makers were in fact looking forward to accelerate the process further. The 11th Five Year Plan (2007-12) thus targeted a GDP growth rate of 9% per annum. The first year of the Plan did achieve this growth rate.

IMPACT OF CRISIS ON INDIAN ECONOMY

Then came the global crisis. Initially, it was thought that the magnitude of the crisis would be small and its impact would be limited to US and EU. Given their restricted operation abroad, Indian banks had limited exposure to structured financial market involving sub-prime loans. But as the crisis intensified and its severity became clear, it was not confined to the banking sector alone. As the effect considerably spread to the real sectors in US and EU, it was realised that the 'decoupled' hypothesis did not hold. The Indian economy could not remain immune to the global crisis.

The overall impact may be judged in terms of the fall in GDP growth to 6.7% in 2008-09 from 9% in the previous year. It looked as if the crisis put the Indian economy back on the pre-2003 growth trajectory. However, the whole of the fall of 2.3 per centage points should not be attributed to the global crisis. Agricultural income grew by only 1.6% in 2008-09 as against 4.9% in 2007-08 (Figure 2). This sharp fall, not related to the global crisis, might have contributed to about 0.8 per centage point fall in GDP. Given the current share of agriculture in GDP, direct effect of 3.3 per centage fall in agricultural income on GDP would be 0.6 per centage point and the rest indirect.

The effect of global crisis on the Indian economy basically operated through the balance of payments channel affecting both current and capital accounts. Contraction of trade flows and capital flows in turn affected the exchange rate and the stock market prices.

FIGURE 2

India's Real GDP Growth by Broad Sectors

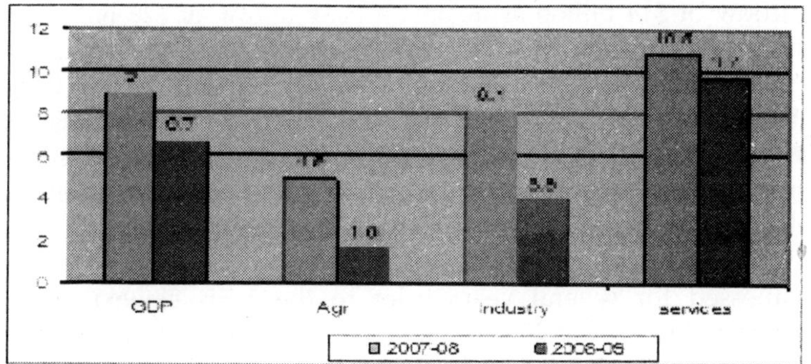

Trade Flows

Taking advantage of considerable expansion in world trade, merchandise exports and imports of India had recorded impressive growth of 21.7% and 29.7% on an average during 2003-04 to 2007-08. Merchandise exports fell sharply to 3.3% in

2008-09 as a result of demand contraction due to global recession. Sectors most affected in India are gems and jewelry, textiles and garments, leather products and handicrafts. Contraction in output growth was accompanied by large scale job losses in these employment intensive sectors. Imports growth too fell to 14.3% in 2008-09, though oil price rise in the first half of FY 2008-09 had an impact on raising the import bill. The effects were very severe from the third quarters of 2008-09 onwards. On a monthly basis, exports and imports growth rates became negative from October 2008 and November 2008 respectively and remained so till at least October 2009. Service exports, which maintained a sustained rapid growth of about 30% for several years, moderated to 16% during April-December, 2008.

Capital Flows

In the initial phase of the crisis, when the 'decoupled' hypothesis was debated, India was thought to be a relatively attractive destination. As a result, foreign institutional investment (FII) increased till January 2008. As the crisis in US and EU grew, the flows reduced and considerably reversed later to meet cash commitments and cover losses in their 'home' countries. During the year 2008-09 as a whole, there was net outflow of $14 billion as against a peak inflow of $29 billion in the previous year. This had strong impact on the stock market index which witnessed sharp fluctuations and fell sharply from about 21000 in January 2008 to about 9000 by March 2008. Stock market certainly went through turbulence and settled for some orderly behaviour at low level of the index. In recent months, FIIs have returned back to India with positive inflows.

The rising trend in net foreign direct investment (FDI) witnessed for several years prior to the crisis slowed down considerably during 2008-09. It stood at $17.5 billion in 2008-09 compared to $15.4 in 2007-08. Net external commercial borrowings came down substantially from $22.7 billion to $6.9 billion. All these developments meant that overall balance of payments turned negative at $20 billion leading to decrease in foreign exchange reserves. Additionally, reserves fell by $40 billion due to revaluation, thus, leading to total fall by as much as $60 billion during 2008-09. No doubt, comfortable levels of

FIGURE 3

FDI and Port Folio Investment in India

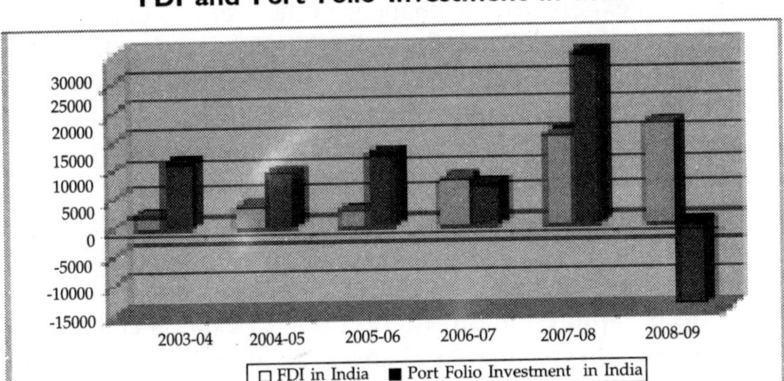

forex reserves built up over the years, which peaked at $316 billion in mid-2008, helped India to tide over this as well as several other problems by permitting flexibility on trade policy decisions without resorting to restrictive measures.

The trade and capital flows put pressure on exchange rate of the rupee. It depreciated by more than 25% with respect to US dollar and Japanese Yen, though changes with respect to Euro and Pound Sterling was similar to previous year. Depreciation of the rupee in dollar terms has raised the cost of imports and of commercial borrowings.

INDIAN POLICY RESPONSE

In response to the crisis, the government of India adopted several fiscal and monetary counter measures to limit the adverse effects. This involved increased government expenditure on infrastructure and other projects, reduction in indirect taxes, reducing interest rates, easing the liquidity available with the banks, etc. How much of the adverse effects due to global crisis might have been countered by the government? This question has been addressed by Kumar and Panda (2009) by carrying out a series of simulations using a computable general equilibrium (CGE) model of the Indian economy. The CGE framework determines only relative prices and does not incorporate monetary variables. Hence, we examined effects of only "real" shocks and "fiscal" counter-measures leaving out effects of "monetary" policy responses such as increased access to credit and reduced interest rate. Specifically, we looked at the impacts of (a) fall in exports due to changes in the world economy, (b) a reduction in the foreign inflows into India, and (c) the fall in global oil prices that happened in the second half of fiscal 2008-09. On the response side, we examined effects of two fiscal measures—(i) a rise in government consumption, and (ii) a cut in indirect taxes—undertaken to mitigate the crisis effect.

The effects on real GDP in the various simulations are given in Table 1. The simulation results show that a 10% fall in exports of goods and services causes a real GDP loss of 3.3%. The total effects capture the direct effect due to exports change and the induced effects due to changes in all other endogenous variables of the model. Given the current share of exports of goods and services in GDP, a 10% fall in exports could have a direct effect on GDP by about 2.0% and the rest might be considered as indirect multiplier effect since exports in India have low import content and the indirect effects are not insignificant. Note that the GDP effect here is due to export fall alone (partial effects) and not trade flows which also involved sharp contraction in imports whose 'competitive' component would have a favourable impact on GDP. The second simulation refers to fall in capital flows in the form of 10% fall in remittances and 15% fall in foreign savings. The effect on GDP operating through consumption and investment demand elements amounts to 1.8 per centage point decline. Simulation C corresponds to fall in international oil and gas price observed in the second half of last fiscal which turns out to be about 10% on yearly average data over the previous year. As expected, oil price decline had a favourable effect on overall GDP growth by 0.9 per cent. Thus, the adverse effects on GDP of the first three scenarios due to global developments turn out to be 4.2 per centage points. The actual fall in GDP growth rate in 2008-09 was not as sharp in practice because observed change is the resultant of all factors operating in that year including the counter-measures. Yet, it is instructive to note the various potential effects under 'controlled conditions' for policy formulation.

We now turn to the policy measures undertaken to counter the effect involving scenarios D, E and F. Simulation D reflects effect of expansionary fiscal policy across the board government consumption in real terms by 5% from the base scenario. This helps to raise GDP by 0.7 per cent which would mean that GDP fall due to global meltdown is arrested to this extent due to government expenditure. On the indirect tax front, government had announced an average reduction of about 4 per centage points in indirect tax rates in goods and services (except for petroleum products) in the middle of the financial year. We have tried to incorporate this aspect by reducing the indirect tax rates by a quarter of the base value to get a tax rate reduction of about 2 per centage point for the whole year. Simulation E indicates that indirect tax reduction might have helped the economy by raising the aggregate income by 0.8 per cent. These results indicate that the fiscal stimulus undertaken by the government thus possibly helped to counter GDP fall by about 1.5 per centage point.

On the income distribution front, their results showed that all income classes are unfavourably affected by the crisis and the fiscal measures provide only partial relief to all sections. While the richer classes might somehow cope with the income loss, the poor might find it extremely difficult to do so. Hence, in one experiment, Kumar and Panda attempt an experiment that expands the national rural employment guarantee scheme (NREGS) to fully cover all those unemployed among the poorest 70% of the rural population in the last stimulus experiment. It is

TABLE I

Effect of Crisis and Counter Measures on Real GDP (% change from Base)

A	*B*	*C*	*D*	*E*	*F*
Exports of goods and services fall (10%)	*Inflows fall (10% remit-tances and 15% foreign savings)*	*Global oil price fall (10%)*	*Government consumption rise (5% in quantity terms)*	*Indirect tax cut (25% in base rate)*	*NREGS (Full demand of bottom 70% of rural population)*
-3.3	-1.8	0.9	0.7	0.8	0.5

interesting to note that nearly 19 million additional jobs are needed to undertake such a target at a cost of 1.4% of GDP. By design, such a programme significantly increases the welfare of the targeted group. With unemployed resources in the reference case, it increases GDP by 0.5% and provides marginal income gains to other income classes too.

LOOKING AHEAD

It is not clear how soon the global economic crisis will be over. The recent turmoil in Dubai indicates that contagion effect very much persists. So far as India is concerned, a silver line is seen in the turn around of the economic growth during 2009-10. GDP growth was 6.1 in the first quarter of 2009-10, but it picked up considerably to 7.9% in the second quarter. More importantly, the manufacturing sector which contracted in absolute terms with a negative growth (-1.4%) in the last quarter of 2008-09 is showing indications of the revival. It has recorded 3.4% and 9.2% growth in the first and second quarters of 2009-10 respectively.

It would be a mistake to consider early exit of the stimulus package despite the fiscal strains. The withdrawal of the stimulus may be initiated when growth continues for a few quarters and be carried out in stages. Policy measures need to be calibrated taking into consideration the emerging changes in the structure of the economy in favour of non-tradable sectors such as infrastructure and construction.

Cost of coupling is a natural corollary of benefit of coupling. Minimising costs and maximising benefits of globalisation requires careful calibration of policies to suit national interest. For example, the present crisis should not lead to reversing policies on capital flows. Yet, International financial markets are intrinsically highly volatile and regulations need to be in place due to the externalities of these markets. Policy goals should support long-term capital flows (FDI and equity) whereas short-term capital movements should be liberalised in a gradual and limited manner. McKinnon and Pill (1996) note critical role of sequencing of financial reforms: first put in place a well-functioning domestic capital system before allowing capital convertibility. Fortunately, this advice is well recognised in India.

GLOBAL ECONOMIC REBALANCING

Indian should also be ready for a pro-active role in the new international initiatives to correct global imbalances. Safe guarding national interest necessarily calls for understanding implications of policy initiatives at the international level. Critical to this process is the complex question: who bears how much cost of global rebalancing cost. Alternative scenarios can have very different implications for developed and emerging market economies.

Using a global CGE model, Von Arnim (2009) shows some interesting results on the recovery process. First, if US reduces its consumption by 5% and Asia continues to accumulate reserves, global macroeconomic imbalances are likely to rise. Such a scenario would require that Europe acts as "consumer of the last resort"; EU exchange rate appreciates giving rise to small current account deficit and fall in GDP. Second, adjustments induced by large relative prices—possible exchange rate adjustments—to correct global imbalances tend to be very volatile and places the burden of adjustment mostly on Asia. Third, acceptable solutions involve 5% reduction of US consumption (and increase in private savings) and $1.25 trillion increase in government spending across the world involving switch in demand from traded to non-traded goods. His results do not indicate smooth reduction in global imbalances.

References

Bernanke, Ben S. (2005): "The Global Saving Glut and the U.S. Current Account Deficit", Sandridge Lecture, Virginia Association of Economics, Richmond, Virginia.

Cline, William R. (2005): The Case for a New Plaza Agreement, Policy briefs in International Economics, Institute for International Economics.

Data as per RBI, Handbook of Statistics, September 2009.

Eichengreen, Barry (2006): "Global Imbalances: The New Economy, the Dark Matter, the Savvy Investor, and the Standard Analysis", University of California, Berkeley.

Ghosh and Chandrasekhar (2009) show a high degree association between cumulative FII investments and Bombay Stock Exchange Sensitive Index.

Ghosh, Jayati and C.P. Chandrasekhar (2009): "The costs of 'coupling': the global crisis and the Indian economy", *Cambridge Journal of Economics*, 33, P.725-739.

In order to ensure that labour does not move out of the productive sectors of the economy to NREGS, its wage rate was set at 90% of the market wage rate.

It is interesting to note that virtues of counter cyclical fiscal policy measures were suddenly rediscovered, after more than two decades, to counter the recession in the developed world. Indian policy-makers have adopted more balanced view in the past and fiscal and monetary instruments have been active instruments of state policy to promote growth and equity.

Johansen (1961): Multi-sectoral Growth Models, North Holland.

Kim Bang_Han, Hong_Ghi Min, Young_soon Hwang and Judith A. McDonald (2009): "Are Asian Countries' current accounts sustainable? Deficits, even when associated with high investment, are not costless", *Journal of Policy Modeling*, 31, pp. 163-79.

Kumar, A. Ganesh and Manoj Panda (2009): "Global Economic Shocks and Indian Policy Response: An Analysis using CGE Model", in Kirit S. Parikh (ed.), *Macro-Modelling for the Eleventh Five Year Plan of India*, Academic Foundation and Planning Commission, New Delhi.

McKinnon, R.I. and H. Pill (1996): "Credible Liberalizations and International Capiatl Flows: The Overborrowing Syndrome", in T. Ito and A.O. Krueger (eds), *Financial Deregulation and Integration in East Asia*, University of Chicago Press.

Rakshit (2009): observes that industrial production and GDP had started decelerating right from the first quarter of 2007-08, before the arrival of global crisis due to fall in private investment as well as in exports.

Rakshit, Mihir (2009): "India amidst the Global Crisis", *Economic and Political Weekly*, March 28.

Rattso, J. (1982): "Different Macroclosures of the Original Johansen Model and their Impact on Policy Evaluation", *Journal of Policy Modeling*, Vol. 4.

Reddy (2009a) talks of several issues in the context of a new global financial architecture.

Reddy, Y.V. (2009a): India and the Global Financial Crisis: Managing Money and Finance, Orient Blackswan.

Reddy, Y.V. (2009b): "Global Financial Crisis and Asia", Justice Konda Madhava Reddy Memorial Lecture.

See, for example, Bernanke (2005).

See, Johansen (1960) and Rattso (1984): It is interesting to note here that Indian Plan models had relied heavily on Johansen macro closure in the past in their approach to macroeconomic submodel.

The Indian Government had already been undertaken at the beginning of 2008 a large expansionary fiscal package involving farmers' loan waiving, revision of salary of government employees, rural infrastructure, and primary education.

Total indirect tax revenue was 8% of GDP in the Base run.

Von Arnim, Rudigor (2009): "Recession and rebalancing: How the housing and credit crisis will impact US real activity", *Journal of Policy Modeling*, 31, pp. 309-24.

2

Global Economic Crisis: The Ideas of Keynes Reinstated

ARCHNA SINGH

The ideas of Keynes did not seem to be as relevant as they are in the present global economic context characterized by recession and turbulence in the financial as well as real sector. There is almost a consensus among the economist that the world economy is facing its severest crisis since the time of Great Depression of the 1930. However, the present crisis is different from that of 1930's in more than one ways, an important distinction being that the great depression affected mainly the real sector whereas in the present crisis originated from the financial sector.

GREAT DEPRESSION AND THE EMERGENCE OF KEYNES

At the time of Great Depression of 1930's the classical solutions failed to pull the global economy out of depression. At that time Keynes came forward for the rescue of the world economic system. Keynes showed the inability of the "classical laissez faire" to maintain continuous, sufficient total demand and production and employment or its liability to fall at intervals into depression and unemployment. Keynes explained the trade cycle as occurring due to fluctuations in propensity to consume, liquidity preference and marginal efficiency of capital. Marginal efficiency of capital is affected by future yield of capital goods. These expectations are subject to sudden changes. A crisis is not so much due to a high rate of interest as to a collapse of marginal efficiency of capital.

The classical prescription of increasing the money supply failed to save the world economy because the new money created went just to satisfy the increased liquidity preference resulting in failure to increase investment (liquidity trap). Thus Keynes abandoned the hypothesis of self correcting market forces and instead argued to enhance the level of government spending.

Though Keynes criticized the classical ideas and showed the way out of the depression through government intervention at the same time he preserved the market economy from the radical attacks of Marxist idea of state control. Keynes in his General Theory mentioned that "the State will have to exercise a guiding influence through the scheme of taxation. But beyond this no obvious case is made for a system of state socialism."

UNDERSTANDING THE PRESENT CRISIS

The present crisis, originating first in the US subprime mortgage market in August 2007, soon spread to markets for other securities in both the US and elsewhere. In this process, it caused within a few months, a string of bankruptcies and a sharp slowdown in all the industrialized countries. Initially the economists believed that the emerging Asian economies like China and India will remain "decoupled" from the crisis, but soon they proved to be wrong.

The present crisis originated in the financial sector which has become a very important part of the economic framework of any country. In fact a well functioning financial system is the prerequisite of the process of growth with stability. Schumpeter (1971) propounded that financial intermediaries are essential drivers for innovation and growth. Later McKinnon Shaw also supported the Schumpeter's argument.

With the revolution of IT, several innovations have

occurred in the financial system. These innovations, on the one hand have made it possible to reap the economies of scale but on the other hand, have increased the complexity and vulnerability of the financial system.

Hyman Minsky, a follower of Keynes has very elaborately dealt with the financial side of business cycles. In his theory, finance is regarded as the cause of the instability of capitalism. Keynes on the other hand believed that finance can only amplify the fluctuations.

Minsky argued that stability is paradoxically destabilizing; good times encourage experimentation and excessive risk taking ending up in a mess. Minsky stated that a prolonged period of stability would induce some units to migrate from hedge to speculative to Ponzi finance. (a ponzi unit has to constantly borrow more to meet its debt servicing commitments)

In the present financial crisis the complex financial pyramid created through financial innovations emerged as the main culprit. The crisis erupted in the US subprime mortgage markets. With the interest rates rising and home prices falling there was a sharp jump in defaults and foreclosures. However, this could have remained as a purely mortgage crisis, but for the fact that these mortgages were securitized and packaged into products that were rated as investment grade. Once doubt about these assets arose they turned illiquid making it hard to price them. This affected a number of institutions which had invested in these products. The international financial system being highly integrated, the crisis spread to almost all the countries of the world. The crisis in the financial sector has now moved to the real sector resulting in a slump in the growth and employment worldwide.

IMF's estimates of growth in world output indicate that the slowdown is severe and widespread. The estimates are as following are as shown in the following table on next page.

DEALING WITH THE CRISIS: SOME KEYNESIAN PROPOSITIONS

In the light of the current economic crisis many of the Keynesian propositions have once again become relevant, in dealing with the present situation.

	2007	2008	2009	2010
World output	5.1	3.1	-1.4	2.5
Advanced economies	2.7	0.8	-3.8	0.6
United States	2.0	1.1	-2.6	0.8
Euro area	2.7	0.8	-4.8	-0.3
Germany	2.5	1.3	-6.2	-0.6
France	2.3	0.3	-3.0	0.4
Italy	1.6	-1.0	-5.1	-0.1
Spain	3.7	1.2	-4.0	-0.1
Japan	2.3	-0.7	-6.0	1.7
United Kingdom	2.6	0.7	-4.2	0.2
Canada	2.5	0.4	-2.3	1.6
Other Advanced Economies	4.7	1.6	-3.9	1.0
Newly Industrialized Asian Economies	5.7	1.5	-5.2	1.4
Emerging and Developing Economies	8.3	6.0	1.5	4.7
Africa	6.2	5.2	1.8	4.1
Sub-Sahara	6.9	5.5	1.5	4.1
Central and Eastern Europe	5.4	3.0	-5.0	1.0
CIS	8.6	5.5	-5.8	2.0
Russia	8.1	5.6	-6.5	1.0
Developing Asia	10.6	7.6	5.5	7.0
China	13.0	9.0	7.5	8.5
India	9.4	7.3	5.4	6.5
Brazil	5.7	5.1	-1.3	2.5
Mexico	3.3	1.3	-7.3	3.0

The figures are projections for 2009 and 2010.
Source: IMF.

Keynes was a supporter of active macroeconomic policy, involving intervention of Government, in contrast to the free play of market forces as advocated by the Classicals. Keynes influenced the macroeconomic policy after 1930 in a large way. But, in the decade of 70's doubts were raised against Keynesian economics. McKinnon Shaw's hypothesis, which condemned the intervention of the government in the financial sector (termed as "financial repression"), supported the idea of deregulation. With the fall of the Berlin wall and the disintegration of the Soviet Union, popularized as the "End of History" by Francis Fukuyama, the world once again moved towards free market fundamentalism and *laissez faire* ideology of the classical. The ideas of Keynes were sidelined in the over optimism that the market is most efficient when left to itself.

But the conditions under which Adam Smith's "invisible hands" worked as laid down by Gerald Debreu and Kenneth Arrow are unrealistic and do not exist in the real world. Joseph Stiglitz in his research has shown that the conditions like perfect competition and symmetric information do not exist in the real world, which is one of the reason why Adam Smith's invisible hands don't work. Keynes believed that government intervention and regulation can often play an important role in making them work better and in limiting the scope of the conflict of interest that repeatedly appeared in accounting, business and finance.

The latest IMF analysis (Feb. 2009) reflect the same idea in describing the root cause of the crisis in: "market failure ......bred by a long period of high growth, low real interest rates and volatility and policy failures in financial regulation, which are not equipped to see the risk concentration and flawed incentive behind the financial innovation boom; macroeconomic policies which didn't take into account systemic risks in the financial system and in housing markets, and global architecture where a fragmented surveillance system compounded the inability to see growing vulnerabilities and links."

Thus one policy prescription which derives from the current experience and supported by Keynesian theory is that of efficient regulation of the financial system. It is all the more important for financial sector which is more fragile and influenced by expectations. The exogenous and spontaneous shift in the moods—optimism or pessimism is at the heart of fluctuations in stock prices. Keynes called it as "animal spirits" in the General Theory. He argues that "Even apart from the instability due to speculation, there is instability due to the characteristic of human nature that a large proportion of our positive activities depend on spontaneous optimism rather than on a mathematical expectation, whether moral or hedonic or economic. Most of our decisions to do something positive, the full consequences of which will be drawn out over many days to come, can only be taken as a result of animal spirits of a spontaneous urge to action rather than inaction and not as the outcome of weighted average of quantitative benefits multiplied by quantitative probabilities."

Thus it becomes important that the government should intervene and there should be an efficient and transparent regulatory system to check the market inefficiencies and failures.

REFORMING THE REGULATORY SYSTEM

The present crisis has glaringly made it clear that there were flaws in the regulatory framework. The Geneva Report has highlighted two crippling weaknesses in the system of regulation. First, it is excessively micro prudential, containing not a hint of recognition that the major problem arises due to the correlation of risks. Second, it concentrates entirely on the composition of a bank's assets and neglects completely whether those assets are financed in inherently stable ways or by borrowing short-term loans in the interbank market.

The Geneva Report proposed a system of macro prudential regulation to the existing system of micro-regulation. This would increase bank's capital asset ratios during boom and reduce them in the period of crisis, providing a deterrent to increasing credit when there is an abundance of credit available and an incentive to lend more at times when the system as a whole is short of lending. The second fundamental change to the regulatory system it proposes addresses the observation that banks and other financial intermediaries engage in risky practice of borrowing short and lending long. The answer to this is to penalize the maturity mismatches through increased CAR's.

Some other measures to enhance the resilience of the global system as proposed by Y.V. Reddy are as following:

1. Risk management frameworks including the governance arrangement in banks and financial institutions need to be reviewed by the managements.

2. Supervisors need to play a more active role in scrutinizing the risk management practices, including stress testing and governance arrangements, off balance sheet entities and structured products
3. Supervisors should encourage institutions to develop more robust models that use more prudent and reliable assumptions and stress testing methodologies and monitor more closely the internal processes and controls for managing risks.
4. There is need to rationalize the regulatory and supervisory prescriptions with a view to reducing the scope for arbitraging.
5. Greater transparency is needed so as to make the markets more efficient and optimize the allocation of capital.
6. There is a need to review and resolve the element of procyclicality in prudential regulations, accounting rules and attitude of the authorities that tend to apply these.
7. The supervisors should be given the clear authority to intervene at the first signs of weaknesses, preferably much before the institutions net worth become negative.
8. The deposit insurance systems should aim to limit the likelihood of retail depositor runs in the troubled banks through adequate coverage and have the ability to pay the depositors quickly.

There is also a need of international co-operation in this direction. Keynes himself was a supporter of international co-operation for the proper functioning of global economy and in this spirit he recommended the formation of international institutions (IMF, World Bank). Bank of International Settlement is also an important supranational institution. There should be a co-ordination among different institutions regulating trade and finance across borders.

2009 Discretionary Fiscal Stimulus Around the Globe

Country	*Per cent of GDP*	*Country*	*Per cent of GDP*
Argentina	1.4	Korea	3.7
Australia	2.2	Mexico	1.4
Brazil	0.5	New Zealand	2.0
Canada	1.7	Norway	1.2
China	2.6	Poland	0.8
Czech Republic	1.6	Russia	2.9
France	0.6	South Africa	2.2
Germany	1.5	Sweden	1.4
India	0.6	Switzerland	0.6
Indonesia	1.4	United Kingdom	1.5
Italy	0.1	United States	2.0
Japan	2.4		

FISCAL STIMULUS PACKAGES: A TYPICAL APPLICATION OF KEYNESIAN THEORY

The world economy is in the grip of serious recession. The growth rates of almost all countries have declined, underemployment increasing to unprecedented level, financial sector under severe stress. Keynesian prescription for such a situation would be that the government should step in to increase the aggregate demand which can help the system to move towards the full employment level of equilibrium. Taking a cue from the Keynesian theory, the governments of countries throughout the world announced fiscal stimulus packages aimed to stimulate the aggregate demand. IMF suggests a stimulus of 2% of GDP for the developed countries. Model stimulations by National Institute of Economic and Social Research suggest that such a coordinated developed country stimulus could lead to a GDP rise of around 1-1.5% in 2009 and early 2010. There is also need for coordinated international approach (advocated by Keynes) to fiscal stimulus. Robert Zoëlick, the President of World Bank, advocated that all the developed countries should pledge 0.7% of their stimulus packages to vulnerability fund for assisting the developing countries.

The stimulus packages of some selected countries are as following:

The fiscal stimulus and/or targeted transfers announced by the governments across the world is expected to have considerable multiplier effect on the economy and would help reverse the negative expectations. In an ideal scenario where fiscal stimulus is both global and supported by monetary accommodation, and where financial sectors that are under pressure and being supported by Governments, every dollar spent on government investment can increase GDP by about $3, while every dollar of targeted transfers can increase GDP by about $1. In countries in which fiscal space is limited, it will be essentially important to focus fiscal stimulus on those measures that will have largest impact on aggregate demand, like targeted transfers and government investment, where possible.

Many studies have shown that both tax cuts and government expenditure have strong impact on macroeconomic variables (studies by Valerie A. Ramey and Mathew Shapiro, 1998, Oliver Blanchard and Robert Perotti, 2002, Craig Burnside, Eichenbaum and Jones D.M. Fisher, 2004, Valerie A. Ramey, 2008).

GLOBAL FINANCIAL CRISIS AND INDIA: IMPACT AND LESSONS

The Indian economy initially seemed to be insulated from the global financial crisis that started in August 2007 in the US. But with the collapse of Lehman Brothers on 23rd September 2008, the financial meltdown turned into a global economic slowdown, impacting the Indian economy also.

The impact of the global economic crisis has been transmitted to the Indian economy through three distinct channels, viz. the financial sector, exports and exchange rates.

Global financial troubles have not so far triggered a major banking crisis in India as they did in the UK and other countries. Whereas banks in the UK and other European countries were exposed heavily to the mortgage backed securities offered by the US financial system, banks in India avoided such exposures. Still there are some worrying factors. First, there has been an outflow of foreign institutional investments starting in Feb. 2008 (Figure 1). The withdrawal of FII investments has created other problems in its wake. India's stock markets have witnessed a collapse. Indian Rupee has been losing steadily against the US Dollar since April 2008 (Figure 2). With the withdrawal of FIIs

FIGURE 1

Monthly Inflows of Portfolio Investment into India, July 2006 to September 2008

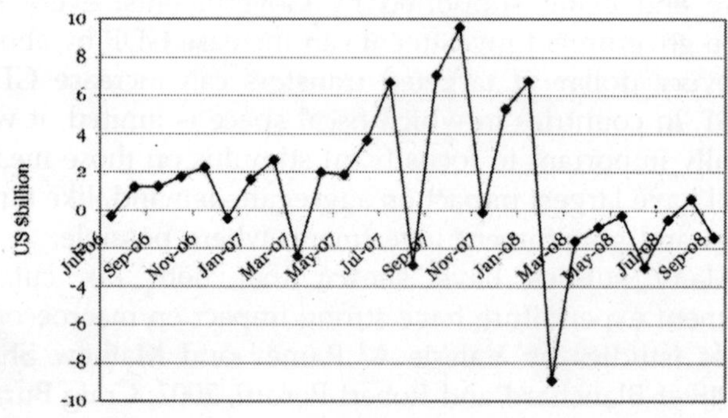

FIGURE 2

Indices of Real Effecive Exchange Rate (REER) and Nominal Effective Exchange Rate (NEER) of the Indian Rupee (Base Year = 2006-07) (6-Currency Trade Based Weights)

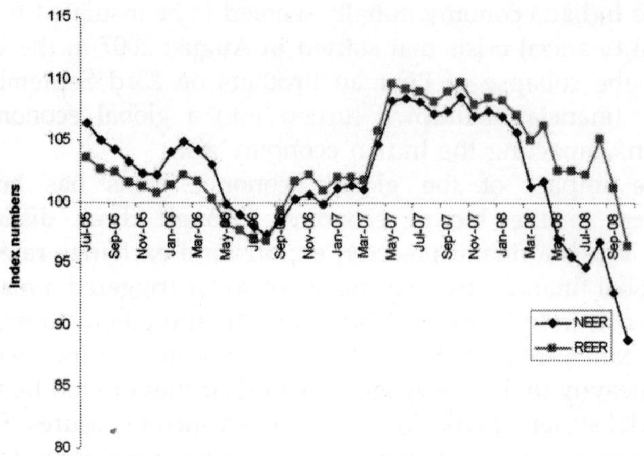

and depreciation of Rupee, RBI stepped in to defend the rupee by selling dollars which resulted in depletion in foreign exchange reserves (Figure 3).

FIGURE 3

India's Total Foreign Exchange Reserves in Billions of US Dollars, Weekly Data, April 2007-October 2008

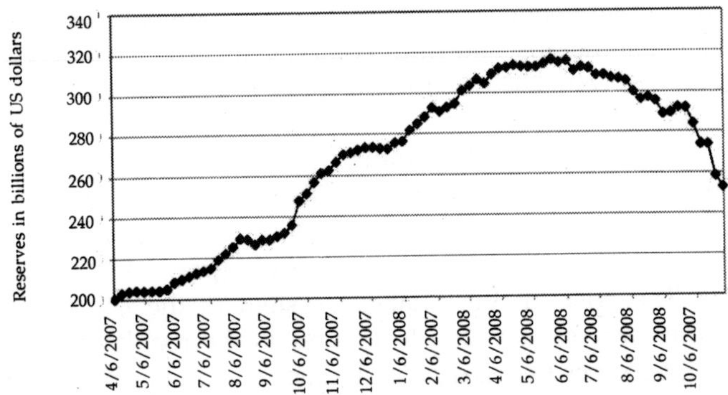

The crisis has led to a serious recession in the real economy, which is evident from the CSO's estimates of growth of real GDP for the last quarter of 2007-08 and the first quarter of 2008-09. GDP for the first quarter of 2008-09 slowed down to 7.9%. (Table 1)

TABLE I

Rates of Growth of Real GDP (at 1999-2000 prices) at Factor Cost, in per cent

	2000-01 to 2007-08	2005-06	2006-07	2007-08	2007-08				2008-09
					Q1	Q2	Q3	Q4	Q1
Agriculture & allied activities	2.9	5.9	3.8	4.5	4.4	4.7	6.0	2.9	3.0
Industry	7.1	8.0	10.6	8.1	9.6	8.6	8.6	5.8	5.2
Mining & Quarrying	4.9	4.9	5.7	4.7	1.7	5.5	5.7	5.9	4.8
Manufacturing	7.8	9.0	12.0	8.8	10.9	9.2	9.6	5.8	5.6
Electricity, gas & water supply	4.8	4.7	6.0	6.3	7.9	6.9	4.8	5.6	2.6
Services	9.0	11.0	11.2	10.7	10.6	10.7	10.0	11.4	10.2
GDP at factor prices	7.3	9.4	9.6	9.0	9.2	9.3	8.8	8.8	7.9

Source: Central Statistical Organization reported in RBI (2008).

As far as the exports are concerned there has been a steep decline in demand for India's exports in the world market. The first to be hit is the Gems and Jewellery, where there has been a sharp rise in unemployment. The negative impact has since covered other export oriented sectors like garments and textiles, leather, handicrafts and auto components. The 21% decline in exports in Feb. 2009 is the steepest decline in the last two decades.

Thus it is clear that Indian economy is not "decoupled" from the economic crisis though the impact has not been as devastating as in some other countries. It is high time for us to take lessons from the current crisis so as to prevent such crisis in India. The crisis in the financial system in the US and other countries was mainly due to failures in the regulatory system. Thus it becomes necessary that Indian regulatory system should be strengthened so as to avoid any such situation in Indian financial system. The Raghu Ram Rajan committee also talks about lessons from the current financial turmoil some of them are as:

1. It is not sufficient for regulators to only look at the part of the system under their immediate purview. Because markets are integrated, any unregulated participant can infect markets and thus contaminate regulated sectors also. For instance, there is some evidence that unregulated mortgage brokers originated worse loans than regulated ones, contaminating the securitization process. While the immediate conclusion is not to regulate everyone to the same degree, it does suggest regulators have to be alert to entities that could have systemic consequences, including on markets.
2. Capital regulation is no substitute for ensuring that the incentives of financial institution management are adequate—that the spirit of the regulation is being obeyed rather than just the rule. For example, the off-balance sheet entities of the major banks, including the Structured Investmen. Vehicles (SIVs), met the rules of being off-balance sheet (and hence did not require a charge on capital), but in practice

turned out to be effectively on balance sheet. Indeed, there is increasing debate about whether the Basel II capital norms are adequate, both in good times in preventing excessive risk taking, and in bad times when strict capital norms can hold back bank lending and result in a downward spiral.

3. In a market-based system, banks are not the only source of illiquidity risk. Any entity that has mismatched assets and liabilities (mismatched in terms of duration or liquidity) is subject to the risk of becoming illiquid. To the extent that that entity is of systemic importance—either too big, too interlinked, or too many investors to fail—it will have a call on public funds. To the extent that markets started in the US sub-prime sector, in part because of excessive financial exuberance, despite its proximity and exposure the United States financial system has weathered the losses thus far surprisingly well. Indeed, US equity markets have held up better than the Indian stock markets! Part of the reason has to be its openness and variety. US banks could raise capital quickly by tapping into sovereign wealth funds elsewhere. Even while banks are hamstrung by overloaded balance sheets, hedge funds and private equity players are entering the markets for illiquid assets and establishing a bottom.
4. Consumer protection is important. Not every household is fully cognizant of the transactions they enter into. While the line between excessive paternalism and appropriate individual responsibility is always hard to draw, in a developing country like ours, it may well veer to a little more paternalism in interactions between financial firms and less-sophisticated households. It is important to improve consumer literacy, the transparency of products that are sold, and in some cases, limit sales of certain products in certain jurisdictions, especially if they have prudential consequences.
5. There is no perfect regulatory system. The problems

with Northern Rock in the United Kingdom are being attributed to the fact that the United Kingdom had moved to a single supervisor, the Financial Services Authority (FSA), with the monetary authority having no supervisory powers. At the same time, the Bear Stearns debacle in the United States is being attributed to the absence of a single supervisor. What is essential is effective cooperation between all the concerned authorities, which transcends the specifics of organizational architecture.

Another issue which must be dealt cautiously, more so after the financial crisis, is that of capital account convertibility. India has adopted a calibrated approach towards opening of the capital account. Foreign investment inflows are encouraged, debt flows in the form of ECBs are generally subject to ceilings and some end use restrictions. Macro-ceilings have been placed for portfolio investment in government securities and corporate bonds. Capital outflows have been progressively liberalized. There should be a strict adherence to the prudential norms to avoid any crisis. The macroeconomic indicators (like inflation and fiscal deficit) should be put well in place before moving towards full capital account convertibility (as recommended by Tarapore committee, 1997).

As far as the Indian banking sector is concerned it has remained insulated from the financial crisis. The balance sheets of banks have remained healthy and adequately capitalized. The CRAR of all the SCB's taken together was 13% at end March 2008. Asset quality of domestic banks also remain satisfactory with net NPA's being only 1% of net advances.

Detailed guidelines have been issued by the RBI on the implementation of the Basel II framework covering all the three pillars. All foreign banks operating in India and Indian banks having presence outside have migrated to Basel II by March 31, 2008 and all other SCB's have migrated to Basel II by March 31, 2009.

In the backdrop of the current crisis it is important that the regulatory system should be efficient because the growing integration of Indian financial sector with the global system, besides many advantages,also increases the vulnerability of the financial sector.

References

Acharya Shankar, 2009, "India and The Global Crisis", Acadamic Foundation Ltd., Report on Trends and Progress in Banking, 2007-08, RBI.

Dillard Dudley, 1950, "The Economics of John Manyard Keynes", Crosky Lockwood & Son Limited.

Freedman Charles, Michael Kumhof, Douglas Laxton, Jaewoo Lee, "The Case for Global Fiscal Stimulus", IMF Staff Position Note, March 2009.

Keynes, J.M., 1936, "The General Theory of Employment, Interest and Money", Mae Millon & Co. limited.

Keynes, J.M, 1933, "Treaties on Money", MacMillon & Co. Limited.

Mohan, Rakesh, "Global Financial Crisis—Causes Impact Policy Responses and Lessons", *BIS Review*, 54/2009.

Nayak, Pulin B., "Anatomy of the Financial Crisis: Between Keynes and Schumpeter", *EPW*, March 2009.

Rajan, Raghu Ram, "A Hundered Small Steps, Report of Committee on Financial Sector Reforms", Sage Publication.

Rangarajan, C.., 2009, "India Monetary Policy Financial Stability and other Essays", Academic Foundation.

Reddy, Y.V., 2009, "India and The Global Crisis : Managing Money and Finance", Orient Blackswan.

Rostow, W.W., 1990, "The Theorists of Economic Growth from David Hume to the Present with a Perspective on New Century", Oxford University Press.

Taylor, 1960, "History of Economic Thought", Tata McGraw Hill Company.

World Economic Situation and Prospects, 2009, United Nation Publication.

3

Global Financial Crisis and the Indian Economy

R. ARUNACHALAM

THE EAST ASIAN CRISIS

The Crisis in East Asia that occurred in mid-1990s is probably the major crisis following the Great Depression of 1929-30 that occurred in the U.S. What really accounted for the upheaval in nations like Thailand, Malaysia, Indonesia and Singapore should be addressed so as to have a better understanding of the Crisis that has emerged in the U.S. in mid-2006. The problem that occurred in East Asia had its forerunner in Latin American nations in the year 1980 and then in Mexico in 1994 followed by crisis in Norway and Sweden in early 1990s. In these nations there was problem of currency depreciation and speculative attacks coupled with large outflows.

The crisis that broke out in Thailand spread to Malaysia, Indonesia, the Philippines and then to South Korea. The G-7 nations attributed the crisis to domestic ills in the East Asian economies like improper judgment of the banks, and financial institutions, over speculation in real estate and the share market, the collusion between governments and business, the bad policy of having fixed exchange rates the dollar and rather high current account deficits. They avoided blaming the financial markets or currency speculation and the behaviour of huge institutional investors. On the other hand, another view attributed it to the global financial system, the combination of financial deregulation and liberalization across the world, the increasing interconnection of markets and speed of transactions through computed technology and the development of large institutional financial players namely the speculative hedge funds, the investment banks and the huge mutual and pension funds.

A large amount, to the tune of US $184 billion, entered developing Asian countries as net private capital flows in 1994-96 as per the Bank of International Settlements. In 1996, US $ 94 billion entered in and in the first half of 1997 another $ 70 billion flowed in. As the crisis gained momentum, $102 billion went out in the second half of 1997 and the large outflow continued since then. One can understand, based on the large magnitude of the flows, how much volatile they were and how capital flows can be subjected to the tremendous effect of herd instinct.

The crisis situation in Thailand was attributed to the action of financial speculation and hedge funds. The Thai government used up over US $20 billion of foreign reserves to ward off speculative attacks. The speculators seemed to have borrowed and sold Thai Baht receiving the US $ in exchange. When the Baht fell, the speculators needed much less dollars to repay the Baht loans, thus making huge profits. According to the *Business Week,* the hedge funds made around 10.7 per cent net profits on an average for the period January to June 1997. But the average profit rate soared to 19.1 per cent for January-July 1997. Thus there was tremendous windfall of profit in the month of July 1997.

The main causes for the crisis in East Asia may be summarized as: (1) Financial liberalization, (2) Currency depreciation and debt crisis, and (3) Liberalization and debt, the case of Malaysia. In the process of financial liberalization, the nations followed total convertibility both in the current and capital account of the balance of payments. This obviously facilitated large inflows of funds in the form of international bank loans to local banks and corporate purchase of bonds and portfolio investment in the local stock markets.

The increase in the short-term debts was alarming. The sudden depreciation in the currencies of Thailand, Malaysia and South Korea accounted for the crisis. This resulted in huge servicing obligations of their debts. The reserves in foreign exchange also fell simultaneously. The shot-term foreign funds started pulling out sharply. The reserves fell so badly that they could not meet their debt obligations and as a result these nations approached the IMF for help.

Malaysia also adopted financial liberalization speedily with freedom to invest foreign funds in the local market, for conversion between foreign and local currencies and for the exit of funds abroad. The Central Bank of Malaysia maintained a key control-restricting the private companies to borrow foreign currency loans to the tune of RM 5 million and making it obligatory to obtain the permission from the Central Bank. Besides, firms are not allowed to raise external borrowing to finance the purchase of properties in the country. Thus there was a policy of limiting private sector external loans to corporates and individuals with foreign exchange earnings. There seemed to have saved Malaysia from the kind of excessive short-term private sector borrowing that led the other three nations into a debt crisis.

The large inflow of funds into these economies contributed to an asset price boom and stock markets. With the depreciation of currencies and expectations of debt crisis, economic slowdown or further depreciation, substantial foreign funds left suddenly as withdrawal of loans and selling of shares. So share prices fell. With the weakened demand and increasing over-supply of buildings and housing, the prices of real estate fell significantly. The countries which encountered the problems of depreciation and share market declines had to tackle the following issues—

(1) Problem of heavy debt servicing, (2) Fall in the value of shares and buildings and other real estates leding to financial difficulties to the borrowers, (3) Enhanced interest rates caused by the liquidity squeeze and tight monetary policy stance further resulting in financial burden to all borrowers, and (4) Rising import prices caused by currency depreciation adding to the problem of inflation.

Thus the economic slowdown in the East Asian nations

also had its adverse impact on the growth rates of the countries. Though the balance of payments performance was a silver lining it happened at a heavy price as the trade surplus was caused by a fall in imports than a rise in exports.

DEBATE ON THE ROLE OF IMF

The IMF officials justified their severe medicine of high interest rates, tight monetary policy stance and the cut in the government expenditures administered to the crisis ridden nations stating that such measures would instill confidence of the investors in these nations. In any case there were opposite views about the efficacy of these programmes. In fact, the three nations fell in deep depression. These nations which suffered initial problems of currency depreciation and stock market decline, also suffered on account of debt repayment and a great deal of financial weakening of the corporate and banking sectors. The private corporate firms which were not involved in raising foreign loans also got affected by the liquidity crunch and the slowdown. The high interest rates in many of these economies caused them to become bankrupt. Therefore, many argue against the policies of the IMF to mitigate the problems of these nations. They argued that instead of raising the interest rates and cutting the government expenditure, these nations should have been advised by the IMF to reflate their economies through lowered interest rates and increased government spending. *The Financial Times* (London) expressed a strong opinion stating through their article titled "Asian Water Torture" with this sub-heading: "Unless the IMF allows the region's economies to reflate and lower interest rates, it will condemn them to a everlasting spiral or recession and bankruptcy."

Among the critics of the IMF's policies to salvage the problems of the East Asian Economies are Robert Wade of Brown University (US), Jeffrey Sachs of Harvard and Martin Feldstein of Harvard University. While Wade argued for a tougher stance to be taken by the Governments of these affected economies through rescheduling of negotiations with the creditor banks, lower interest rates to near zero and step on the monetary stance, Saches advocated the need for debt rescheduling exercises between the countries and their foreign creditors. Feldstein strongly criticized the short-term macro-economic policies of IMF expected to be followed by Korea.

THE U.S. FINANCIAL CRISIS

The economic and financial crisis that is affecting the global economies since the middle of 2007 had its origin in the United States (US), basically in the housing sector in the name of sub-prime crisis. At this juncture one has to recollect the Great Depression of 1929-30 that cropped up in the U.S. but it had its major impact on the rest of the world economies. The difference between the two economic upheavals is that in 1929-30 depression, global economies were not as integrated either financially or trade-wise as compared to the 2007 situation. Besides, that was time period of controls and regulations unlike decontrols and deregulations being widely followed as a paradigm of development in recent times.

What really caused the meltdown or global recession or the financial crisis as they are frequently reported in various quarters? The sub-prime crisis, as it is known, is the basic reason for the emergence of the financial crisis in U.S. It refers to giving credit facilities to borrowers who have inadequate credit history or inadequate documentation. This involves high stakes in the financial markets under uncertainty with risks associated with holding assets which are disproportionately high as compared to their realized returns. This was referred to as Minskian 'ponzi' that was dealt with by the post-Keynesian economist Hyman Minsky in 1986. Such transactions are unsustainable and hazardous as compared to acts of simple hedging or even speculation on asset prices in markets. (Sunanda Sen, 2008). The rate of interest charged in this market is higher due to higher risk involved in lending to people who do not show the required credit worthiness. The reasons being: (a) During the aftermath of the tech-bubble burst and the impending recessionary tendency in the U.S. the Federal Reserve of U.S. lowered the rate of interest to as low as 1.5 per cent in June, 2003, the lowest since 1958. This was an incentive for borrowers of credit in the housing sector. (b) For the borrowers, the rationale for taking out a mortgage loan was that with home prices in a secular uptrend, in a short span of time itself, the market value of mortgage house would outstrip both the principal and interest payment liability attached to it. The house could be sold in the open market and the excess of the market value of the mortgage house over the liability towards the mortgage would be the potential capital gain to the borrower. For the lenders, the mortgage giving institutions cooked up enticing credit instruments like the adjustable mortgage rate (ARM) to attract borrowers. The ARM is the one in which the rate of interest is lower for the initial two years and subsequently, for every 6 months it was enhanced. The mortgage backed securitization was a strong incentive to mortgage giving institutions to make the loans rampantly.

Mortgage backed securitization refers to the process of issuing securities on the back hand to disburse loans at high sub-prime rates not packaged as ARMs to make expensive loans though the issue of mortgaged backed securities and take the profits equal to the difference between the interest received on the sub-prime loan and the interest paid on the corresponding mortgage backed security.

Eventually, when the housing sector started showing signs of decline (as depicted in Figure 1) the borrowers could no longer think of selling their houses and settling-off their mortgaged liabilities attached to it. So borrowers could no longer benefit from refinancing. After availing the initial low interest rate on ARMs, when they had to pay higher interest rate, it caused a massive burden on foreclosures. Defaults on sub-prime loans had overnight transferred risky mortgage backed securities into junk. In the U.S. context, such junk loans quintupled over the years and found their way into various debt papers, bond and CDOs.

This apart, the U.S. government stood behind Fannie Mae and Freddie Mae and using the Housing and Economic recovery Act of 2008, increased the natural debt from 9.5 trillion to $14.8 trillion. The trouble U.S. Treasury Secretary Hank Paulson faced when working out the problem with Fannie Mae and Freddie Mae was that a sizeable number of mortgages used as collateral for the U.S. mortgage-backed securities markets were not real and did not exist. Catherine Austi Fits also reported that it took nearly 232 years for America to accumulate around $10 trillion in natural debts but only one new bill, bailing out Freddie Mae and Fannie Mae to clean up more housing bubble move to add

EXHIBIT I

Sub-prime Situation

Features of Prime Loans	Fea tures of Sub-prime Loans
➢ The borrower has a high credit score	➢ The borrower has poor credit history with low income and without any collateral.
➢ Borrower fully documents his income and asset	➢ The borrower and the asset do not meet the mandatory criteria for loan. So he has to pay additional interest to makeup for low credit score.
➢ Borrower's debt to income does not exceed 35 per cent.	➢ Borrower's debt income ratio may exceed 35 per cent. These borrowers have a much higher rate default than prime mortgage loans.
➢ The borrower retains two months of mortgage payments in reserves after closing. He also injects atleast 20 per cent equity.	➢ If the subprime borrower defaults which is very likely to happen, than the asset for which loan is taken is fore close.

another $5 trillion overnight. Between 1999 and 2001, anywhere around $10 trillion of private and public funds were pulled out of U.S. by fraudulent methods. If we consider different estimates of what would cost to end global poverty, ensure that all Americans have health care and no home is lost to foreclosure or to solve any other of the major problems we have, what we discover is this $10 trillion is more than enough to make significant inroads into solving most of the world's ills. The collateral fraud also took place on similar lines. Among other factors, it was observed by Pitts that had the U.S. Government produced proper financial statements as required by the law and had also produced such disclosures contiguous to congressional district, the housing bubble and a lot other problems could never have happened.

The US, which has been practicing capitalism with unbridled obsession with market mechanism as a paradigm of development and as an ardent champion of privatization and globalization, probably has paid a price for massive deregulation and mergers. The manner in which the crisis has spread from the financial sector to the external sector, monetary sector and now slowly to the real sector of both the developed and emerging economies has two major implications. They are, to what extent the dichotomy between the monetary sector and real sector as advocated by the classicals and neo-classicals has proved to be an anathema to the current situation and secondly, the basic economic indicator of globalization, deregulation has proved to be questionable as they are analogous to externalities of the adverse type. Indian economy, not-withstanding its reported strong macro fundamentals, and fairly high trajectory growth is not free from the adverse effects of happenings in the US economy. This apart, there are strong views that the Indian economy is affected by domestic as well as external factors thus causing the recessionary trend in the last two years.

REVIEW OF LITERATURE

Literature abounds with interesting empirical studies. The empirical study of Mihir Rakshit (2009) refers to the down trend on Gross Domestic Product (GDP) in the first quarter of 2007-08, and the down trend in primary sector, gross investment, export of goods and services, index of industrial production and the sharp down trend in private sector capital formation since 2004-05. He also refers to the basic weakness of the government policy relating to public private partnership as it relies on private funding of infrastructural investment projects through the provision via grants. Similarly, the slowdown in export growth in the pre-crisis period according to him is due to the type of policy followed.

Enduring the views of Rakshit, Ram Mohan chooses to contend that there is some merit in the decoupling hypothesis. That is emerging markets appear reasonably developed from the advanced economies as along as the downturn in the latter is moderate, though a services recession in the advanced economies has its effect on the developing economies. According to Ram Mohan, even though the corporate sector which relies increasingly upon overseas, the banking sector in India is better placed to manage the adverse effects of downtrend elsewhere. Dilip Nachane referring to the spread of the crisis to Indian economy finds that the crisis has its effects in terms of the decline in exports, foreign institutional investment and industrial investments, crashing of real estate prices, and that of rising unemployment. The government remedial measures, though to some extent safeguard the interest of well-off sections of the society, he doubts very much to what extent such measures would take care of the interest of the poor. The gross domestic savings of India is not affected by the financial crisis.

Amit Bhaduri examines the basic reasons for the crisis. Falling asset prices and shadow banking system which facilitated circular rather than vertical network of audit independence is prone to be vulnerable. According to him in the absence of adequate demand for liquidity from the real economy, the depressive economy conditions may continue. James Crotty is of the view that the present crisis is the latest phase of the evolution of financial markets under the radical financial deregulation process that began in the late 1970s. According to him, the structural flows in the US financial system resulted to bring on the current crisis.

Yet another study by Willi Semmler *et al.* (2009) describes the current credit crisis and explains the aspects of micro and macro features. The study recommends that if private profitability has to be encouraged it has to be along with private responsibility. It does not recommend bailouts for irresponsible, the greatly and the corrupt. If an institution too big is to fail and it is rescued by public funds, an appropriate oversight board is needed to oversee the flow of funds.

The work of Arun Kumar (2007) referring to the depth of the present crisis throws light on the different ways of understanding demand deficiency, which happened to be crucial for the earlier down trends in capitalist economies. Therefore, to retrieve the economy from the crisis, he advocates redistributive measures. In his paper on "Anatomy of the Financial Crisis: between Keynes and Schumpeter" Pulin B. Nayak (2009) argues that the stimulus package to fight the crisis ought to be in terms of long-run solutions addressing the needs of the poor. The paper of Ozlem Onran examines the consequences of the global economic and financial crisis for income distribution and then outlines implications. The policy implications include preventions of socialization of costs; solve the problem of distributional crisis, proper regulatory measures which would ensure avoidance of large private banks.

The work of Ramaa Vasudevan (2009) explores the root causes for the US credit crisis. According to her, the sub-prime crisis basically is responsible for the financial crisis in the US. However, the crisis spread through the shadow banking system which has been built on the shaky edifice of these sub-prime loans. This shadow banking system was fostered by brokers—dealers, investment banks, hedge funds, private equity groups, structured investment vehicles and conduits, money market funds and non-bank mortgage lenders which thrived on huge outcomes generated by the securitization of loans. Depreciation and a low interest rate regime put in place under US federal Reserve Chairman Alan Green Span (1987-2006) facilitated the under pricing of risk and the growth of shadow banking system. Ramaa Vasudevan also contends that financial assets were less than 5 times the size of the US GDP in 1980s, but over 10 times as large in 2007. The US credit market debt increased from around 1.6 times larger than the GDP in 1973 to over 3.5 times GDP by 2007. Added to these, there was the huge outflow of private capital from US to the emerging markets since 1980s. The counter-cyclical pattern of private capital flows to emerging markets, which has been a critical aspect of the financing of US deficit, began to loose traction in the context of sub-prime crisis.

IMPACT OF THE FINANCIAL CRISIS ON INDIA

India is no exception to the adverse effects of the financial crisis of the U.S., particularly, after the opening up of the economy and financial integration because firstly, foreign institutional investors have free play in Indian stock markets; Secondly, speculative flows have their impact on stock markets, and thirdly, there is an extensive use of derivatives as a legal basis in security exchanges. Derivative trading has increased six times the turnovers in spot trading at the National Stock Exchange. The rising level of inflows also faces problems of depletion which appear in the exchange rate of the rupee. The adverse effects will also be on the balance sheets of corporates with global exposures. It may also affect the real sector of the economy like the export sector.

Global Slowdown and Impact on Emerging Economies

The emerging market economies (EMEs) when compared to the developed economies are not that badly affected by the financial crisis of the globe. Domestic demand would be the major driver of growth in the EMEs, though the external risks through trade and financial channels would pose downward risks. According to the IMF, 1 per cent reduction in US GDP leads to 0.5 per centage point decline in the growth in advanced European economies with a six month lag, and about 0.75 per centage point decline in the growth of EMEs, taking into account the joint effect of a slowdown in the US and Europe. World trade is also expected to decelerate in 2008 by 1.2 per centage points as per the IMF and 1percengtage point as per the World Trade Organization, reflecting the expectations of slower global growth.

If China gets impacted from the global slowdown particularly in the US, it could have spillover impact on other economies. The impact through financial linkages in terms of capital flows to EMEs has moderated in recent times. Secondly, the IMF observes that the ability of the EMEs to remain decoupled from the substantial slowdown depends upon their productivity growth and stabilization gains from improved macroeconomic policy frameworks. A study by Akin and Loss, 2007 observes that US slowdown seems to be limited to certain sectors and financial market conditions are restored in a timely manner, spillovers to other economies could remain limited.

TABLE I

Sectoral Growth

	2000-01	2001-02	2002-03	2003-04	2004-05	2005-06	2006-07	2007-08	2008-09
Agriculture	-0.2	5.3	-7.2	10.0	0.0	5.9	3.8	5.1	2.6
Industry	6.4	2.4	6.8	6.0	8.5	8.0	10.6	7.5	4.2
Services	5.7	6.9	7.5	8.8	9.9	11.0	11.2	11.1	9.2
GDP @ factor cost	7.3	-	-	8.5	7.5	9.4	9.6	9.0	-
GDP @ market price	4.0	5.2	3.8	8.4	8.3	9.2	9.7	9.2	7.1

Sources: 1. Akin, Cigdem and Kose, M. Ayhan (2007), "Changing Nature of North-South Linkages, Stylized Facts and Explanations", IMF Working Paper No: 07/280.

2. Inrternational monetary Fund (2008), World Economic Outlook, April.

3. Kose, M. Ayan (2008), "Can Emerging Economies Decouple" as referred in RBI Annual Report, 2007-08, p. 141.

GDP expressed at factor cost as well as market prices exhibit (Table 1) fairly sustained growth rate during the period 2000-01 upto 2007-08, though in 2008-09, it records at 7.1 per cent. This should be attributed to the individual sectoral performance. Agriculture and related sectors, in general during the period of economic reforms measures show unstable growth owing to falling public investment in agriculture, declining capital formation and rising input prices. For example, in the year 2000-01 and 2002-03, the agriculture and related sectors show negative growth and zero rate of growth in 2004-05. Though the industrial and services show uptrend in terms of growth, during 2007-08, 2008-09 and 2009-10, they have recorded downtrend. The impact of financial crisis is felt in these sectors by way of liquidity crunch, crashing stock market performance and general pessimism of the corporate sector.

Table 2 shows the scenario of sources of savings and capital formation for specified selected years. The household sector savings obviously dominate the other sources accounting for 23-24 per cent of the GDP. The public sector saving is hardly a third of the corporate sector savings and around a twelfth of household sector savings. In any case, all these sources are on the rise. The gross domestic savings as a proportion of GDP increased from 30 per cent in 2003-04 to 37.9 per cent 2007-08. The Gross Domestic Capital formation keeps increasing between 2004-05 and 2006-07. However, the gross investment, net of capital imports is not steady as it plunged to 9 per cent in

TABLE 2

Gross Domestic Savings and Investment (as a % of GDP)

Category	*2003 -04*	*2004 -05*	*2005 - 06*	*2006 -07*	*2007 -08*
Household Savings	24.3	23.0	24.2	23.8	24.5
Private Corpo rate Savings	4.6	6.6	7.5	7.8	8.9
Public Sector Savings	1.1	2.2	2.6	3.2	4.5
Gross Domestic Savings	3.0	31.8	34.3	34.8	37.9
Gross Domestic Capital formation	25.2	32.2	35.5	35.9	34.2
Gross investment net of import of capital goods	19.9	19.1	16.8	9.3	19.0

Source: RBI, Annual Report, 2007-08 and Economic Survey, GOI, 2009-2010 as cited in *Times of India*, 3rd July '09, p. 12.

2006-07 from around 20 per cent in 2003-04. This has obvious adverse impact on the performance of investment sector, particularly, during the period of crisis. Though in general the period of crisis is reported to be a time of loss of jobs, in the IT sector and negligible fresh recruitment in the rest of the sectors, the savings trend in India does not seem to be adversely affected. A point noteworthy in this context is that Indian agricultural economy is by and large insulated from the developments in the urban employment as well as the adverse effects of the financial crisis. In addition, labour force engaged in the government sector as well as organized non-IT sector area is also not severely affected and so probably, the savings trend remains fairly steady. The industrial sector did record slow growth with falling employment.

Table 3 brings out the performance of selected infrastructural industries. Read interms of both the index and growth rates, it is observed that the electricity sector shows consistent growth rates. Of course, we do not compare here the growth rate of demand for electricity and its supply growth rate as the excess demand for electricity is a persistent problem in almost all part of India. In the same way, the coal industry also shows fairly consistent growth rate. The steel industry is consistent upto 2006-07, but recorded as 5.1 per cent growth rate during 2007-08. The unstable performance is seen both in regard to crude petroleum and petroleum refinery products. But it has its critical adverse effect on the industry and services sectors. The

TABLE 3

Growth of Selected Infrastructural Industries

Industry	*Index*		*Growth Rate*				
	2006-07	*2007-08*	*2003-04*	*2004-05*	*2005-06*	*2006-07*	*2007-08*
Electricity	204.7	217.7	5	5.2	5.2	7.3	6.3
Coal	172.8	183.2	5.1	6.2	6.6	5.2	6.0
Finished Steel	330.2	347.1	9.8	8.4	10.8	13.1	5.1
Cement	281.4	304.1	6.1	6.6	12.4	9.1	8.1
Crude Petroleum	125.8	126.2	0.7	1.8	-5.2	5.5	0.4
Petroleum Refinery Products	274.8	292.5	8.2	4.3	2.1	12.9	6.5

Source: Office of Economic Adviser, Ministry of Commerce and Industry.

unprecedented rise in oil prices during the middle of 2006-07 and 2007-09 had its effect on inflation, which shoot upto 12-13 per cent towards the end of 2008.

TABLE 4

Trade Sector

Category	*2003-04*	*2004-05*	*2005-06*	*2006-07*	*2007-08*	*2008-09*
Export growth (US $)	21.1	30.8	23.4	22.6	28.9	3.6
Import growth (US$)	27.3	42.7	33.8	24.5	35.4	14.4
Current a/c deficit % of GDP	2.3	-0.4	-1.2	-1.1	-1.5	-4.1
Foreign exchange reserves US $ billion	113	141.5	151.6	199.2	309.7	252

Source: Economic Survey, GOI, as cited in *Times of India*, 3rd July '09, p. 10.

Table 4 brings out the growth of exports, imports and current account balance. For the period from 2003-04 upto 2005-06, the export growth is sustained but subsequently it shows down trend. The magnitude of decline in export growth is quite pronounced during the period of the crisis namely 2007-08 and 2008-09. The fiscal year 2009-10 started on a dismal note with exports plunging by a massive 33.2 per cent during April and by 29.2 in May. In the same way the growth of imports which has recorded a rising trend upto 2007-08, fell significantly to around 14 per cent during 2008-09, thus recording more than 50 per cent decline. The gap between export growth and import growth is obviously reflected in the current account balance which has increased four fold between 2004-05 and 2008-09. However, foreign exchange reserves have increased more than 200 per cent during the above period. In the Indian context, large amount of investments have been made in the 100 per cent export-oriented units and special economic zones. The reduction in export growth rate would obviously cause slowdown. For example, exports of goods declined by 25.3 per cent between 2004-05 and 2006-07 and by around 12 per cent between 2006-07 and 2007-08. In the same way, imports also declined by 27 per cent and 15 per cent respectively during the above periods. The current account deficit increased by 3.7 per cent between 2005-06 and 2006-07, but by 55.2 per cent between 2006-07 and 2007-08.

The global slowdown has its impact on emerging economies (EMEs) too. Though the EMEs have so for remained insolated from the global slowdown, the growth prospects will also be affected by external factors. Rise in the risk aversion has already dampened private bond issuances in several EMEs and there remained the possibility of capital inflows drying up in present scenario. Besides, in the developing countries the recent increase in headline inflation caused by higher energy and food prices is of concern India is no expectation to this. In fact, though the rate of inflation is running single digit, food prices in India have sizably increased. This has tremendous adverse effect on the middle income and lower income groups.

The impact of US slowdown should also be considered in the trade front. According to the IMF, one per cent reduction in US GDP growth leads to 0.5 per centage point declining growth in advanced European countries with a six-month lag, and about 0.75 per centage points decline in the growth of EMEs, taking into account the joint effect of a slowdown in the US and Europe. The effect of US slowdown on the EMEs mainly takes place through trade linkages and financial linkages. Since China's trade with US is sizable, if China gets impacted from the global slowdown, particularly in US, it could have spillover effect on the other emerging economies. In the Indian context, large amount of investments have been made in the 100 per cent export-oriented units and special economic zones. The reduction in export growth rate would obviously cause slowdown.

Table 5(a) brings out the flows of FDI, portfolio and FII. Of course, FIIs are the major constituent of portfolio flows. We examine these flows for the three periods from 2006-07 to 2008-09. Going by the monthly flows, one can observe significant fluctuations in all these flows. However, after mid-2007, there are negative flows of portfolio, particularly, FIIs. During atleast 4 months in 2007-08 and 10 months in 2008-09, there are negative flows of portfolio and FIIs.

If we examine the net annual flows as shown in Table 5(b) we get the magnitude of decline in the flows of portfolio and FIIs. For example, as regards FDI, the total of the same in 2006-07 was $15585 million and it surged to $27307 million in 2008-09. In other words, in per centage terms FDI increased to 57.7 between 2006-07 and 2007-08, but fell sharply to 11.1 between

TABLE 5(a)

Foreign Capital Inflows (month-wise)

Category	April	May	June	July	August	Sept.	Oct	Nov	Dec	January	February	March	Total
	2006-07												
FDI	661	538	523	1127	619	916	1698	1151	5130	1921	698	603	15585
Portfolio	3711	-3334	-903	-309	1212	1238	1755	2236	-429	1602	2603	-2406	7405
FIIs	174	-1473	193	285	1173	1318	1879	2213	-599	-370	1834	82	+6409
	2007-08												
FDI	1643	2120	1238	705	831	713	2027	1864	1558	1767	5670	4438	24574
Portfolio	1974	1852	3656	6713	-2875	7081	9564	-107	5294	6739	-8904	-1600	29387
FIIs	1752	1265	269	5545	-1772	4609	5684	-1567	2204	-2747	1049	-250	16041
	2008-09												
FDI	3749	3932	2392	2247	2328	2562	1497	1083	1362	2733	1466	1956	27307
Portfolio	-880	-288	-3010	-492	593	-1403	-5243	-574	30	-614	-1085	-889	-13855
FIIs	-1432	-734	-3011	-459	464	-1403	-5240	-574	30	-614	-1085	-909	-15007

Source: RBI Monthly Bulletin, May 2009.

Note: Represents inflow of funds (net) by foreign institutional investment.

TABLE5(b)

Foreign Capital Inflows (Annual)

Category	*2006 -07*	*2007 -08*	*2008 -09*
FDI	15585	24574 (57.67)	27307 (11.12)
Portfolio	7405	29387(296.85)	-13855 (-147.17)
FIIs	6409	16041 (150.29)	-15007 (-193.55)

2007-08 and 2008-09. The impact of the crisis on FDI is thus pronounced. The scenario of portfolio and FIIs is still worse. The rate of increase in portfolio was nearly 300 per cent between 2006-07 and 2007-08, but the same nose-dived to minus 150 per cent between 2007-08 and 2008-09. FIIs alone, though increased to 150 per cent between 2006-07 and 2007-08, but fell steeply to (-)200 per cent. Thus, the impact of the financial crisis seems to be severe on the financial market.

IMPACT OF THE CRISIS ON THE INDIAN INSURANCE SECTOR

The impact of the global financial crisis on the Indian Insurance sector is not severe unlike the share market and to certain extent the banking sector. Insurance companies are generally financed by the premiums paid in advance and payments are subject to the occurrence of insured events. As long as they have built up reserves and investments which are calibrated to match the statistically anticipated claim amounts, there is no liquidity risk. They do not leverage to enhance expected investment returns, a fact that makes them less vulnerable when financial markets collapse. The insurance companies are very well diversified which adds as further shield. Most insurers have market-to-market losses on their asset portfolios. In the case of non-life, the losses will ultimately be borne by shareholders. In the life savings products, losses are usually shared between policy-holders and shareholders.

The relationship between the growth rate of GDP in nominal terms for India and the insurance premiums collected both life and on non-life is shown in Table 6.

The actual trend in the movements of GDP, Non-life and Life insurance premiums is also shown in Figure (Exhibit 2). It may be observed that over the different quarters, the movements in the different variables exhibit similar trend. In fact in the Indian context the impact of the financial crisis is not felt very much in the insurance sector. This does not mean that the crisis will not affect the insurance sector at all. As long as the insurance sector is part of the financial sector, if the crisis is prolonged and if the growth rate of the economy were to be affected seriously then its resultant impact will be on the insurance sector too. The

TABLE 6

Growth Rates of GDP, Non-life and Life Insurance Premiums

Year	*GDP*	*Non-life Ins. premium*	*Life Ins. premium*
2004-05:Q1			
2004-05:Q2	3.06	-11.25	30.62
2004-05:Q3	15.07	1.00	-0.86
2004-05:Q4	2.36	5.00	126.04
2005-06: Q1	-6.36	19.58	- 58.47
2005-06:Q2	1.52	- 1.02	50.63
2005-06:Q3	16.58	-1.09	24.44
2005-06:Q4	3.23	-5.54	86.07
2006-07:Q1	-7.38	41.25	-91.38
2006-07:Q2	4.50	-9. 13	15.95
2006-07:Q3	16.23	7.57	20.63
2006-07:Q4	4.07	3.83	38.16
2007-08:Q1	-8.32	14.90	-52.83
2007-08:Q2	1.66	12.41	65.03
2007-08:Q3	15.95	6.50	-11.23
2007-08:Q4	5.34	6.48	44.10
2008-09:Q1	-6.53	15.10	-63.60
2008-09:Q2	3.68	-15.03	41.69

Source: Computed from Insurance Regulatory and Development Authority and The Reserve Bank of India.

work of Aashim Joy (2009) brings out the positive association between gross domestic saving and that the total premiums collected for the period 1990-91 and 2006-07. It also shows the rate of return on insurance investments—both life and non-life insurance investments during the middle 2000 which are positive over the period, particularly during the financial crisis period.

CONCLUSION

The East Asian Crisis of 1997 is the fore runner of the financial crisis that has emerged basically in US economy, particularly in the form of sub-prime crisis during the middle of 2007 and has its adverse effects both in the developed and emerging economies. Recent empirical works on the US financial

EXHIBIT 2

The Growth Rates of GDP, Life and Non-Life Insurance Premiums

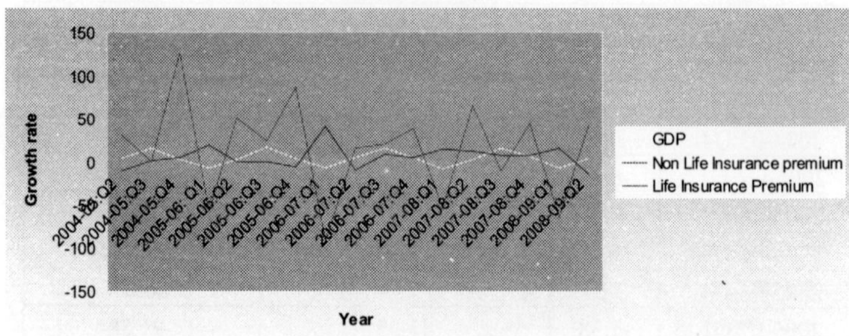

crisis attribute its emergence to sub-prime crisis in the housing sector, failure of Fannie Mae and Freddie Mae, shadow banking radical financial deregulation and the failure of the big financial companies. This study reveals that the global crisis has its adverse affects on the stock market, trade sector in terms of declining exports and increase in current account balance, growth rate of the industrial sector and fall in net flows of foreign capital both foreign direct investment and foreign institutional inflows. At the same time, the growth of savings and capital formation, infrastructure industries and insurance sector have not been affected. However, the growth rate of the economy and sub-sectoral growth rates have suffered, though not significantly, after the outbreak of the global crisis.

If suitable remedial measures are undertaken without mach of time lag, depending upon the effectiveness of such measures, the recovery would take place. In any case, the pace of recovery in the US economy would be very slow as it happens to be the place where the impact of the crisis is severe.

REFERENCES

Aashim Joy (2009), Ramification of the Financial Crisis on the Insurance Industry: Predominantly Indian Insurance Sector, Unpublished Project Report, submitted to Madras School of Economics, May 2009.

Amit Bhaduri (2009), Understanding the Financial Crisis, *Economic and Political Weekly*, Vol. XLIV, No.13, March 28-April 3, p. 123.

Arun Kumar (2009), "Tackling the Current Global Economic and Financial Crisis:

Beyond Demand Management", *Economic and Political Weekly*, Vol. XLIV, No. 13, March 28-April 3, p. 151.

Catherine Austin Fitts, "The Housing and Economic Recovery Act of 2008", http://www.goldseek.com accessed on 23rd August, 2008.

Dilip Nachane, (2009), "The Fate of India Unincorporated, *Economic and Political Weekly*, Vol. XIIV, No. 13, March 28-April 3, pp. 115-22.

James Crotty (2009), Profound Structural Plans in the US Financial System that helped causes the Financial Crisis, *Economic and Political Weekly*, Vol. XLIV, No. 13, March 28-April 3, p. 127.

Martin Khor, Director, The Economic Crisis in East Asia (largely adopted), www.google.co.in accessed on 30th July 2009.

Mihir Rakshit (2009), "Indian Amidst Global Crisis", *Economic and Political Weekly*, Vol. XIIV, No. 13, March 28-April 3, pp. 94-106.

Ozlem Onaran (2009), "A Crisis of Distribution", *Economic and Political Weekly*, Vol. XLIV, No. 13, March 28-April 3, pp. 171-78.

Pulin B. Nayak (2009), "Anatomy of Financial Crisis: Between Keynes and Schumpeter", *Economic and Political Weekly*, Vol. XLIV, No. 13, March 28-April 3, p. 158.

Ram Mohan, T.T. (2009), "The Impact of the Crisis on the Indian Economy', *Economic and Political Weekly*, Vol. XIIV, No. 13, March 28-April 3, pp. 107-14.

Ramaa Vasudevan (2009), "The Global Meltdown: Financialisation, Dollar Hegemory and the Sub-Prime Market Collapse", *Economic and Political Weekly*, Vol. XLIV, No. 13, March 28-April 3, pp. 193-99.

RBI, 2007-08, Annual Report p. 141.

Sunanda Sen (2008), Global Financial Crisis: A Classic Ponzi Affair, Main Stream, October 24-30, pp. 11-14.

The Hindu Business Line, August 5, 2009, p. 9

Willi Semmler and Lucas Bernard (2009), "Banking complex securities and the credit crisis", *Economic and Political Weekly*, Vol. XLIV, No. 13, March 28-April 3, p. 143.

India's Revival Agenda and Global Economic Crisis

AMALESH BANERJEE

I. INTRODUCTION

Although originated in the USA, the current global economic crisis has affected the economies of both developed and developing countries in varying degrees. Those countries that have deeper economic relations with advanced countries, particularly USA, are affected more than those who maintain a closed economy status. However, under the present globalized economic structure of the world no country can remain immune from this global downturn. Continent-wise, Europe is more affected than the countries of Asia. In Asia, China, Japan and East Asian countries are relatively more affected than other Asian countries. They have open economies and since late last century have been building open economy trade relations with United States and other advanced countries. They have already withstood the onslaught of Asian crisis of 1997. However, India is in a unique position. The present paper initially in section II makes some observations on the genesis of depression in general. Section III deals with the current global crisis and its causes and ramifications. How Asian countries, particularly India and China are affected is also discussed. This section also deals with how the present crisis is different from the past events. Section IV deals with India's revival agenda and its limitations. Section V offers some conclusions. It is observed that India is successfully combating the present economic crisis as she did during the East Asian financial crisis of 1997. The current revival agenda of the Govt. of India is likely to revamp the economy in the growth path.

II. GENESIS OF DEPRESSION

Economic recession that took place over last century had provided interesting inputs for theoretical debate among the economists to formulate the recovery agenda. The fundamentalists argue that recession takes place due to technological shocks. Real business cycle theorists, the hard core fundamentalists find explanation of downturn in capital erosion and prescribe, in Walrasian form work, that the recession will pass through the natural process of creative destruction and then the equilibrium will be restored. They consider the recession as a necessary remedial process of the capitalist economy which is prone to short run and long-run fluctuations. Real business cycle theories point out that output fluctuation results from changes in technology that bring about changes in production function from period to period. Contemporary evidence shows that technology shocks and propagation mechanism of real-business cycle models are of little relevance to actual fluctuation. Actually it is the nominal disturbances and failure of the nominal prices and wages to adjust to those disturbances that are central to fluctuations.

As against the real business cycle theories, Keynesian and New-Keynesian theories are based on analyses of the demand shocks and also on various non-Walrasian features such as externalities, asymmetric information, imperfect competition and market failure. While the real business cycle theories point to the supply shocks due to change in production technology, the Keynesians point to the demand shocks that arise due to various asymmetries and imbalance between savings and investment. Keynesian explanations of Great Depression of 1936 reverberated during the rest of the century and do so even today. Over last quarter of the last century, recession surfaced several times in 1973s, 1978 due to oil shocks. It is also explained that unrealistic monetary policy of Fed had contributed to the deep recession in 1982 and in 1991. In 1993 the Fed came to realize that there were fundamental weaknesses in the financial system that restricted the revival of the economy.

The asymmetric exchange rate, currency crisis, the contagion effect and the fallout of banking crisis are all the live events of financial crisis. A side issue of that is the asset bubble of Japan which caused slowdown in Japanese economy. This is different from the broad money supply of the Monetarists which has a different kind of explanation of business cycle, emphasizing squarely the importance of the Central Bank in business cycle. East Asian crisis, the contagion effect over a broad region of countries, brought to the fore the importance of finance capital and the impact of IMF sponsored liberalization. It thus appears that under the current liberalized and globalized capital market, economic crisis are very likely to originate in financial world which percolate down to the real sector, resulting in decline in output and rise of unemployment.

III. CURRENT GLOBAL CRISIS AND INDIA

During the current global crisis, India is doing economic management effectively. Indian economy is affected like the many advanced country economies, but the effects are limited.

The current economic meltdown originated in the financial sector of the US. In 1970's the US adopted tight monetary policy in order to control inflation. US financial sector devised many new instruments in order to avoid the credit crunch.

Such devices are swaps, securitization and derivations which are outside the regulatory mechanism of the Fed. However, these instruments facilitated the corporates and households to take credit for property acquisition on the basis of mortgage. This is called sub-prime lending as the borrowers are not rated as prime and do not have sound track record, but are given loans as long as property prices continue to rise. With the fall of property prices payment of instalments stopped and the sub-prime mortgage crisis began to surface in August 2007. The collapse of Lehman Brothers in September 2008 was followed by closure and bankruptcy of financial institutions such as mortgage banks and investment banks holding these toxic assets. Credit flow dried up, money market interest rates scored up and business confidents slumped. In the process the global meltdown began and the financial institutions were severally hit in many countries. When credit flow dried up, industrial houses and multinationals were equally impacted. This scenario was followed by closure of businesses, loss of jobs, deferment of investment plans. Since the global economic scenario is inter-connected through financial sector, trade connections and exchange rate, any strain developed in any of these are transmitted to other countries connected with these channels. Millions of job loss and collapse of financial institutions in all developed and developing countries had become almost rampant.

This global phenomenon had hit India also. Our information technology sector was severally hit India's major exports such as textile, carpet, leather, gems and jewelries, all labour intensive industries were equally affected. There was a huge loss of jobs. The IT sector also witnessed job losses. Therefore, both the organized and the un-organized sectors have been bitten. Effect on India's financial sector was not direct but indirect. As industries were affected and unemployment developed, credit delivery was restricted. With low confidence in industry, the credit market was also shaken and the financial institutions restricted credit for expansion. Liquidity crunch developed as the financial institutions held toxic assets and were not ready to part with liquidity.

China has been also affected. Millions of Chinese urban labour force have become jobless as Chinese exports have fallen significantly affecting Chinese balance of payments. This urban jobless labour force has been shifted to the rural sector with billions of bail out package.

Before we turn to the revival agenda of India for the present economic crisis, let us remember the events of 1936 when India suffered severely during Great Depression.

The Great Depreciation hit India's export trade seriously. Agricultural price had fallen and export of agricultural products declined. This had serious effect on farmers and farmers indebtedness increased abnormally. Gold exports supplemented the export of other merchandise and saved the situation for the government which was determined to keep the exchange rate fixed at ____. The Reserve Bank (1935) was not yet born. The then government maintained protectionism and was not in favour of government running budget deficit for public works or pump priming which were Keynesian method of defeating depression. In fact the Keynesian recovery agenda had not yet become popular and government maintained *lassiez faire* attitude to gold exports, even though the economists did favour cheap money policy and planned policy of public works in order to meet the depression. Rather, the government policy was strong to maintaining exchange rate and weak in respect of combatting depression.

The depression period was divided in three phases: (1) October 1929 to June 1930, (2) the fourteen-month period from July 1930 to August 1931, and (3) sixteen months from September 1931 to December 1932. During the first phase, primarily the producing countries were affected, with filthy exports and export prices and consequent balance of payment difficulties. During the second phase, depression spread to manufacturing countries and affected employment, income, prices, stock markets, government budgets and balance of payment. During this phase Britain and some other countries suspended gold standard. During the third phase the depression deepend and monetary measures were found wanting. Banking crisis were in many countries including India. Depression in Indian economy resulted in rise in overdues of loans of agricultural cooperative societies, fall of railway freight, fall of coal and cotton production.

By second half of 1930, output of jute, cotton, paper, cement, iron and steel made some progress. At the international level also recovery programme began to take place. Roosevelt came to office in March of 1933 and came out with New Deal which suspended gold payments by banks and by implication gold standard. Direction action came in effect through National Recovery Act in the USA.

IV. INDIA'S REVIVAL AGENDA

Although not as seriously affected by current global recession as the USA and other advanced countries, India has taken a strong 'Mission 2010 Reforms and Revival' agenda in order to attain economic growth of 9 per cent again. The one point revival programe is composed of augmenting demand which has been struck off both in domestic front as well as in the external front. Hence the revival programme of India, declared in different phases, is directed to increase external export and generating demand in the rural and urban sector of the economy. Following the Keynesian strategy of pump priming, the government has embarked upon a huge expenditure for generating new employment and infrastructure in the rural and urban sector. This has been aimed at meeting double challenges—the impact of global recession and daunting drought throughout the country.

Government of India has taken the following strands of action to bail out the economy : (a) Several fiscal measures have been announced to encourage the export industries and to encourage the inflow of external capital. (b) Host of monetary measures have been announced by the RBI in order to increase the liquidity in the country. Monetary instruments such as SLR, Repo and reverse repo have been related to enhance the flow of credit to the industries. (c) Specific booster doses have been announced for housing, textile, steel and leather. (d) Huge amount of money has been sanctioned for several items of infrastructure front in the rural as well as urban sector. (e) Large amount of money has been announced for National Rural Employment Guarantee Scheme (NREGS) and several other on going programmes for rural infrastructure and housing. (f) Special focus has been given to farmers who are debt-ridden and poor. Apart from farmers debt waiver scheme, other schemes also have been given for farmers' development. Thus stimulus (i) for export, (ii) relaxation of monetary policy for regular flow of liquidity to the industry, and (iii) extensive expenditure by the Government to support the farmers and infrastructure have created a dynamic process for growth.

India is now in the forefront of recovery, along with Germany, France, US and China. India's economic base is strong such as high rate of saving, high rate of growth, protected monetary structure and vast domestic market with expanding demand.

It is expected that the huge recovery agenda taken by the Govt. of India will enable it to overcome the twin challenge of drought and depression. When inflation has come down, the course is easy to augment supply and demand so that economy reaches to the high level of growth again.

V. CONCLUSION

Current global recession is the outcome of mismanagement of the complex and irrational financial activities of capitalist worlds of which the USA is the central point. In a globalized financial world, the fallout of the activities of greedy financial institutions and manipulators has overcast the economies of different countries. Keynes has long ago correctly diagnoised the ills of the system and also shown the positive path for correction. The monitory authority has failed again and again to contain this diseases of capitalist economic structure. He had prescribed the positive stimulus of the government because the monetary authority will be unable to lead the economy to high growth path free from fluctuations.

Unlike the advanced capitalist economies, India has certain advantages. The high rate of savings, protected monetary sector, high rate of growth and growing information technology industry are the silver line for India's success. The current survival agenda with particular focus on augmenting domestic demand and inclusive growth will energize the rural sector, encourage export and will enable sustainable development. The present steps taken for infrastructure development and rural employment will generate more employment and income. With inflation regulated, the stimulus agenda will open the broad channel for robust growth. However, the leadership of steering the economy should not be left to the free market forces. Rather, the government must regulate all sectors in order to promote a balanced growth free of serious dislocation from international and domestic forces.

References

Banerjee, A. (2009), India's Inclusive Growth in the Age of Globalization. Kanishka Publishers and Distributors, New Delhi.

Banerjee, A. (2003), Issues of Financial Reforms, Kanishka Publishers and Distributors, New Delhi.

Galbraith, J.K. (1987), Economic in Perspective, Houghton, Rifflin Company, Boston.

Mankiw, N. Gregory (1992), Macroecoomics.

Montial, Peter J. (2003), Macroeconomics in Emerging Markets, Cambridge University Press.

Rai, Gobinda M. (2009), The Fiscal Situation and Reform Agenda for the New Govt., *EPW*, June 20.

Romer, David (1996), Advanced Macroeconomics, The McGraw Hill Companies Inc.

State Bank of India (2003), The Evolution of the State Bank of India, Vol. 3, Sage Publications of India Pvt. Ltd., New Delhi.

Stiglitz, Josheph E. and Bruce Greenwals (2003), Towards a New Paradigm in Monetary Economics, Cambridge University Press.

5

Global Financial Crisis and its Impact on the Indian Economy

S.B. Mishra

INTRODUCTION

On 15th September 2008 the global economy contemplated the worst financial turmoil since the Great Depression of 1930's being triggered by the ideosyncratic spurt in mortgage delinquencies and foreclosures in the United States with adverse consequences for banks, financial markets, exports, employment, wages and salaries, consumer expenditures and tax revenue collections all over the world. The sprawling financial contagion across the globe was marked by the debacle of the major US Investment Bank, Lehman Brothers Holding Inc. The genesis of the crisis can be traced back to the recklessness or financial profligacy of the US banking system that disbursed loans to sub-prime borrowers who had no track record of redemption of loans from their income; sub-prime lending was advanced with speculative bubbles or with the extrapolation that the real-estate boom would enable the debtors even with dodgy credit backgrounds to reimburse the loans as domestic prices escalate at an unprecedented rate. The global financial crisis germinating from 15th September 2008 not only shattered US economy but the global economy was entrapped in the cobweb of depression. The crisis originated when Lehman Brothers, the fourth largest US Securities House established in 1850 plunged into bankruptcy position in New York when it failed to survive the global financial turmoil and lost colossal amount of $ 639 billion. Synchronizingly its rival Morgan Stanley was purchased by Bank of America at half the prevailing market capitalization to save the ailing company. The world's biggest Insurance Company American Investors Group (AIG) sought financial assistance to the tune of $ 85 bn.

The causes of the crisis include mortgage repayment defaults, high risk lending, excessive speculation during boom period, high personal and corporate debt level, large scale sale of risky securities on the support of dubious credit ratings, lack of proper financial regulation in US and European countries, international trade imbalances and lack of proper government regulations. The present study makes an ingenious endeavour at exploring the genesis of global financial crisis, impact of the financial contagion on the Indian economy and policy paradigms to tide over the depressionary pangs on the Indian economy.

The entire study is based on secondary data and information elicited from *EPW*, competition Refresher Publications, Standard Books, *Economic Times*, *Times of India* newspapers and Economic Survey of Govt. of India.

The present Study has been schematized into four sections. Section I encompasses introduction, objectives, methodology and plan of the study. Section II incorporates genesis of the global financial crisis. Section III delineates the incidence of global financial crisis on different sectors of Indian economy and Section IV focuses on policy paradigms to tide over the crisis.

GENESIS OF THE GLOBAL FINANCIAL CRISIS

Global financial crisis was triggered by sub-prime lending. The two important catalysts of the sub-prime crisis were the influx of large funds from private sector and banks entering into the mortgage bond market and predatory lending practices of mortgage brokers especially the adjustable rate mortgage loans. The credit rating agencies assigning investment grade ratings to Mortgage Based Securities (MBS) were instrumental in influencing large scale sale of such risky securities. The rating agencies suffered from conflicts of interest as they were paid handsomely by Investment Banks and other firms that organise and sell structured securities to investors.

Lehman Brothers Holding Inc., filed for bankruptcy protection, making it the largest casualty of the global credit crisis and surrendered its assets at the time of filing. Lehman surpassed World Com as the biggest US bankruptcy filing till date. The Investment Banker had $ 639 bn. assets at the time of filing, while World Com had about $ 107 bn. when it filed the same in 2002. The chapter II filing did not include Lehman's broker-dealer operations and other units such as asset management from Neuberger Berman and these will continue to operate although Lehman is expected to liquidate them. Lehman is among the biggest investment banks to collapse since 1990. The chapter II filing represented the end of 158 years old company that survived World Wars, Asisan Financial Crisis and the collapse of long-term capital management, though not the global credit crunch. Financial Institutions globally have recorded more than $ 500 bn of write-downs and credit losses as the US sub-prime mortgage crisis has engulfed other markets. Lehman had $ 600 bn. of assets financed with just $ 30 bn. of equity at the end of August 2008 which implied that a 5% decline in assets would wipe out the value of the Company which investors contemplated as a real risk of billions of dollars of mortgage securities. The bankruptcy filing comes after plenty of heated negotiations among regulators and wall street firms about Lehman's fate. The US Government had refused to back Lehman's worst assets, the way it did for Bear Stearns Cos Inc.'s sale to JP Morgan chase.

Lehman Brothers Holding Inc was a global financial services firm which conducts business in investment banking, equity and fixed income sales, research and trading investment management, private equity and private banking. It is a primary dealer in the US Treasury securities market. Its primary subsidiaries include Lehman Brothers Inc., Neuberger Berman

Inc., Aurora Loan Services Inc., SIB Mortgage Corporation, Lehman Brothers Bank FSB, Eagle energy partners and the Crossroads group.

Sub-prime Mortgage Crisis

In August 2007 the firm closed its sub-prime lender BNC Mortgage eliminating 1200 positions in 23 locations and took an after tax charge of $ 25 million and $ 27 million reduction in goodwill. Lehman stated that poor market conditions in the mortgage space necessitated a substantial reduction in its resources and capacity in the sub-prime space. In 2008 Lehman faced an unprecedented loss in the continuing sub-prime mortgage crisis. Lehman's loss was apparently a result of holding large positions in sub-prime and other lower rated mortgage tranches when securitising the underlying mortgages. Huge losses occurred in lower rated mortgage backed securities throughout 2008. In the fiscal quarter, Lehman reported losses of $ 2.8 billion and was forced to sell off $ 6 billion in assets. In the first half of 2008 alone, Lehman stock lost 73% of its value as the credit market continued to tighten. In August 2008 Lehman reported that it intended to release 6% of its work force, 1500 people just ahead of its third quarter reporting decline in September 2008. On 15th September 08 in New York, Lehman Brothers Holdings announced the filing of chapter II bankruptcy protection citing bank debt of $ 613 billion, $ 155 bn. in bond debt and assets worth $ 639 bn., the filing of mark which the largest bankruptcy in US history. Barclays announced its agreement to purchase, subject to regulatory approval.

Merrill Lynch

In 1907 Charles Merrill arrives in New York to work for a textile company. In 1914 the company opened its door. Edmund Lynch joins him and jointly opened an office at 7, Wall Street. In 2006 Merrill added billions of dollars of mortgage to its balance sheets, by first Franklin Financial Corp, a sub-prime mortgage lender. In 2007 Merrill expunged its chairman Stanley O' Neal and John Thain look over. In 2008 losses began cumulating at $ 19.2 bn. In June, 2008 Merrill scrambled to raise capital and sell risky assets. In September, 2008 Merrill agreed to be acquired by Bank of America for $ 29 per share.

AIG

American Investors Group accumulated $ 18.5 bn. losses upto September, 2008 and required $ 75 billion capital to compensate loss. When US Federal Reserve declined to provide financial support, AIG was forced to seek government rescue before rating agencies slashed its ratings and forced it to post-billions of dollars in additional collateral on derivatives contracts it insured.

The global financial crisis can be attributed to macro-economic management and financial sector regulation.

MACROECONOMIC EXPLANATIONS

Firstly, US built up large current account deficits, whereas some countries in Asia built up current account surplus and lent to US. Since these recurring imbalances persisted over the years, correction was warranted by the markets.

Secondly, in many countries, macroeconomic policies resulted in gross inequalities in income and wealth. For example median wage was constant in real terms despite the growth of output in US. Consequently there has been deficiency in aggregate demand which did not manifest as long as the illusion of economic activity was maintained by the excessive development of the financial sector. These excesses in the financial sector created an illusion of sustainable activity in the real sector for quite some time, but it could not last. The sub-prime crisis in the US was only one of the symptoms of the lack of aggregate demand, coupled with excessive financialisation of the economy and excessive leverage, i.e. utilizing a far larger proportion of borrowed or others money relative to one's own in undertaking risky business.

Thirdly, in view of the underdeveloped nature of financial markets in some developing economies, the domestic savings in those economies could not be fully channeled into the required domestic investments and hence there was a surplus of savings in these countries.

Fourthly, the monetary policy, especially in the US, was excessively accommodative, i.e. allowing the supply of money to be plentiful and interest low, relative to appropriate level, for several years resulting in excess liquidity. This excess liquidity caused investors to search for yields and other under price risks. Such excess liquidity found its way into speculative activities causing asset bubbles. Such real estate boom was based on the contention that housing prices will be sky- rocketed in future.

Fifthly, some Central bankers were focused exclusively on price stability and many of them were mandated to focus on this through inflation targeting regimes. In addition, there was no formal mandate to any particular institution to maintain financial stability and hence the relatively low emphasis of such stability in public policy. Financial stability implies the existence of uninterrupted financial transactions as well as an acceptable level of confidence in the financial system and an absence of excess volatility that unduly adversely affects the normal real economic activity.

Sixthly, many Central banks were persuaded to be very transparent and provide forward guidance to financial markets on their policy stance, especially on the future course of monetary policy. Such forward guidance provided excessive comfort to financial markets and enabled them to under price risks.

Seventhly, even when some of the central banks perceived the under pricing of risks, financial market agents asserted that the central banks could not adjudge prices set by a competitive market and assured policy-makers that markets would correct themselves automatically. The central banks were informed by financial market agents time and again that the dangers of policy mistakes were more than the prospects of markets not correcting themselves smoothly. The central banks were obviously persuaded by these arguments and as a result did not act or intervene.

Eighthly, some of the central banks perceived that there were excessive risks in the system, but concluded that due to the emergence of new intermediaries like hedge funds and new derivative instruments, such risks were dispersed widely, especially among those who could afford to bear them with no impact on the financial system as a whole even though the risks did not disappear. Overall the central banks seem to have ignored the economic imbalances and asset bubbles that were building up and thus failed to act in a counter cyclical fashion to moderate though not eliminate the boom bust cycle.

Ninthly, multilateral institutions like IMF which were

charged with the responsibility of surveillance, gave warnings about macroeconomic imbalances. However they did not bring out the extent of the vulnerabilites of the global economy in general and the systemically important economies in particular. The multilateral institutions were constrained partly because they were dominated by select countries that were unwilling to subject their economies to objective surveillance and infact encouraged the institutions towards an excessively market oriented ideology.

Tenthly, there is dollar hegemony. The global economic system was subject to the undue influence of the polices of one country. This dependence of the global economy on one currency by itself had the potential for instability and in any case could have facilitated excessive risk taking by the public policy in the US. This could also partly explain the smooth financing of the twin deficits in the current account of the balance of payments in the external sector and the fiscal account of the government of the US by the rest of the world for several years, resulting in a huge build up of global imbalances.

REGULATION OF THE FINANCIAL SECTOR

A second set of explanations relate to the regulatory environment in which financial markets were functioning. It is well recognised that the problem of sub-prime lending for housing in the U.S. was only a proximate cause or simply a trigger. The sub-prime lend was also a case of irresponsible lending and ignorant borrowing, rather than a programme of financial inclusion. Such lending was facilitated by regulatory environment that was driven by vested interests which benefited excessive lending in the deregulated financial environment. The explanations most commonly advanced in respect of financial sector are epitomized below:

(i) The regulators in the financial sector did not have the adequate skills to cope with the rapid growth in the variety and complexity of market innovations in financial products.

(ii) The principle based regulation adopted by some of the regulators left too much of discretion to the regulated entities to manage their own risks.

(iii) The regulators concentrated on mitigating the entry level risks in the individual-regulated institutions through micro-prudential regulation, rather than the risks to the system through macro-prudential monitoring and regulation. The regulators did not recognize the need for counter cyclicality in regulation, thus amplifying the boom and bust cycle, i.e. the need to tighten regulation when the economy was experiencing an excessive exuberance and relaxing it during a period of unjustified pessimism.

(iv) The liquidity risks in the operations of financial entities were ignored and this was also not built into the Basel II prudential norms. While the prudential norms focused on the quality of assets, they did not reckon the pattern of funding of such assets, e.g. there are consequences of funding long-term assets with short-term funds.

(v) The off-balance sheet items and investment vehicles and their potential impact on capital adequacy were not fully captured by the regulators.

(vi) The regulators focused on regulating commercial banks, ignoring the development of shadow banking system. Non-bank entities such as investment banks, hedge funds, private equity firms, etc. remained unregulated and hence turned out to be sources of risk.

(vii) The regulators relied heavily on ratings assigned by credit rating agencies, particularly in implementing Basel II. They failed to adequately regulate the Credit Rating Agencies even though they were relying heavily on the ratings. The ratings proved to be unreliable and possibily motivated by the prevailing framework of incentives and conflicts of interests.

(viii) The regulatory structures were inadequate since multiple regulators facilitated regulated arbitrage by the market participants and thus exacerbated the risks.

(ix) The global framework for cross border institutions regulation and supervision was weak, although the financial markets and institutions were globalised.

(x) In a bid to attract the financial services industry to their jurisdictions, regulators in international financial centres such as London and New York adopted a policy of relatively soft regulation named as light touch regulation.

It is generally accepted that the environment in which market participants operated also contributed to the crisis.

(i) The accounting standards were pro-cyclical, especially due to the policy of mark to markets rules of valuation of assets and liabilities. The mark to market rules require that the assets and liabilities be valued from time to time as per the prevailing market values which tend to give a high valuation when the economy is in boom and depress values when the economy is in a bust.
(ii) The incentive framework especially investment banks, hedge funds and private equity funds, etc. encouraged excessive risk takings. The remuneration policies for senior management in particular were set in such a way that gave no incentive to encourage prudent behavuour. Since they got hefty bonuses based on short-term performance irrespective of the long-term risks assumed in the process.
(iii) The banks developed a business model wherein they originated loans but distributed the credit risks inherent in such loans to others. This led to manifold increase in the leverage. The securitization was a convenient tool to avoid additional regulatory capital. These practices were carried to excesses resulting in a huge increase in the overall leverages in the financial sector.
(iv) Greed became an accepted and generally respectable norms of behaviour in the financial sector resulting in a build up of excessive risks.
(v) Complexity in financial instruments helped profit-seeking by ensuring savings on regulatory capital requirements and defeated the purpose of transparency prescribed by the regulator.

(vi) The global financial system was dominated by a few large financial conglomerators and these were fully aware that they were too big to fail. Such awareness by itself provided incentives to be big enough and then take up risky ventures. The crisis originated in large globally significant financial institutions.

(vii) The tax havens and bank secrecy laws provided opportunities for maximizing profits through tax avoidances and the avoidance of applicable regulations.

There are three sets of inter-related facts which seem to capture the nature of this financial vulnerability.

Firstly, there emerged a set of financial institutions and companies that were in the lending business unlike commercial banks but had no lender of last resort. They resembled instead a shadow banking system which lacked the explicit backing of monetary authority on the one hand and escaped largely its regulation on the other hand.

Secondly, without a lender of last resort at the top, innovative shadow banking resulted in circular rather than a vertical network of credit interdependence in which shadow bankers especially large investment banks went into securitization of these debts by mixing them in different ways.

Thirdly, by treating each others debts as assets in the capital base for lending, the volume of lending could be expanded enormously. Low margin, high volume by pushing loans to more risky borrowers named as sub-prime lending. However, this circular credit structure was subject to two opposing magnifying effects from the beginning. On the one hand, the capital base itself became increasingly vulnerable due to magnifying effect of each defaulted loan, as each loan was linked or correlated with the asset base of several other shadow bankers in whose asset structure those securitized loans had entered. This double magnification largely accounted for the fragile circular credit structure on the supply side. Continuous innovations in credit instruments rapidly raised leverage while increasing the number of layers raised both the proportion of non-performing loan and reduced the capital base in a magnified way in case of each default through its correlation effect on the shadow banking system as a whole.

These ideas can be made more precise through a formal model comprising the demand and supply of credit in the shadow banking system as mentioned above. Let 'n' denote number of layers leveraged on the capital base B and 'q' denote proportion of performing loans,

$$(1>q>0),\ q = q\ (n)\ q'\ (n) < 0 \qquad \text{....(1)}$$

The capital base 'B' depends positively on the level of economic activity 'Y'. It also depends on 'n', but the nature of dependence is more complicated. The variable 'n' depends on financial innovations and could be looked upon as an index of the degree of quantity rationing of credit. The typical index of price rationing of credit is the interest rate 'i' which is assumed to be at its minimum value and left out from the model upto some threshold value of 'n'. More assets might be created through securitisation to augment the capital base so that 'B' increases with 'n' but beyond that threshold value, a further increase in 'n' through high risk securitisation makes the effect on capital base negative. A credit supply function can be postulated as

$$S= n.q.\ B(y,n)\ B_y > O,\ B_n > O \text{ or } < O \qquad \text{....(2)}$$

depending on whether 'n' is below or above the threshold value.

The demand for a loan depends positively on both the level of economic activity and the ease with which credit is made available, i.e.

$$D = D\ (y,n)\ D_y > O \text{ and } D_n > O \qquad \text{....(3)}$$

with the interest rate assumed to be given at some minimum value analogous to Keynesian liquidity trap, in the credit market quantity rationing takes over. Any excess demand is attempted to be met by increasing leverage of credit layers 'n', i.e.

$$\frac{dn}{dt} = a, \left[D(Y,n) - nqB(Y,n)\right] a > 0 \qquad \text{....(4)}$$

For any given y which allows us to focus exclusively on the credit market, the stability of the adjustment equation (4) requires

$$K = D_n - qB - nB\ (dq / dn) - nq.\ B_n = D_n - qB\ (1+\in) - nqB_n < 0,\ \in = (n/q)\ (dq/dn) \qquad ....(5)$$

Stability requires that the stimulation to supply is greater than that of demand as a result of increase in leverage 'n' as measured by the slope of the demand and the supply curves of credit. From eqn (5) it is clear that if the negative elasticity of q with respect to n exceeds unity in absolute value, i.e. $\in < 1$ and leverage is sufficiently high to exceed the threshold value to make $B_n < 0$, the stability of credit market is sufficiently violated. The necessary and sufficient condition for violation of stability is less stringent. With an over extended leverage in the credit market through various innovative credit instruments in place, it is no longer possible for the credit market to stabilize on its own.

Injection of funds by the government would be needed to satisfy stability condition (5). The higher the leverage, the greater the volume of funds needed for injection. Assuming injection is proportional to leverage for simplicity, the term 'B' is sufficiently large to the slope of supply of credit to stabilize the system, i.e.

$$k = D_n.\ qB\ (1 + \in).\ nqB_n,\ b<0,\ b>0 \qquad ....(6)$$

The impact on the real economy of stabilizing an unstable credit market through injecting funds only to the financial market can be studied through standard comparative static exercise. Now totally differentiating the equilibrium condition of demand equals supply of credit and rearranging terms

$$\frac{dy}{dn} = K / nqB_y, D_y \text{ where } K<0 \qquad ....(7)$$

by the fulfilment of stability condition (6) with injection of funds eq (7)

IMPACT OF GLOBAL FINANCIAL CRISIS ON INDIAN ECONOMY

Economic Growth Rate

The global financial meltdown and consequent economic recession in developed economies have been the major factor in India's economic slowdown. The overall growth of GDP at FC at constant prices in 2008-09 as estimated by CSO was recorded at 6.7% as against 7.1% projected mid year review and 9% target fixed by 11th quinquennium (2007-12). 6.7% growth rate achieved in 2008-09 represents a declaration from high growth of 9% and 9.7% in 2007-08 and 2006-07 respectively. The declaration of growth in 2008-09 was spread across all sectors except mining and quarrying and community, social and personal services. The growth in agriculture and allied activities decelerated from 4.9% in 2007-08 to 1.6% in 2008-09, mainly on account of high base effect of 2007-08 and due to a fall in the production of non-food crops including oil seeds, cotton, sugarcane and jute. The manufacturing, electricity and construction sectors decelerated to 2.4%, 3.7% and 7.2% respectively during 2008-09 as against 8.2%, 5.3% and 10.1% respectively in 2007-08. The slowdown in manufacturing could be attributed to the combined impact of a fall in exports followed by a decline in domestic demand, especially in the second half of the year. The manufacturing sector growth was adversely affected by the impact of global recession. There was an increase in the cost of construction due to rise in prices of inputs like steel and cement. In certain segments of the industry, there was an excessive price build up in the form of speculative bubbles related to limited supply of urban land for those segments. The rise in interest rates and the slowdown in housing loans also moderated demand. The double squeeze on the cost as well as the demand side and fall in the liquidity in mid-Sept. 2008 precipitated a sharp downturn in this sector.

Financial Sector

The sub-prime crisis that surfaced around August 2007 had affected financial institution in the US and Europe including the shadow banking system comprising inter-alia investment banks, hedge funds, private equity and structured investment vehicles. The collapse of Lehman Brothers on 15th September 2008 further aggravated the situation, leading to a crisis of confidence in the financial markets. The resulting hightened uncertainty cascaded into a full blown financial crisis of global dimensions that stymied prospects of an early recovery. India could not insulate itself from adverse developments in the international financial markets. The effect on the Indian economy was not significant in the beginning. The initial effect of the sub-prime crisis was positive as the country received accelerated Foreign Institutional Investment (FII) flows during September, 2007 to January 2008. This contributed to the debate on 'decoupling' where it was contended that the emerging economies could remain largely insulated from the crisis and provide an alternative engine of growth to the world economy. The argument soon proved unfounded as the global crisis intensified and spread to the emerging economies through capital and current account of BOP. The net portfolio flows to India soon turned negative as FIIs rushed to sell equity stakes in a bid to replenish overseas cash balances. This had a knock on effect on the stock market and the exchange rates through creating the supply-demand imbalance in the foreign exchange market. The current account was affected mainly after Sept. 2008 through slowdown in exports.

The global crisis revealed that the economy experienced extreme volatility in terms of fluctuations in stock markets prices, exchange rates and inflation level during a short duration necessitating reversal of policy to deal with emergent situations.

The direct impact of the crisis on financial sector was primarily through exposure to the toxic financial assets and the linkages with the money and foreign exchange markets. Indian banks had very limited exposure to the US mortgage markets. The deepening of global crisis and the subsequent deleveraging and risk aversion affected the Indian economy leading to slackening of growth momentum.

Foreign exchange reserve declined from $309.7 bn. in 2007-08 to $ 252.0 bn. in 2008-09. Money and credit markets have been affected indirectly through the dynamic linkages. The drying up of liquidity, fallout of repatriation of portfolio investment by FIIs affected credit market in the second half of 2008-09. This was compounded by the risk aversion of banks to extend credit in face of general downturn. The extent of the external financial and monetary shock on the Indian monetary financial system is best captured by the precipitous contraction in reserve money by more than 15% between August 2008 and November 2008. Reserve money growth collapsed from 26.9% in August 2008 to 10.3% in November 2008 and further to 6.4% in March 2009. M_1 growth decelerated from 19.4% in August 2008 to 10.3% in November, 2008 and further to 8.2% in March 2009 while M_3 growth decelerated from 21% in August, 2008 to 18.7% in March 2009. Bank credit growth decelerated sharply from 26.9% in November 2008 to 17.1% in March 2009, partly because of transmission of OECD recession effects to Indian exporters and organized manufacturing.

Impact on Banking System

Indian banking sector has been considerably less affected by the on going crisis than banking system in US and Europe. In respect of bank credit towards the later part of 2008-09, credit growth declined abruptly, reflecting the slowdown of the economy in general and the industrial sector in particular. Bank credit growth declined from 22.3% in 2007-08 to 17.3% in 2008-09. It was observed that average PLR declined marginally from 12.5% to 12% in March 2009. Flow of financial resources to the commercial sector revealed that from banks it increased from Rs. 2,24,921 cr. to Rs. 2,93,243 cr. but from other sources it declined from Rs. 274563 cr. to Rs. 191470 cr. Growth of non-food credit declined from Rs. 284456 cr. (April-January, 2009) to Rs. 2,73,303 cr. The key policy rates of RBI moved to signal of contractionary monetary stance. The repo rate (RR) was increased by 125 basis points in three tranches from 7.75% on 1st April 2008 to 9% with effect from 30th August 2008. The reverse repo rate was however left unchanged at 6%. The CRR was increased by 150 basis points in 6 tranches from 7.5% in April 2008 to 9% in August 2008.

Exchange Rate

The nominal value of the rupee declined from Rs. 40.36 per US dollar in March 2008 to Rs. 51.23 per US dollar in March 2009 reflecting 21.2% depreciation during 2008-09. The annual average exchange rate during 2008-09 worked out Rs. 45.99 per US dollar compared to Rs. 40.26 per US dollar in 2007-08.

BOP

The overall BOP situation remained resilient in 2008-09 despite signs of strain in the capital and current accounts due to global crisis. The current account deficit was 4.1% of GDP during the first three quarters of 2008-09 as against 1.8% of GDP for corresponding period of 2007-08. The capital account balance declined significantly to 1.8% of GDP from 9.8% of GDP in 2007-08.

Trade

The adverse effect of the global financial crisis was felt on the export sector on account of the drying up of international financing and trade credit followed by a fall in global demand. Export growth was robust upto August 2008. But in September 2008 export growth dipped and turned negative till March 2009. The persistent decline in export growth was due to the recessionary trend in the developed markets where the demand had plummeted. The growth in merchandise exports during 2008-09 was 3.6% in US dollar terms and 16.9% in rupee terms as against 28.9% and 14.7% respectively in 2007-08. Import growth began to decline from October 2008 and became negative over the period January to March 2009. For 2008-09 the overall import growth was subdued at 14.4% in US dollar terms and 29% in rupee terms. Growth of POL and non-POL imports was 16.9% and 13.2% respectively in US dollar terms. During 2008-09 (April-Feb.) fertilizers and edible oils registered high import growth to meet domestic demand. The trade deficit increased from US $ 88.5 bn. in 2007-08 to US $ 119.1 bn. in 2008-09.

Price Index

A positive fallout of decline in demand and fall in commodity prices due to the crisis was a sharp decline in headline inflation as indicated by WPI which was 0.8% in March 2009 and further declared to -1.26% in July 2009 and -1.61% in August 2009. However, CPI for rural and industrial workers remained at 9.7% and 8% respectively in March 2009. The average inflation on CPI-(RL) and CPI-(IW) remained 10.2% and 9.1% respectively during 2008-09. The elastic demand for consumer goods revealed that global recession has marginal effect on consumer goods sector.

Employment

The Indian Government official survey of the unemployment impact of the global crisis was conducted by the Labour Bureau with a focus on eight sectors. The survey estimated a total job loss of 50,000 over the quarter September-December 2008. Extrapolating this trend in conjunction with the official growth projections in EAC (2009), the estimated job loss approximately would be about 1.5 million over the entire recessionary phase (September 2008 to December 2009).

The impact of global financial crisis was less severe because of lower dependence of the economy on export markets and the fact that a sizeable contribution to GDP is from domestic sources. India's trade reforms since 1991 have moved, progressively towards a neutral regime for exports and imports eschewing tax and other incentives for exports.

POLICY PARADIGM TO EFFECTIVELY TACKLE THE CRISIS

Decoupling Theory

This theory asserted that growth in Asia was driven mainly by domestic factors, that these factors were decoupled from trends in the West and that the growth engines in Asia would not only continue to chug along but also serve as shock absorbers for the Western economies and might even help to pull them out of the recession. The strength of the Asian economies was contemplated to stem from their recent shift to market-oriented policies in a big way, their regional consolidation via trade and investment relationship and the benefits they derived from global inflows of capital. However recent data from IMF and other international organizations as well as national sources is seriously at variance with the decoupling thesis. IMF World Economic Outlook (January 2009) concedes that financial market conditions have remained extremely difficult for a longer period than envisaged in November 2008. In the WEO update, despite wide ranging policy measures to provide additional capital and reduce credit risks, growth estimates for 2008 and projections for 2009 and 2010 have been scaled down perceptibly *vis-à-vis* November 2008 update. The advanced economies are estimated to have grown by 1% in 2008 and projected to grow at -2% in

2009 and 1.1% in 2010. ASEAN growth rates would be at 2.7% in 2009 and 4.1% in 2010 in contrast to 6.3% and 5.4% in 2007 and 2008 respectively.

To counteract the negative fallout of the global slowdown on the Indian economy, the government responded by providing a substantial fiscal expansion in the form of tax relief to boost demand and increased expenditure on public projects to create employment and public assets. The net result was an increase in fiscal deficit from 2.7% in 2007-08 to 6.2% to GDP in 2008-09. The differential in fiscal deficit constituted the total fiscal stimulus not withstanding the fact that some expenditure was on account of the implementation of the Sixth Pay Commission award and the agriculture debt relief scheme announced in the budget of 2008-09. About 0.5% of GDP was committed prior to the dramatic deterioration of international financial markets in September 2008.

For implementing the fiscal stimulus, the government increased its spending on the plan, both for central sector as well as on central assistance to states and Union Territories plans by nearly 1% of GDP. There was an increase of nearly 2.5% of GDP on non-plan expenditure that included increased spending on fertilizers and food subsidies, agriculture debt waiver, defence, salaries and pensions. The government renewed its efforts to increase infrastructure investment in telecommunications, power generation, airports, ports, roads and railways. Policy response to the financial crisis on the basis of time frame objectives, policy options and government response have been enumerated below.

(a) Immediate Measures

Objectives of these measures relate to addressing financial panic and uncertainty and trade policy. Policy options relate to guaranteeing of bank deposit, interbank loans, providing liquidity to banks and forbearance on regulations. In case of trade policy, policy options are maintaining competitive exchange rates and encouraging free trade. Reversing protective measures introduced during the year for inflation, management and government response are not required due to the limited direct exposure of Indian financial institutions to the US financial markets. Top policy-makers and RBI reassured the market in right earnest. Government did not intervene in the foreign exchange market and rather allowed the market to determine the rupee exchange rate.

(b) Short-term Measures

With the objective of monetary policy, policy options relate to reductions in the cost of borrowing, improving market liquidity and credit flows. Government response relate to RBI's successive policy announcements (between August 2008 and March 2009), reduced reverse repo and repo rates from 6% to 3.5% and 9% to 5% respectively, CRR reduced from 9% to 5% which helped in improving liquidity in the system. In case of fiscal policy, policy options relate to expansionary fiscal policy with increase in public spending on works, social safety nets and employment. Government response relates to overall fiscal stimulus of nearly 3.5% of GDP. Institutional measures relates to recapitalization of banks and consolidation of financial sector institutions. The Central Government contributed to recapitalization of RRBs, i.e. 196 RRBs merged into 85 RRBs. Government recapitalizing public sector banks over two years to maintain CRAR of 12% NPAs for these banks declined from 7.8% in 31st March 2004 to 2.3% in 31st March 2008.

(c) Medium-term Measures

With the objectives of domestic financial sector reforms and other measures, policy options relate to increasing access to finance, improving efficiency of banking sector by domestic resource mobilization, avoiding financial repression, improving supervision and regulation, strengthening property and contract rights, judiciary and rule of law. Government response relate to interest subvention extended on pre and post-shipment credit for specific sectors, improving regulatory over sight of capital markets, putting a divestment plan for PSEs in place. In case of reforms of international financial architecture, policy options relate to deepening of financial markets and reforms, moving towards a more inclusive system of global financial governance, satisfactory conclusion of Doha WTO Round and improving aid effectiveness and development cooperation architecture reform of Bretton Wood Institution. Government response relates to initiatives under the G-20 forum of which India is an active participant.

CONCLUSION

A democratic agenda for coming out of the recession must have at least five elements. Firstly, the nationalisation of financial institutions in the leading capitalist countries where they have basically become insolvent. Secondly, controls on cross border financial flows. Thirdly, protection introduced to defend peasants and other petty producers of primary commodities (ideally through agreements among producing countries) in the case of all commodities whose world prices are demand determined as opposed to cost determined. Fourthly, coordinated fiscal stimulus to the world economy provided by a group of leading countries. Fifthly, a system of grants where by the increased surpluses generated by such a stimulus are given as grants to the less developed countries on the condition that they do not merely add these to their reserves.

There is imperativeness for several prudential and fire fighting measures such as--

(i) A switch over to a system of risk-based deposit insurance relying on a system of Fair Value Accounting.

(ii) A raising of the deposit insurance coverage from the current Rs. 1 lakh to Rs. 5 lakh which will provide a much needed safety net for the savings of the middle classes.

(iii) The role of rating agencies in the perpetration of the current crisis has come under heavy scrutiny from economists like Buiter, Portes, Gio Vanni and Spaventa, Such criticisms have prompted the financial stability forum, through the International organisation of Securities Commissions (IOSC) to offer a code of conduct for credit rating agencies. RBI should see that this code of conduct for credit rating agencies should be accepted and adhered to in their Indian operations.

(iv) A strict monitoring of balance sheet items and structured product Vehicles (SPVs) of banks and financial institutions.

There is some merit in the decoupling hypothesis. Emerging markets appear reasonably decoupled from the advanced economies as long as the downturn in the latter is moderate. Recession in advanced economies tend to drag down emerging markets as well. This is because emerging markets got affected initially mainly through the trade channel. When economic conditions in the advanced economies worsen, the financial channel also tends to be activated.

India will not escape unscathed in the present crisis because its economy has become more integrated with the rest of the world. Over the past decade and half, overseas finance has become relevant for Indian corporates and the drying up of such finance is bound to tell on their fortunes. Monetary and fiscal stimulus packages would help the Indian economy to recover from the morass of global recession most probably by December 2009 as Indian economy is not trapped by demand recession in respect of consumer goods sector. Implementation of Sixth Pay Commission award would bring recovery from the pangs of depression.

References

Bernanke, B.S., M. Gertler and S. Gilchrist (1999): The financial Accelerator in a Quantitative Business Cycle Framework in J.B. Taylor and M. Woodford (ed.) Handbook of Macroeconomics, Vol. IC North Holland.

Bose, A. (1989): Short period Equilibrium in a less developed economy in M. Rakshit (ed.) Studies in the Macroeconomics of Developing Countries, New Delhi, Oxford University Press.

Bhaduri Amit (2009): Understanding the Financial crisis, *EPW*, March 28-April, 3, 2009.

Economic Survery, Govt. of India, 2008-09, Oxford University Press, New Delhi.

Global Economic and Financial Crisis, *EPW*, March 28-April 3, 2009.

Global Economic and Financial Crisis (2009): Orient Blackswan Pvt. Ltd., in association with Sameeksha Trust, Hyderabad.

Gupta, K.R. (2009): World Financial Crisis, Atlantic Publisher, New Delhi.

Hamiltor, J.D. (2008): Understanding Crude Oil Prices, NBER Working paper, Cambridge.

IMF (2008): World Economic Outlook, update 6th Nov. 2008 and 28th January 2009

Lahiri, A. (2009): Indian Financial Reforms, National Priorities Amidst an International Crisis.

Nachane, DM (2007): Liberalisation of Capital Account Perils and Possible Safeguard, *EPW*, 8-14 Sept. 2007.

Nachane, D.M. (2009): The Fate of India Unincorporated, *EPW* March 28-April 3, 2009.

Patnaik, Prabhat (2009): The Economic Crisis and Contemporary Capitalism, *EPW*, March 28-April 3, 2009.

Rakshit, M. (1982): The Labour Surplus Economy, Macmillan Press, New Delhi.

Rakshit, M. (1989): Studies in Macroeconomics of Developing Countries, Oxford University Press, New Delhi.

Rakshit, M. (2006): On Liberalising Foreign Institutional Investment, Oxford University Press, New Delhi.

Rakshit, M. (2008): The Subprime Crisis; A Primer, Money and Finance.

Rakshit, M. (2009a): Understanding the Indian Macroeconomy, Oxford University Press, New Delhi

Rakshit, M. (2009b): Global Economic Crisis, Stagflationary Phase, Money and Finance.

Ram Mohan, T.T. (2009): The Impact of the Crisis on the Indian Economy, *EPW*, March 28-April 3, 2009.

Reddy, Y.V. (2009): India and the Global Financial Crisis, Managing Money and Finance-oriented, Blackswan Pvt. Ltd., Hyderabad, India.

6

Globalization, Global Meltdown and the Indian Economy

RATAN KUMAR GHOSAL AND SAIKAT BHATTACHARYYA

INTRODUCTION

One of the most conspicuous aspects of the on-going process of globalization has been the stupendous growth of international finance. As a consequence there has been a tremendous increase in the private daily trading of foreign currency in the global market amounting to about 1.8 trillion dollars. Surprisingly, only 2% of this is related to trade of goods and services, and a minor proportion is in the form of FDI and the rest, i.e. the majority proportion is in the form of portfolio investment, i.e. investment in stocks, shares, etc. for short-term speculative gain. Considering the case of India one can easily find that about 75% of the total inflow of foreign investment has been in the form of portfolio investment, of which the lion's share comes from private financial institutions, popularly known as Foreign Institutional Investment (FII henceforth). The policy of Neo-liberalism has made relentless cross country movement of corporate capital possible. Further, it is striking to note that the protagonists of this on-going process of globalization is not the Nation State but the multinational corporations, international financial institutions, etc. on which the Nation States hardly have any control. It is the consideration of the relative rate of return on capital determined by the market forces which dictates their cross country movement as well as the nature of investment to be undertaken. So there is every possibility of withdrawal of such investment from any country depending not only on the macro fundamentals of the country but also on any trivial exogenous disturbances which they think could affect the short-term capital flow. Obviously, the country wherefrom such rapid withdrawal takes place is likely to face tremendous crisis as has happened in East Asian countries in late 90s, thanks to indiscriminate liberalization of financial markets coupled with the information asymmetry, causing moral hazard driven fictitious growth of the asset price without any increase in the productivity of factors. Even after the financial crisis in the East Asian countries, the community of policy-makers of other EMEs did not learn any lesson. The process of financial liberalization continued at a robust speed in these countries. India has been of no exception to this. Actually, the crisis of East Asia could not penetrate into India because of poor financial integration at that time. However, with gradual full-fledged integration of the economies of the globe and as a fallout of the globalization of finance, the possibility of financial crisis in almost all the countries including the emerging market economies have become much more prominent. In fact the liberalization of finance has brought the third world assets into the ambit of the first world wealth holders in such manner that the likely impact has been the unleashing of the financial crisis in the third world. This time the global financial meltdown had started since the middle of 2007 and it has led to the global depression, leading to the tremendous fall in employment, output and market demand, etc. The global growth rate of output has plummeted from 4% in 2006 to 2.5% in 2008 and the World Bank expects it to be 0.9% in 2009. Actually the root of the global crisis was in United States and it started its germination in 2007. Some may identify it as a short-run business cycle fluctuation, which is very common in capitalistic economic system which the market force with mild government intervention will cure. But some questions crop up. Is it really a short-run problem? Can the market cure it? What role the state should play? Is it the crisis of capitalism? This paper highlights the origin of this crisis and its possible impact on Indian economy and the potential role of the state to combat the evil effect of the same.

GENESIS OF GLOBAL FINANCIAL MELTDOWN

The present global financial meltdown has actually had its origin in USA since the second quarter of 2007 and then gradually continued to disperse in almost all the countries in the globe in varying degrees. It is, in fact, a fallout of the indiscriminate and impersonal securitization of toxic assets backed initially by the weak or shaky financial architecture of banking system and then through the involvement of even the non-bank financial institutions like insurance companies, mutual funds, etc. In one word, it is actually the outcome of the securitization multiplier backed by the prime motivation of reaping maximum profit through the instant diversion of risk factor by the transfer of the mortgages within a short span of time. Of course there was information asymmetry which has caused adverse selection and generated moral hazard problem. But the flaws in the government policy and the lack of governance were no less responsible to sub-serve this crisis. This crisis had surfaced in the name of "sub-prime crisis", the genesis of which runs as follows.

Not only in USA but also in almost all the western countries there is a system of housing loan against the mortgage of the house in the banks. But what has happened in USA since the second quarter of 2007 has been the massive non-repayment of loan instalments by the people taking the house loan from the banks. In fact by that time a very large volume of house loan was issued by the banking system at a very low rate of interest even to the non-credit worthy people in view of releasing the large volume of accumulated reserve with the banking system. With the gradual accumulation of the loan defaulters and its substantial volume, the confiscation process of mortgage started at a rapid speed, thereby leading to create shaky mortgage market and the plummeting of prices of houses in USA.

Consequently, the credit markets based on this shaky mortgage structure gradually got shocked by severe jolt with a strong devastating effect. Its effect continued to pervade among the mortgage-based financial institutions like banks, insurance corporations, and other investment banks thereby leading to their bankruptcy, the most important of which are the Lehman Brothers, City Bank, etc. This is actually termed as *sub-prime crisis* having the following anatomy of functioning.

The shaky credit market with its complex accounting system has given the opportunity of transferring the risk of mortgage from one lending bank/institution to other banks and non-bank financial institutions without ensuring normal return on capital. Actually the financial institution giving the house mortgage loan continued to sell the mortgage to other banks in Wall Street for profit and also for transferring risk to that bank. The concerned bank after purchasing this mortgage and combining it with other risky assets has fabricated a new higher risky asset known as "Toxic Asset" and sold the same to other banks, and non-bank institutions like insurance corporations, mutual funds, pension funds, etc. for reaping quick profit by transferring risk. This process of reaping short-term profit with minimum risk through risk transferring continued to take place at a robust speed. The ultimate effect of cumulative risk of non-repayment of loans fell on the end purchaser of the mortgage security. So the banks and non-bank financial institutions in other countries like the countries in Asia, Europe, Japan and South America who had purchased such toxic assets too fell into this risk trap leading to the generation of tremendous financial crisis. The effect of this process gradually had its spread over all the countries of the globe.

One can have an insight about the density of this crisis by considering the dollar value of the amount of mortgage-based CDO of ninety thousand crore in 2007 in USA. The dollar value of the amount of toxic assets was of the order of fifty thousand crore. To counter the effect of the tremendous falling trend of the price of mortgage based bonds as well as its risk factor, some credit related derivatives in the name credit default swap were issued, the total dollar price of which amounted to about sixty two lakh crores in 2007. But the eventual impact of this fell on real economy.

On the employment front, there had been a tremendous cut. In USA the unemployment rate increased to 6.7% and the number of job loss had been to the order of 19 lakh in 2008. The prices of house in USA continued to plummet at a robust speed. People continued to bring down their consumption expenditure tremendously which had led to a precipitous fall in market demand, thereby leading to an overall fall in the output, employment, growth rate (from 5.7% to less than 2%) in USA. The same effects were produced in other countries too. As a result of this sub-prime crisis, the call money market has also been afflicted so that mistrust between the banks has been in operation. All these have led to generate a great depression not only in the US economy but also in other economies because of their tie up with not only the US economy but also the global economy, thanks to the on-going process of globalization. There has also been a devastating effect of this crisis on the stock markets countries across the globe. Actually this crisis has gradually taken the shape of global crisis and it is partly the outcome of the Neo-liberal policy. To save the US economy from this crisis, the US Government had supplied about seventy thousand crore dollars to the banks on basis of the vague assumption that it is a short-run problem. The governments of other countries including India had also come forward through the adoption of various demand management policies in terms of undertaking large volume of deficit financed public expenditure in various infrastructural constructions and also by pursuing cheap money policy for the provision of large volume of credit for real estate development through banks at a very low rate of interest.

Now the most fundamental question which may crop up is that why has such crisis occurred first in the US economy and then spread over other countries? The quick look at the anatomy of the crisis leads us to highlight two proximate explanatory factors responsible for such catastrophic collapse of the financial system in USA.

First, it is the bursting of the housing bubble or the real estate bubble which was formed on the basis of the misperception about the prices of houses that they would continue to increase in the long-run. This had led to form a belief that housing investment ensures financial security and even a source of wealth accumulation thereby leading to the tremendous increase in the housing mortgage loan issued by banks. The demand for housing continued to increase thereby leading to the circular causation towards the further increase in price of houses and triggering further investment in housing industry thereby forming the housing bubble. Alongside there has been unbridled expansion of securitization. The overt recognition of the assessment of the rating agencies which were based on their own perception instead of reliable statistics has expedited this process of the securitization of toxic assets. This massive investment in real estate development at lower rate of interest indeed brought about an upswing in the US economy for some time. This was also accompanied by rise in inflationary rate. Consequent to this, the Federal Reserve raised rate of interest in view of controlling demand and inflation. So the massive default in the loan repayment continued to occur since the second quarter of 2007 which was followed by a fall in the demand of house ownership as well as the price of house. So the basic belief that the price of house would rise perennially was actually proved wrong and the bubble burst. Eventually the entire financial structure had been on the verge of collapse and it started afflicting the real economy.

Secondly, the easy money policy of the Federal Reserve in US during the 90s and the first four years of this new millennium coupled with the policy towards facilitating and encouraging the house ownership have helped generating and sustaining the housing bubble thereby leading to the persistence of the sub-prime mortgage multiplier and sub-prime bubble through securitization as a way out for reducing risk of individual financial players. The misperceptions about the speculative bubble and the Federal's failure to assess the risk factor have eventually caused bursting of the bubble. Since the policy of liberalization especially the financial liberalization, pursued by the US Government since the 70s followed by the policy of cheap money policy in the 90s and first four years of the new millennium eventually caused tremendous erosion to the financial system, one can safely attribute the present crisis as a partial outcome of the Neo-liberal policy.

GLOBAL CRISIS AND THE INDIAN ECONOMY

In this section we will focus on the routs of penetration and the impact of the crisis on the Indian economy. To judge this, one has to have clear insight about the macro fundamentals of our economy. It is well known that we have been able to achieve a noticeable growth rate of GDP (7-8%) during the last five years, which has placed our economy among the frontier ranking countries in the world. But the country remained miserably unsuccessful to convert the growth rate into a commensurate human and social development through reducing unemployment and inequality. As a matter of fact both unemployment and inequality increased even during the years of high economic growth.

The trickle down effect of this growth has been negligible because the share of the poorest 20% of our total population remains only 8.2% and the Gini ratio of income distribution has increased from 0.25 to 0.27 in case of the urban area and from 0.31 to 0.35 in rural areas between 1993-4 and 2004-05. So the growth process has bypassed the poor and vulnerable section of our total population and it has merely become a solace to the common people. Further, 35% of our total population still lie below the international poverty line, i.e. they have income less than $1 per day. The employment effect of this conspicuous growth is highly pessimistic such that the 7-8% growth of GDP has been accompanied by only 1% increase in employment. Actually the employment elasticity of GDP has fallen from 0.52 to 0.12 in 2004-05. If one considers the sectoral growth rates, one finds deplorable condition of both the industrial and agricultural sectors such that the industrial growth rate has fallen remarkably well below 5% and the growth rate of agriculture has become well below 2%. Further, the growth rates of rice, wheat and food grains have become negative during the first five years of the new millennium while the growth rate of population reads the figure of 1.96% per annum. The supply side deficiency has already created the problem of food security. This, coupled with the high rate of inflation during the last year, has put our economy at the state of stagflation. One should keep in mind that the present global financial crisis had actually been preceded by severe global food crisis also. Under this backdrop one has to judge the likely impact of the present global crisis on Indian economy.

The growth rate of GDP, as shown in Figure 1 has come down to 1.1% in the fourth quarter of 2000-01. After that it has increased and maintained a quite steady rate around 9% till 2005-06. But since the 2nd quarter of 2007-08 it is falling almost monotonically. The reason of the deceleration can be found in the falling growth rate of investment expenditure which started from the 1st quarter of 2006-07, that is, prior to the surfacing of the sub-prime crisis in August 2007. Further, the deceleration of investment expenditure has started in the 4th quarter of 2005-06 and the fall in industrial growth rate has started in the 4th quarter of 2006-07, i.e. before the premier financial institutions started to collapse. The downswing in the Indian Economy was initiated almost simultaneously with, if not earlier than, the commencement of the crisis led by bursting of the housing price bubble. Later, the situation became severe as the contamination embarked on. So, one cannot blame the sub-prime crisis solely for the deceleration of the Indian Economy. Indeed the crisis has worsened the situation.

FIGURE I

Growth Rates of GDP, Industry and Gross Investment

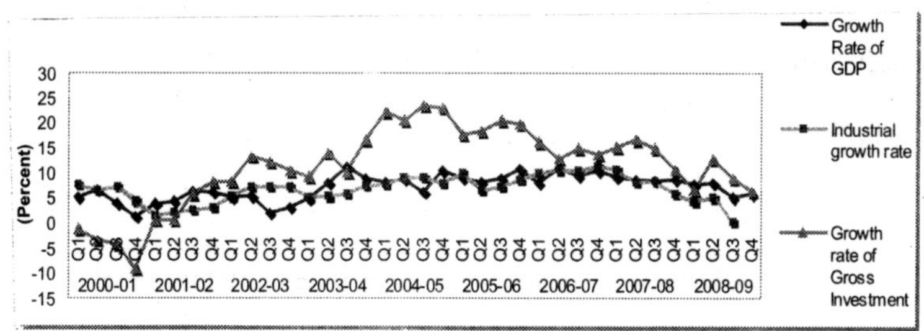

Let us identify the factors which are generally seemed to be responsible for the contagion effect. Conventional wisdom suggests some important channels, through which a financial crisis generated in a developed world gets transmitted. Here we will analyze these factors and try to find out the relative strength of each of these factors.

Firstly, the contraction of export demand is perhaps one of the most important factors. The logic is quite simple to understand. With the outbreak of the global crisis, the export market especially in USA and in other European countries has already started squeezing and so the demand for our exportables has already started falling. This has led to the reduction of overseas demand for our exports and also the employment in our export sector through a negative multiplier process. As seen in Figure 2, though the growth of export demand remained very volatile, at least since 2000-01, from the first quarter of 2004-05 to the second quarter of 2006-07 the country was maintaining quite a high growth rate (at around 25 to 30 per cent) of exports of goods and services. This growth of exports is primarily attributable to stupendous, if not abnormal, growth of export of services, particularly IT enabled services. During the years 2004-05, 2005-06, 2006-07 the growth rate of export of services were 48.9%, 26.8% and 24% respectively. Further it is seen that the down turn of our economy came well before August, 2007, especially when the sub-prime crisis was perceived. In fact the global meltdown has accelerated the down turn of our export sector. Although after the second quarter of 2007-08, the growth rate of export started to revive following a period of negative growth rate, it again started to fall from the second quarter of 2008-09. No doubt, this downward trend of export due to global down turn has affected our economic prospect very badly Thus the cascading effect of the export demand on the economic performance of the country unambiguously nullifies the 'decoupling theory'.

FIGURE 2

Growth Rates of Internal and External Demand

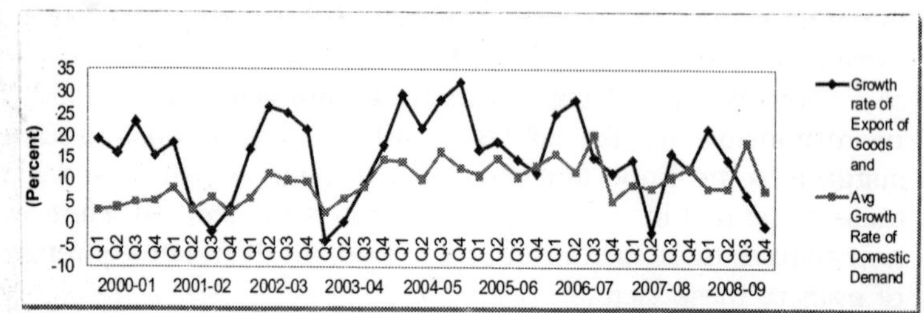

Secondly, another important factor which could affect the Indian economy like that of many other emerging market economies is the drying down of inward remittances due to global financial slowdown. Figure 3 shows the behaviour of inward remittances since 2000-01. As far as the inward remittance is concerned we do not see any uniform relationship between the growth rate of GDP and the inflow of remittances. So, it is plausible to conclude that inflow of remittances, affected by the global slowdown has not provided any impact on the growth performance of our economy since the beginning of the new-millennium. In fact the following diagram reveals that the behaviour of inward remittances do not follow any systematic pattern over time. Even during the midst of the crisis the growth rate of the inward remittances is seen to be increasing. During 2004-05 the growth rate of the inward remittances has fallen significantly, which is mainly attributable to the disturbances created in the Middle East during the Gulf War II.

FIGURE 3

Growth Rates of GDP and Inward Remittances

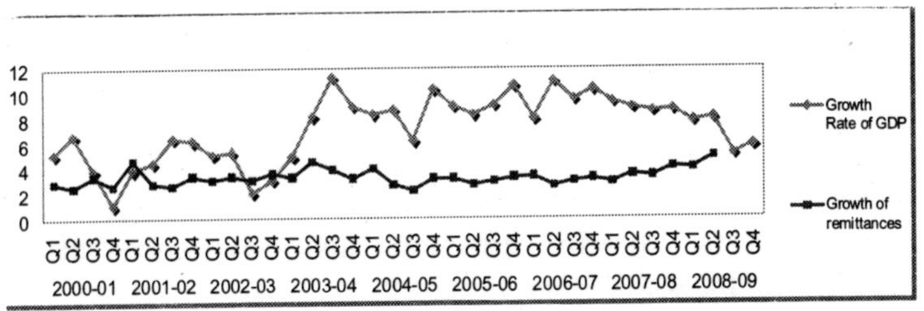

Thirdly, the other avenue through which a financial meltdown could affect an emerging economy like us seems to be the financial one. During the process of financial liberalization the inflow of foreign institutional and direct investment has increased in our economy. This seems to have helped the pattern of conspicuous growth of our economy. But with the outbreak of sub-prime crisis and following the collapse of top financial institutions in USA, the reverse flow has been found to operate, thereby inflicting our economy through the creation of tremendous pressure on our balance of payment, which is characterized by perennial current account deficit. Figure 4 shows the trend of net FII inflow in India. It is clear from the Figure that the flow of FII has revealed a declining trend after the second quarter of 2007-08 and by the 4th quarter of the year it has become negative. This rapid decline in FII flow has indeed produced a massive adverse effect on the stock market leading a tremendous fall in the stock prices.

FIGURE 4

Net FII and FDI Inflows

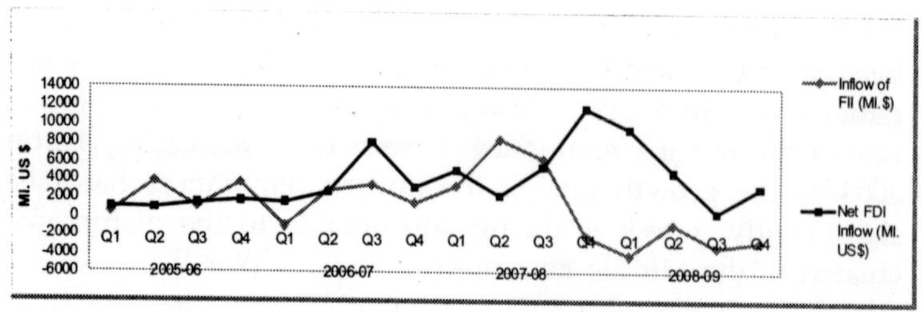

On the other hand, the reverse flow of FII from our country caused by the increased demand for finance for mitigating the domestic demand for liquidity in US and other European countries has led to a gradual rising trend in the rupee value of dollar. With the increase in the rupee value of dollar due to massive withdrawal of FII, our import competing sector seems to have been tremendously affected due to the rise in the import cost. This has affected the import of technology and the capital goods, thereby affecting the production of our manufacturing sector. As a fallout there is an overall decline in the output, employment, income as well as the aggregate demand in the economy, which results in a further fall in the demand for the goods produced in the manufacturing sector.

Finally, the other ways by which the global crisis has already started afflicting our economy are as follows. Since in most of the cases the loans of the corporate sectors are unsecuritised in the sense that they are collateralized by the value of their own shares and their balance sheet position, with the fall in the share value there will be pressure from the banks to cover the loss. Obviously the large corporate borrowers with sound financial position would be able to cope with this pressure.But small scale corporate sector will have to undergo distress sale of their assets. This will raise their cost of production. The eventual outcome is likely to be the fall in industrial production thereby affecting our real economy through the reduction of income, employment, etc.

As a fallout of the global depression there has been a tremendous cut in the employment created through the BPO and KPO in our economy. This would eventually lead to produce a contractionary impact on the aggregate demand for the industrial and agricultural goods and also for the informal services. The result of this overall demand deficiency would obviously cause the terms of trade to disfavour agriculture thereby aggravating the agrarian crisis that we were facing since the beginning of this millennium. On the whole this demand constraint as an outcome the global crisis will lead to a fall in the aggregate output of all the sectors (i.e. the agricultural sector, manufacturing sector and the service sector) and employment and income. Obviously the informal service sector activities driven by the demand created out of the output and employment in the agriculture and industrial sector will be reduced due to fall in demand. So the economy as a whole is likely to fall in the crisis such that it will suffer from depression.

POLICY OPTIONS

Until August 2008, the Reserve Bank of India adopted a tight Monetary Policy to control inflation. With the collapse of Lehman Brothers and other premier financial organizations, there has been a massive outflow of Foreign institutional investment, which has led to a sudden drop in all major domestic stock indices. Another problem that arose due to the sudden fall of FII is that of stress on the foreign exchange rate of the country. The RBI has started selling its forex reserve in order to keep the stability in the foreign exchange market. As foreign funds are going out of the country very fast a serious illiquidity problem has emerged. Since September 2008 the RBI is taking care of the problem by reducing different policy rates and thereby injecting liquidity into the system.

The Indian banking system, unlike many other Emerging Market Economies, was not exposed to the toxic assets and as a consequence remained almost unaffected by the crisis.

Moreover, all the banks even during the crisis were successfully meeting their capital adequacy norm of 9%.

As we have already highlighted that the impact of the global crisis has already been reflected in our real economy in terms of the fall in demand for our exportables, the tremendous fall in the rupee dollar exchange rate to a five year low figure of Rs. 49.94, the rise in the import cost of technology and capital goods causing damaging impact on our import competing sector, tremendous fall the forex reserve in 2008-09 by the magnitude of 53937 million US$ over 2007-08, the tremendous deficiency in the demand for manufacturing goods, depression in the stock market, and finally the substantial fall in the agricultural and industrial output. On the whole, our economy is also on the verge of depression. The global depression and its impact on our economy is not a short-run phenomenon, rather it has a deep rooted impact which has already had its mechanism of action. So some short-run patch working measures will not be able to tackle this deep rooted crisis. The following policy options may prove useful.

First, so far as the monetary policy is concerned the government has already introduced cheap money policy to increase the flow of credit to the development of real estate, expansion of infrastructure and also to the corporate sector and small scale sector in view of giving a boost to the output, income and employment *vis-à-vis* aggregate demand by sustaining the growth without paying heed to the distributive impact of the growth. But the massive flow of credit for investment in real estate development without being backed by sufficient demand generation may be self-defeating, thereby leading to massive default in loan repayment and the increased magnitude of non-performing assets with the banks. The introduction of CDS by RBI may also prove dangerous through the generation of moral hazard problem as has happened in USA. Actually what is needed is to have close look at the end use of the credit so that the flow of the credit has had its productive utilization. It is well known that our agricultural sector, small and micro-enterprises, the SHGs, benefitted from institutional credit since a long time. The recent All India Debt and Investment Survey conducted by NSSO has revealed that the small and marginal farmers and the small and micro enterprises are again getting trapped under the clutches of the traders, moneylenders, etc., i.e. under the unorganized credit market. So the banks should be directed rigorously to increase the flow of credit to these sectors so that the said sectors can be given a boost for the increase in output and employment in these sectors. This will in turn create market for the domestic manufacturing goods and also demand for various informal activities in both the rural and urban areas thereby helping the economy to get disentangled from the recent crisis.

Secondly, instead of increase in the public investment and the flow of credit for the infrastructural development of the economy as a whole, the region specific increase in investment in the said sector may be thought of. For instance more investment is to be directed to the region with backward infrastructural facilities and also towards the rural agricultural sector especially for the development of irrigation power, roads, warehouses and marketing infrastructure.

Thirdly, it is well known that the creation of infrastructure involves a very long gestation lag in producing its final impact on the society's output, income and employment. So massive public investment in those projects which have very short gestation lag and the output of which are directly consumed by people employed in such projects may be much more helpful in overcoming the demand deficiency through the proper working of income generating multiplier. So the increased flow of credit to the small, micro and large corporate sectors and massive public investment for the installation of the agro-based industries may prove helpful in reviving our economy from the evil impact the global crisis.

Fourthly, since the growth rate that we have achieved is overwhelmingly a service sector driven growth, government should pay more emphasis through the channelisation of more investment and credit to sustain the growth of this informal service sector as a major source of employment and income generation.

Fifthly, it is well known that although our economy is overwhelmingly dominated by agriculture, the policy induced and the patrilineal property relation induced transformation of our agrarian structure has made it marginal farm dominated economy without time to time consolidation of land holdings and market friendly diversification of cropping pattern. This has led to generate agrarian crisis since the beginning of the present century by making agricultural operation non-profitable. So increased flow of credit to this sector should be made available on a group lending basis instead of individual basis so as to induce cooperative process of farming through mutual conciliation among the farmers through the active involvement of the *panchayat* system.

Sixthly, one of the important failures of our development strategy has been the failure to divert the majority proportion of our total population who are exclusively dependent on agriculture to industry through the process of industrialization and then to the service sector even if the productivity of the agricultural sector has fallen tremendously and it has now become abysmally low. So for the revival of the agricultural sector, industrialization process should be boosted depending on the domestic market demand base and also through expansion of the size of the market keeping in view the backward and forward linkages of the process of industrialization. This will obviously help reviving our economy from the evil impact of the global crisis thereby helping the economy to sustain the growth process.

Finally, it is well known that in the era of globalization the monetary and fiscal policies of any individual country can not work independently without having any counter effect form the global market. So to tackle the problem of external sector (i.e. the demand constraint) of our economy the reorganization of the domestic production structure suitable to global demand may be necessary. Further the global consciousness for chalking out the global fiscal and monetary policies for the revival of the global economy from such severe crisis may prove to be a good solution.

CONCLUDING OBSERVATIONS

(This paper actually investigates the genesis of the global crisis and it also explores the likely impact of the same on our economy. It also tries to find out the avenues of disentangling our economy from the evil effect of the global crisis which had its origin in USA and continued to disperse over almost all the countries in the globe in varying degrees.) It is, as shown in this paper, a fallout of the indiscriminate and impersonal securitization of toxic assets backed initially by the weak or shaky financial architecture of banking system and then through the involvement of even the non-bank financial institutions like insurance companies, mutual funds, etc. The shaky credit market with its complex accounting system also gave the opportunity of transferring the risk of the mortgage from one lending bank/ institution to other banks and non-bank financial institutions without ensuring normal return on capital.

In this paper it is also shown that the down turn in Indian economy had started before the sub-prime crisis and the resulting financial crisis came into light. The global economic crisis has surely aggravated the pace of downswing. So, one cannot hold solely the sub-prime crisis responsible for the deceleration in Indian economy.

The fundamental problem is essentially internal and has to be sorted out domestically. The problem relating to Indian economy is principally a supply side problem unlike the case of advanced countries. So, only Keynesian "pump priming" will hardly help in long-run. It is imperative to break the supply side bottle necks to come out of the crisis.

References

Bhaduri, Amit (2008), "Predatory Growth", Lecture Delivered at the Department of Economics, University of Calcutta, March 28.

Bank for International Settlements (BIS) (2008): 8th Annual Report (2007-08).

Chandrasekhar, C.P. (2008), "The Problem as Solution" Book Review, *Economic and Political Weekly*, Vol. XLIII, No. 42, October.

Ghosal, Ratan Kumar (2004), "GDP Growth and Feel Good Factor", *Economic and Political Weekly*, Vol. 39, No. 20, May 15, 2004.

———(2006), "Globalisation and the Nation State" in Occasional Papers, Vol. 14 March, Rabindra Bharati University, Kolkata. Also in Open Eyes, Vol. 2, Nos. 1 and 2, June.

Lahiri, A (2009), Indian Financial Reforms National Priorities Amidst an International Crisis", Sir Pusushattamdas Thakurdas Memorial Lecture, Mumbai, 16th January.

Nachane, D.M. (2009), "The Fate of India Unincorporated" Global Economic and Financial Crisis: Essays from *Economic and Political Weekly*, Orient Blackswan Pvt. Ltd.

Sengupta, Arjun (2008), "A Monetised Deficit for Sustaining Growth amidst the Meltdown", *Economic and Political Weekly*, vol.XLIII, No. 42, October.

Subbarao, D. (2009), "Impact of Global Financial Crisis on India: Collateral Damage and Response", Speech delivered in Tokyo 18th February.

7

Global Economic Crisis: A Macroeconomic Explanation of Structuralist Theory and Verification of "Decoupling Hypothesis" on the Indian Economy

DHIRAJ KUMAR BANDYOPADHYAY

INTRODUCTION

In the twenty-first century the global financial crisis, the worst since the depression of the 1930s, is unlikely to end soon. In fact, since it began early in 2005, the United States (US) economy has had tepid growth with the world's largest economy had started to borrowing heavily on international capital market rather than lending and subsequently depreciation of US dollar against the major international currencies. Some economists say the US is currently in a recession, together with Japan, China and the European Union (EU). Some mainstream economists think that since the crisis was triggered by collapsing home prices in the US, it is likely to come to an end only after prices reach a bottom. That crisis is now unrolling. The year 2008 has seen the failure of as many as 19 banks—exactly half the number of all publicly listed banks in India. So the number of bank—failures in the past eight years has grown to 46—which is more than the total of 38 banks listed on the Indian bourses. With one great blast, the US Federal Reserve has fired off all that remains in the monetary canon, reducing the Fed Funds rate to an unprecedented zero to 0.25 per cent. The British economy has already lurched deep into recession and is heading for the worst downturn seen in any advanced economy since the Second World War. The GDP growth rate of Japan has reached at the low level of about zero per cent. The economies of Germany, France and China have been facing serious recession. On 26th January, 2009 about eighty thousand employees lost their jobs in US and EU. In the month of January 2009 about 20 lakh employees were retrenched in US and EU. In the year 2008 about 26 lakh employees lost their jobs in US and EU. International Labour Organization's Global Employment Trends Report 2009 has said that globally unemployment in 2009 could increase over 2007 by a range of 18 million to 30 million workers, and more than 50 million if the economic situation continues to deteriorate, particularly in developing countries. In response to the crisis management US, EU, Japan, China and some of the developing countries have announced bail out packages and stimulus plans worth more than $2000 billion to combat the growing economic slowdown. On 29th January 2009 the US House of Representatives had passed the $819 billion mega stimulus package, which is aimed at reviving the US economy that is reeling under the worst ever crisis since the great depression of last century. This global economic crisis has been characterized by a sharp slowdown in GDP growth, culminating in recessions in quite a few countries and rising unemployment and job losses practically everywhere. The financial turbulence and the downturn in the real sector were compounded during August 2007-August 2008 by sharply rising inflation, especially of oil and other primary commodities. The two most important features were: (i) unabated deceleration of GDP growth with growing unemployment; and (ii) sharply rising inflation.

Having said this, in Section-II we like to present a

macroeconomic explanation of structural causes of global economic crisis. In Section-III we like to revisit John Maynard Keynes' explanation as well as prescription of depression economies of the World. Section-IV seeks to explain pre-global economic crisis development in India and intend to verify how far "decoupling hypothesis" could be valid example for India. Section-V finally concludes.

MACROECONOMIC EXPLANATION OF STRUCTURAL CAUSES OF GLOBAL ECONOMIC CRISIS

The British Broadcasting Corporation's Radio Four listeners voted Karl Marx as the "greatest philosopher of the millennium." We know that the "greatest philosopher" propounded dialectical materialism. He is the great economist who discovered "surplus value" in the capitalist mode of production and the built-in factors leading to recurring crisis in capitalism. He is the economist who surpassed Adam Smith and David Ricardo in uncovering the place of money in present day of World economy. The biggest as well as greatest revolutions of human history—the 1917 Russian socialist revolution, led by the Bolsheviks headed by Lenin, the Chinese anti-feudal, anti-colonial revolution led by the Chinese Communist Party headed by Mao Zedong, Vietnam's anti-colonial and anti-feudal revolutionary Wars under Ho Chi Minh's leadership, revolutions in Latin America such as Cuba and Venezuela—have all been products of Marxian thought and the ideological concepts Marx formulated. The collapse of the Communist-led regimes of Russia and Eastern Europe was naively conceived by many to be the end of Marxism—such as a leading Japanese economist Francis Fukuyama tried to convince the World by saying that this is the end point of mankind's ethiological evolution. But the critics have been proved terribly wrong. At the dawn of 21st century, Marx returned with a vengeance, bigger and more relevant than ever before. Globalisation and the new shape of the capitalist economy have come, as Marx predicted. At this moment we can recall of his most crucial predictions—recurring crisis in the capitalist financial system—is now a hard reality as well as relevance and depth of Marxian thinking. His relevance possibly is even greater now. We think that two aspects need to be under-scored: (i) Marxism's basic formulation on economics and the technological level of production reached being the key to societal edifice; (ii) the role of the financial sector under capitalism.

We know that the roots of the current global economic crisis lie in the particular solution that was proposed to sort out the previous systemic capitalist crisis (especially in the US) in the late 1960s and 1970s. Being experienced with the "Golden Age of Capitalism", between 1945 and the late 1960s, the capitalist class in the advanced capitalist world began to witness another crisis in profitability by the mid-1960s. Then the national Keynesian structure of accumulation was dismantled and a new regime was instituted in its place during the 1970s that has come to be known as "neo-liberalism." Besides dismantling the fixed exchange rate system in 1971, this new regime also witnessed the restructuring of capitalism in significant ways. It targeted the welfare dimension of the state. The state also had to vacate its productive economic role, to become mainly a facilitator for the improved profitability of capitalist enterprise. This led the state to alienated its properties at throwaway prices to private players. Finance capital that was kept under strict control after the Great Depression escaped the clutches of regulation, separated itself from and dominated over other kinds of capital such as the industrial and merchant varieties, and began to play a crucial role in restructuring the global economy in its own interests. Labour was disciplined in terms of its ability to bargain for better wages and benefits. Then this process deepened in the 1980s as several developing economies were brought under this regime with the helping hand of the Bretton Woods twins—the International Monetary Fund (IMF) and the World Bank. Mainstream macroeconomic theory made a big switch from the Neo-classical-Keynesian synthesis to monetarism and new classical macroeconomics to support the so-called "free market" model of the economy as the most efficient way of organizing an economy.

That new regime, while addressing the profitability crisis of capital, never fully addressed the crisis in the sustained realization of surplus value. Even other means were resorted to, such as rapid dispossession and transfer of assets from the state and various vulnerable groups (such as peasantry) to capital, creation of unprecedented levels of credit so that consumption growth could proceed uninterruptedly even as capital found means to its own profitable deployment, creation of a precarious international macro-balance, and through the generation of temporary bubbles/booms.

The current crisis is not merely a financial crisis but a broader economic crisis, first and foremost in the US economy and by extension in all those economies that followed the US neoliberal model of capitalist accumulation and also those economies that were closely connected with the US economy in terms of linkages in trade of finance.

We know that Marx points to two modes of capitalist accumulation in *Capital*, Volume 1. With regard to first one what he termed as a "process of primitive accumulation", through which the incipient capitalist class forcibly dispossessed productive groups such as the peasantry and artisans, thereby creating a class of people without any means of production and another that possessed these means. The former became the class of wage workers, and the latter the class of productive capitalists. The next one what he termed as "extended reproduction", whereby money capital is invested in a process of production wherein means of production and labour power are put through a process of production in order to produce a new commodity. During the process of production, workers add more value than what they are compensated for and this gives rise to what Marx termed as surplus value. So, once surplus value is produced, it needs to be realized by selling the new commodity. Once this is done, a higher quantum of money capital accrues to the capitalist than what he possessed at the beginning of this cycle. The whole process has two stages—production of surplus value and the realization of it. If this process is arrested in either of these stages, it leads to a crisis of devaluation of capital or commodities.

Unlike in the Golden Age, when productivity gains were shared with the workers, this time around, these gains were distributed among the different sections of the capitalist class, shareholders, landlords, and importantly the managerial people. Therefore, this implies that the previous crises in accumulation were largely resolved at the source, i.e., at the level of the production of surplus value. Then accumulation proceeded at a faster pace due to improved strategies of appropriation and improved productivity and this in turn gave rise to two other problems. First, sustained conditions of realizing the generated surplus were never put in place. Basically, this means that sufficient purchasing power was not created in the new regime.

We have observed that the US working class witnessed a decline in its real wages from 1973 onwards until the late 1990s (Dean Baker, "The Productivity to Paycheck Gap: What the data show", April 2007). What this meant is that when real wages began to decline, the working class could not (and may be was also unwilling to) adjust its spending/consumption patterns. The working class adopted several strategies. They worked much harder, worked more jobs, women joined employment in bigger numbers, and they also resorted to borrowing in order to fulfil their needs. The next savings rate of the household sector in the US became close to zero (Figure 1). For the capitalist class that saw the growing accumulation of capital, this was a boon. Now they could resort to lending the surplus capital to workers and extract interest out of it instead of paying them wages, The entire housing boom and collapse that acted as a precursor to the current crisis needs to be located in this context as well.

To reiterate an important point, one of the crucial fallouts of this situation is that the already precarious domestic realization problem became further compounded since the burden of solving it (clearing the excess supply in the global markets) for the entire global economy was taken on by seemingly willing US consumers (mainly the working class). This eventually (especially towards the late 1990s) led to an explosion in their borrowing with the terms fairly liberally defined since there were massive capital inflows (especially from China, Japan and other Asian economies) into the US economy, creating easy liquidity. Between 2000 and 2004 US households' mortgage debt and total debt as ratios of household disposable income soared from 67% and 98% to 90% and 122% respectively (Figure 1).

The neo-liberal regime, especially in the last 15 years or so, also witnessed, on a large scale, an explosion of what Marx refers to as fictitious capital in Chapter 29 ("Components of Banking Capital") on *Capital,* Volume 3, that further exacerbated the problem of over accumulation of capital as well as generated

FIGURE 1

US Household Disposable Income, Saving and Debt in Per centage (1995-2006)

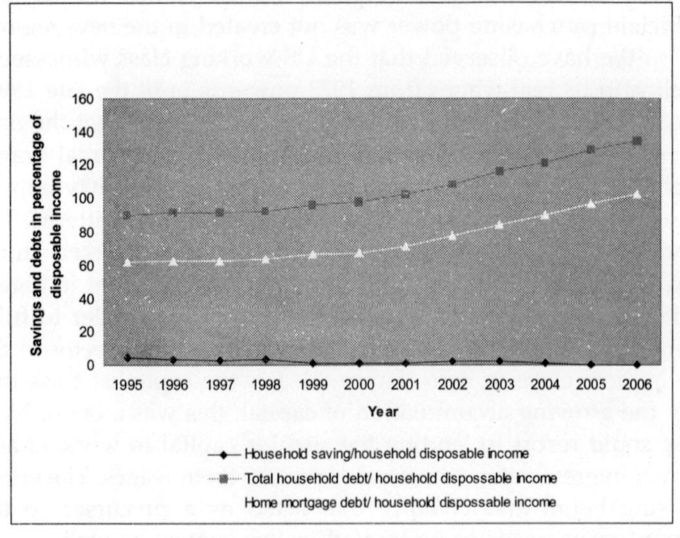

Sources: 1. Bureau of Economic Analysis, US Department of Commerce (http://www.bea.gov/)

2. Federal Reserve Statistical Release (http://www.federalreserve.gov/releases/h15/data.htm)

solutions to the deployment through the creation of asset bubbles. Fictitious capital is different from real capital in that it is usually not engaged in the production of current surplus value or incomes but has a claim over future surplus value or income. When money is lent out to borrowers in lieu of collateral, lenders holding on to paper titles themselves begin to circulate them as capital, making it fictitious in Marx's understanding. The collateral might be in the form of fixed capital or a durable commodity. When the value of the collateral changes drastically, or if the production of surplus value or incomes does not keep pace with the future claims of fictitious capital, the accumulation regime-based on this fictitious capital ends up in a state of crisis.

Again, a significant chunk of all the various forms of derivatives, collateralized debt obligations, mortgage-backed securities and credit default swaps, etc. that have been part of the recent explosion in finance are examples mainly of fictitious capital. These have been developed usually by various institutions that received a boost after the 1970s under what has been called the "shadow banking system"—investment banks, special investment vehicles, hedge funds, and so forth. Securities representing this fictitious capital circulated not only in the US and other advanced economies but also all across the world.

Marx and Keynes can not be cited together on ideological as well as philosophical ground but can be cited on the question of role of state intervention in economic development, particularly in an economic environment where capitalists seeking or making abnormal profit by deceiving majority of the people of World economy. So, we can revisit Keynes not for solution of damaged economics but by principles as instruments for macroeconomic development.

REVISITING KEYNES' THEORY OF DEPRESSION ECONOMIES OF THE WORLD

At present, most of the affected economies of the World (due to US economy meltdown by following neo-classical paradigm of monetary policies) have been injecting more liquidities in their economies and planning for higher borrowing, tax cuts, reduced interest rate and more spending. With the World economy as a whole sliding into depression, it is not surprising that the old Keynesian tool kit is being ransacked. But Keynesian economics is not just about fixing damaged economies. We don't need very sophisticated economics to spend our way out of a depression. In one form or other—usually by war or war preparations—governments have been doing it throughout history.

We do require very sophisticated economics to prove that depressions cannot happen. This was the economics Keynes set out to challenge in his great book, *The General Theory of Employment, Interest and Money* (1936, London), written during the Great Depression of the 1930s. His own ideas, he wrote, were "extremely simple, and should be obvious." Economies were inherently unstable; governments had a vital role to play in establishing them.

We argue that these heresies were too simple and obvious

for the economics profession. In fact, after a long and rather successful trial run, Keynesian economics was obliterated by the free-market revolution which swept the Anglo-American world under former UK Prime Minister Margaret Thatcher and former US President Ronald Reagan. Then in a notable comeback, updated versions of the theory Keynes had challenged "proved" that unregulated or lightly regulated market economics were very stable, and that government intervention only made things worse. In apparent disregard for mathematical demonstrations to the contrary, crises and crashes, booms and busts continued to occur, and politicians continued to try to mitigate their consequences, common sense being stronger than logic. This is more or less the situation we are in now. Neo-classical economic theory points to non-intervention: politics points to intervention. Keynes's attempt to marry the two in the notion of "practical statecraft" failed.

What is more, Keynes's "simple and obvious" ideas can be summed up in two propositions. The first is that large parts of the future are unknowable. He wrote (in chapter-12, section-III), "The outstanding fact is the extreme precariousness of the basis of knowledge on which our estimates of prospective yield have to be made. Our knowledge of the factors which will govern the yield of an investment some years hence is usually very slight and often negligible." The "unknowability" of the future imparted an inherent instability to financial and investment markets, leading to periodic outbreaks of "hard behaviour", when "new fears and hopes will without warning take charge of human affairs." He called the economics of his day a "polite technique which tries to deal with the present by abstracting from the fact that we know very little about the future."

But the question was how was this "abstraction" achieved. By assuming, Keynes wrote, that uncertainty could be "reduced" to calculable probability, and therefore to the same status as certainty itself. This underlies today's "efficient market hypothesis" which treats uncertainty as measurable risk. The intellectual basis of deregulation of the late 1980s and early 1990s can be traced to this sort of efficient market hypothesis. Among the major economists who have contributed to this idea are Milton Friedman, Eugene Fama and Robert Lucas of the Chicago school. It essentially says that prices of stocks, bonds and other speculative assets reflect everything that is known about economic fundamentals, such as corporate profitability, inflation and export possibilities. Consider for a moment that stock prices have risen above the levels justified by the fundamentals. Then rational economic agents would step in and sell them, causing the relevant stock prices to go down. The process would continue till stock prices are restored to the levels that are justly warranted by the fundamentals. If stock prices were to fall below their fundamentals, then the reverse process would be expected to operate.

The efficient market hypothesis has an interesting corollary. It is that if stock prices already reflect everything that is known and knowable, then rational investors cannot hope to outperform the market using trading strategies based on publicly available information. There are two implications to this. First, rather than waste time and pick individual stocks; investors would be well advised to place their savings in broadly diversified mutual funds. Largely owing to the work of Fama and some of his followers, the so-called mutual or index funds today play a key part in the retirement planning of millions across the world. Second, if there are some agents who are privy to insider information and are willing to use it, then they can potentially make a huge profit.

The idea is that the prices prevailing in a market make it impossible to earn abnormal economic profits by trading in that market on some specified amount of information. The hypothesis is invariably applied to financial markets. Here, it says that if the price of an asset is expected to rise tomorrow, traders, anticipating this, will buy the asset today. This will drive the price of the asset up until it is no longer expected that it will rise further tomorrow. Thus no quick capital gain could be expected to be made. If the markets were not efficient, the possibility of making arbitrage profits would exit and a clever trader could make quick speculative gains. Its acceptance explains the explosion of the derivatives market since the 1980s, which has brought the financials system crashing down.

Now, Keynes's second proposition is that depressions can last a long time, longer than it is politically safe to tolerate. He did not doubt that markets worked "in the long-run." "But this long-run", he wrote in his best-known remark, "is a misleading guide to current affairs. In the long-run we are all dead."

Keynes offered a number of reasons why economies did not simply "bounce back" after a great shock (the Dow Jones index did not recover its 1929 prices till 1952). Besides this, his clinching argument in his 1930s debates with free market economists such as Friedrich Hayek was political. It was much too risky to allow economies to slide into deep depression. We could recall the example of Hitler which was vivid in the minds of all democratic politicians. In 1928, at the height of Weimar Germany's prosperity, the Nazis got 2 per cent of the vote. By 1930 they were up to 18 per cent. In 1933 Hitler was in power. During that time, German unemployment had risen from two million to six million. Hayek and the free market economists never had an answer to this argument. So what should the governments of affected economies do now? In 1931 Keynes favoured the devaluation of major currencies, but this is now irrelevant: the currencies are not fixed to gold as it was in his day, and are sinking quite naturally. The suggestion most favoured by neoclassical economists is to cut interest rates and go on cutting them. Keynes was certainly not against his, but "cheap money" to counter depression is not specifically Keynesian, and he doubted the efficacy of monetary policy on its own.

The Bank of England and Federal Reserve of US might flood the market with money, but this would not necessarily produce lower interest rates—and therefore greater lending—if the tendency to hoard money was going up at the same time. "The possession of actual money", Keynes wrote, "lulls our disquietude; and the premium which we require to make us part with money is the measure of the degree of our disquietude." As the adage has it: you can bring a horse to water but you can't make it drink.

The final question is this: Will we be content simply to take Keynes out of his cupboard from time to time, dust him down, and put him in charge of rescue operations, before putting him back firmly in his cupboard? Or will we now try to run our affairs paying proper attention to his insights into financial instability so as to prevent these alternations of mania and panic from periodically seizing control of our lives?

It might be instructive to see at this point how the issue of business cycles was looked upon by John Maynard Keynes.

Keynes' substantial formulation on the issue of instability of capitalism is contained in his *Treatise on Money,* published in 1930. Prior to writing the *Treatise,* Keynes had written *A Tract on Monetary Reform* (1923) which contained a systematic statement of his view on the means of economic policy as well as a presentation of his abiding interest in the stabilization of economic activity. This was further definitively elaborated upon in the *Treatise.* In both these works, Keynes, like Malthus before, was interested to understand the forces that determine the level of savings and investment in an economy. In the phase of early capitalism after the onset of the industrial revolution, the individuals who saved were also the ones who invested. Large-scale, mass-producing monopolistic units were still not the order of the day. As production became more roundabout and technological progress enabled and even necessitated large scale, mass-production units to come into being, there was a possibility for investment and saving activities to be delinked. This also concomitantly created the need for banking and financial intermediaries to mobilize savings that could be canalized to the investors. The savers and investors were now typically two distinct sets of economic agents. But this also implied that the manner in which Ricardo-Mill-Say had presumed the savings-investment identity to always necessarily hold could no longer obtain. There could now be the very real possibility, for example, of savings exceeding investment, thereby bringing in the possibility of gluts. As a result, national income and employment would not be set to shrink.

Both the above works created the stage for Keynes' tour de force, *The General Theory of Employment, Interest and Money.* The revolutionary breakthrough consisted of the recognition that there could now be a possibility for the equilibrium level of income to be strictly below the full employment level of national income. This is an outcome that could not possibly have occurred in the Ricardo-Say-Mill system. If employment were to be at less than the full employment level, then wages would go down till full employment is restored.

Keynes suggested that since wages are typically sticky downwards, this would eliminate the possibility of self-adjustment below certain level of institutionally agreed upon nominal wages. The economy could then settle for equilibrium at a less than full employment level of employment and income. The idea that the equilibrium could possibly occur at any level other than the full employment level itself constituted a revolutionary departure from the essential stance of classicism wherein full employment of all factors was regarded to be axiomatic.

Keynes diagnosed the problem as one of lack of effective demand. The problem that he was addressing was that being faced by mature capitalist economies. It was not a problem of any supply constraint. Factories were all there; only that they stood idle because there was no demand for their produce and labour was not being hired, and the ones who still had jobs faced the imminent possibility of being fired. Keynes showed that if somehow the level of aggregate demand could be triggered, possibly by the government printing currency notes to employ people to dig holes and fill them up, the wages that would be paid out would resuscitate the economy by generating successive rounds of demand through the multiplier process. The higher the marginal propensity to consume of the workers, the greater would be growth of national income. Since there was idle capacity, the system could immediately set to work. There would be no problem of a gestation lag.

The difficulty however with this hypothesis is that it does not and cannot adequately account for the fact that stock markets are at least as much driven by investors' expectations and exuberance as by market fundamentals. It is this exogenous and usually spontaneous shift in moods—optimism or pessimism—that is at the heart of the fluctuations in stock prices. Keynes called them "animal spirits" in *The General Theory.* He argues, *Even apart from the instability due to speculation, there is the instability due to the characteristic of human nature that a large proportion of our positive activities depend on spontaneous optimism rather than on a mathematical expectation, whether moral or hedonistic or economic. Most probably, of our decisions to do something positive, the full consequences of which will be drawn out over many days to come, can only be taken as a result of animal spirits—of a spontaneous urge to action rather than inaction, and not as the outcome of a weighted average of quantitative benefits multiplied by quantitative probabilities (Keynes 1936, 161).*

The aforesaid dilemma over economic crisis cast a long

shadow over the policies pursued by the authorities during the stagflationary phase of the crisis. The important point to note in this context is that, despite the worsening financial and real sector scenario during the first year of the crisis, in no country, other than the USA, policy-makers deemed it prudent to implement expansionary fiscal measures. Even in the USA, the fiscal stimulus package, announced on 13 February, 2008, was one of $170 billion, quite paltry for a $14-trillion economy. It is useful to start with the widely prevalent perception relating to factors behind the stagflationary tendencies in the global economy. As we have seen, while the GDP slowdown is attributed to demand deficiency caused by the bursting of the housing-*cum*-mortgage bubble and its rapid contagion, the rise in inflation is traced to excess demand conditions in the markets for food and petroleum.

According to the consensus macroeconomics that has emerged out of the debate between the Keynesians and Neo-Classical over the last three to four decades, a deficiency of aggregate demand, whatever be its source, will tend to reduce output and employment as also the general price level in the short-run. The opposite will be the effect of an increase in aggregate demand. For explaining the stagflationary experience at the global level, the mainstream framework requires substantial modification. Unlike in the open economy models considered above, oil and food prices are not exogenous for the global economy. Hence it is not clear why a positive demand shock or a negative supply shock in the oil market should raise all nominal prices; such a shock could as well have led to a fall in other nominal prices, with prices of petroleum falling less than that of other goods. Nor is it possible to say anything regarding the impact of the shock on aggregate demand without considering the income distributional consequences of the shock and the relative marginal propensities to spend of the gainers and the losers. What is most important, even though the shock might have led to excess demand in some markets, in view of the widening (global) output gap, the mainstream macro-model would predict a downward drift of the general price level, not its accelerated increase for a year or so. As per such model it is only when the fall in the full employment (NAIRU) output due to shocks in the agricultural or the oil sector is larger than the decline in aggregate demand resulting from the meltdown in the housing and financial markets that the world economy would be afflicted with stagflation.

For an adequate explanation of the economic consequences of sectoral and aggregate demand or supply side shocks we need to look to "Structuralist Hypothesis" as it was initiated by M. Kalecki (1976). Under the structuralist hypothesis, prices of foodgrains, minerals and other primary articles are flexible and markets clear even in the short-run, but those of industrial products are sticky and set on a cost-plus basis. Thus while there is near instantaneous adjustment of product prices to changes in demand or supply in the primary sector, the adjustment in the manufacturing sector is as in the consensus macro model. An important implication of such a dual adjustment process is that, macroeconomic analysis in terms of aggregate demand and aggregate supply may often be inappropriate, especially when the primary sector constitutes a significant part of the economy. Hence arises the need for examining the interaction between (i) the agricultural (including the mineral) sector where prices are fully flexible; and (ii) the industrial sector, characterized by cost-plus pricing. This in fact is the hallmark of structuralist models, designed for studying the macro-behaviour of developing economies.

The foregoing analysis sets the stage to examine the implication of crisis on Indian economy that has now been treated as emerging economy and could play an important role to moderate the crisis.

PRE-GLOBAL ECONOMIC CRISIS DEVELOPMENTS IN INDIA—VERIFICATION OF "DECOUPLING HYPOTHESIS"

In this section we seek to explain pre-global economic crisis development in India and intend to verify how far "decoupling hypothesis" could be a valid example for India. India's gross domestic product (GDP) growth, it needs to be emphasized, had started decelerating in the very beginning of 2007-08 (Figure 2), about six months before the outbreak of the US financial meltdown and considerably ahead of the surge of recessionary tendencies in all developed countries from August-September 2008. That the beginning of the deceleration of the

Indian economy predates the global meltdown is also attested to by the sharply downward trend since April 2007 if we closely observe the Index of Industrial Production (IIP), which has been reduced from 11.3 per cent in 2007 to -2.0 in December 2008. In fact, the slowdown in industries during 2007-08 was much more pronounced than that in GDP growth; while the latter registered a 0.5 per centage fall to 9.2 per cent from the earlier year, the decline in industrial GDP amounted to as much as 3.1 per centage points (CSO, Govt. of India, *website*).

FIGURE 2

Year to Year Growth Rate of India's GDP and its Components (2001-09 Constant Prices)

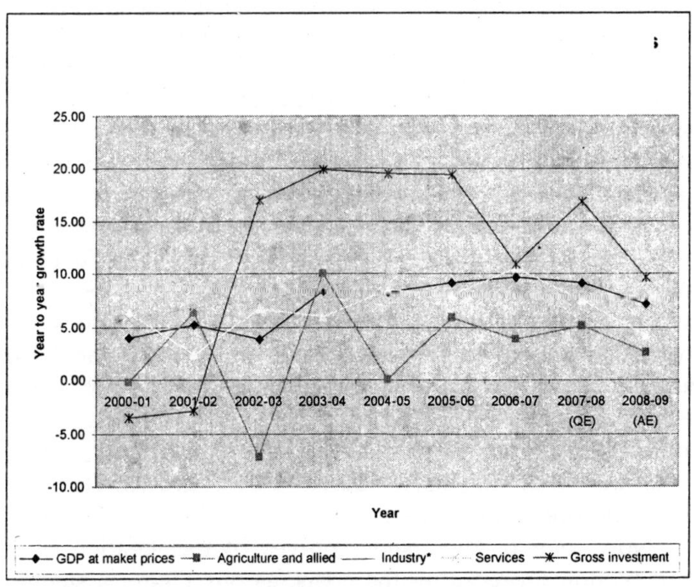

Source: Central Statistical Organization (CSO), GOI, National Accounts Statistics, 2008 and various press releases; RBI's web site.

It is important to note that the economic slowdown occurred despite a significant increase in agricultural (GDP) growth, from 3.8 per cent in 2006-07 to 5.1 per cent in 2007-08. In contrast, the growth in the secondary and the tertiary sectors declined from 10.6 per cent and 11.2 per cent in 2006-07 to 7.5 per cent and 11.1 per cent, respectively in 2007-08. As agricultural output is primarily supply determined, and production in industries and service is 'demand-driven' in the short-run, then the deceleration was obviously due to demand-side factors operating in the markets for non-agricultural products. One of the important factors governing the demand for these products is agricultural income; but since its effect was positive during 2007-08, the effects of other demand-side factors must have been sufficiently adverse to outweigh the impact of a good harvest. Let us examine the most important of these factors.

In order to analyze variations in demand, it is customary in macro-economic analysis to focus on the relatively autonomous components of demand which do not depend significantly on current levels of output. Then logically, as a first approximation investment, government expenditure and exports are treated as autonomous, while imports and household consumption are considered endogenous. This standard classification of the components of autonomous demand in the Indian context requires modification in two respects. First, it is necessary to differentiate between public and private investment since (i) their variations, being governed by separate sets of consideration, often differ widely, and (ii) unlike in developed countries, public sector capital formation, despite its loss of pre-eminence compared with the pre-reform era, still remains fairly significant. Second, in the Indian economy, remittances from non-resident Indians are non-negligible sources of private consumption and to that extent have to be treated as an autonomous factor driving domestic demand (Rakshit, 2009). Let us examine what the major sources of the growth slowdown were in the pre-crisis period.

Now, one of the major sources of deceleration of the Indian economy preceding the crisis, as our Figure 3 suggests, was the declining trend in capital formation, particularly in the private sector. After its prolonged slump from the mid-1990s to 2001-02, investment recovered in 2002-03 and clocked an average growth of nearly 19 per cent over the four-year period 2002-06 (Figure 3). Private investment, accounting about 75 per cent of aggregate capital formation, grew at an average rate of nearly 20 per cent and constituted the principal driver of the economy's GDP growth during this period. However, since 2005-06, there

FIGURE 3

Year to Year Growth Rate of India's Macroeconomic Indicators

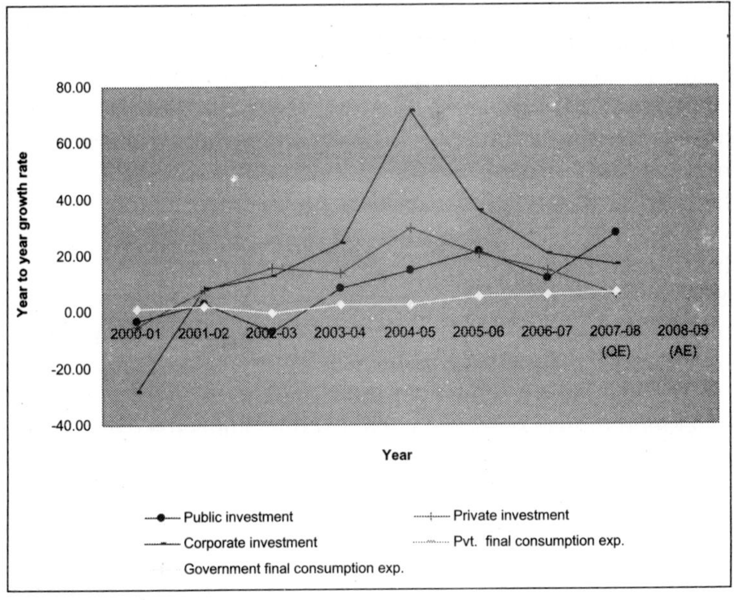

Source: Central Statistical Organization (CSO), GOI, National Accounts Statistics, 2008 and various press releases; RBI's web site.

has been a marked deceleration in aggregate investment; its average growth during 2006-09 has fallen by about 8 per centage points from that in the preceding period. In fact, the sharply downward trend in private investment started in 2005-06 itself. In this respect there is an interesting analogy between the current slowdown and the deceleration of the Indian economy in 1996-97. In the earlier instance too the onset of deceleration was preceded by a sharp slowdown in private investment. We argue that the quantitative significance of the downturn in private capital formation in pulling down GDP growth well ahead of the global financial turmoil is undoubted. There are two important points that could be taken into consideration: (i) in 2006-07, private investment constituted more than one-fourth of GDP and nearly 40 per cent of total autonomous expenditure, and (ii) between 2006-07 and 2007-08, the fall in the growth of private investment was as much as 8.9 per centage points. The implication is that ceteris paribus the growth reducing impact of private investment amounted to a huge 3.36 per centage points in 2007-08. Though this impact was more than outweighed by the 17.6 per centage point jump in public investment in the last year of 2008-09, which is almost certainly due to the continuation of the downward trend in private investment from 2005-06.

What is more, another most important demand-reducing factor operating in the pre-crisis period was the sharp slowdown in exports. According to Central Statistical Organization (CSO) data, 2007-08 saw export growth plummeting to 7.5 per cent from 18.9 per cent registered in the earlier year (Figure 4). Even this constitutes an underestimation of the decline in external stimulus to the domestic economy. The CSO estimates of export growth are obtained by deflating nominal export earnings by the export price index. This yields the per centage change in the volume of export. However, for estimation of the demand generation impact of exports, what is relevant is the command of export earning over domestic consumption and investment. So, the need is for using the GDP deflator rather than the export price index. Again, to the extent some exports directly involve

FIGURE 4

Year to Year Growth Rate of India's Exports nd Imports

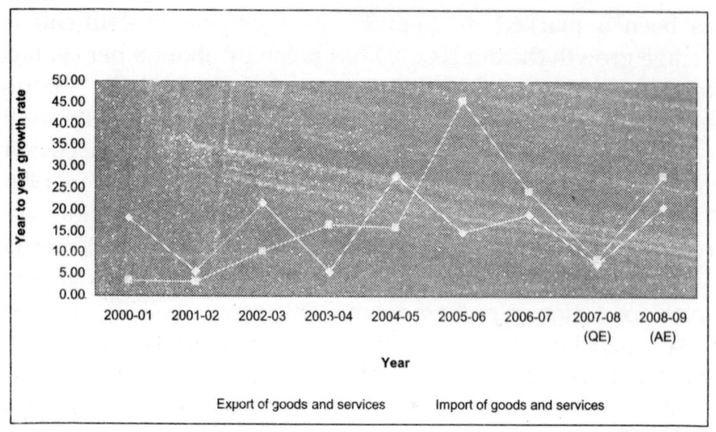

Source: Central Statistical Organization (CSO), GOI, National Accounts Statistics, 2008 and various press releases; RBI's web site.

use of imported items, it is export earning less the value of the items that denote the autonomous component of domestic demand arising from trade. It is interesting see how important export slowdown was in causing the decline in GDP growth in general and industrial growth in particular during 2007-08. Exports less export-related imports (ELEM) were a little over 20 per cent of GDP in 2006-07, but their share in total autonomous expenditure was nearly 30 per cent. Then this, together with the fact that between 2006-07 and 2007-08 there was a 15.8 per centage fall in ELEM attests to the enormous significance of exports in engineering the GDP deceleration.

In fact, the decelerating trends of industrial and GDP growth started from April 2007 and the first quarter of 2007-08, respectively. Our estimates of export growth (gross of export-related imports) indicate how closely this turning point corresponds to the behaviour of export earnings. Export growth started decelerating from the third quarter of 2006-07, decreased from 13.2 per cent to 0.6 per cent in the first quarter of 2007-08, and declined further to -3.1 per cent per cent in the second quarter of 2007-08. We argue that the two most important factors behind the deceleration of GDP in general and industrial production in particular were in operation well before the onset of the global crisis.

Again, the slowdown in GDP growth in the pre-crisis period was significantly less than what the precipitous fall in the growth of private investment and exports. The reason lay partly in the enhancement of public expenditure. Between 2006-07 and 2007-08, the growth of public investment and government consumption went up by 15.6 and 0.8 per centage points, respectively. Given their shares in autonomous expenditure at 11.4 per cent and 15.1 per cent respectively, the accelerated increase in public expenditure helped greatly in preventing a sharper slide in GDP growth. Then the more important mitigating factor was perhaps the 1.3 per centage point rise in the growth of agricultural GDP. Therefore, apart from its direct contribution to overall GDP growth, the increase in farmers' income also helped in raising the demand for industrial goods and services and triggering off a multiplier process in the non-agricultural sector.

Our foregoing analysis brings to the fore a significant

difference between the growth-debilitating and growth-enhancing factors operating before the crisis. While the former is related to structural features of the economy, the latter are either primarily policy instruments or largely random, at least in the short and medium-run. It is for this reason that in the absence of sustained expansionary policy measures, the downward drift of the Indian economy, we believe, would have continued, albeit at a slower pace, even without the global meltdown. The pre-crisis trend in household consumption also lends support to our viewpoint.

What is more, in recent years there appears to have occurred a significant change in the propensity to consume which has an important bearing on GDP growth. Since the first quarter of 2005-06, there has been a marked deceleration in household consumption expenditure that cannot be accounted for by the behaviour of GDP (Figure 3). Between 2005-06 and 2006-07, growth of private consumption expenditure declined by as much as 1.6 per centage points even though there was a 0.5 per centage point rise in GDP growth. There is one catch here to explain why the slowdown in consumption growth was larger than that in GDP in 2007-08. The point to appreciate in this context is that since private consumption accounts for around 60 per cent of domestic income, the downward trend in the consumption expenditure ratio is of major macro-economic significance when GDP growth is "demand-driven." Our calculated ratio had shown a relentlessly downward trend since 2001-02, registering a huge 9.4 per centage falls over the period 2002-07. One reason behind the slowdown of consumption in relation to aggregate income was the decline in personal disposable income as a ratio of GDP. However, as per estimates from CSO data (GOI, 2008), between 2002-03 and 2006-07 the ratio of private disposable income to GDP came down from 84.3 per cent to 77.6 per cent, and that of private consumption expenditure to disposable income 75.0 per cent to 71.9 per cent. This reflects the operation of other factors in curbing household expenditure. The most important of these was the worsening distribution of income between those engaged in the sunrise sectors and the vast and growing majority of the population working in unorganized enterprises. The other important factor was the rise in prices of commodities entering the consumption basket of rural and urban workers. Since April 2006 there was a significant rise in consumer price index (CPI-IW and CPI-RL) inflation due to an increase in food and other commodity prices, and this tended to have a restraining impact on consumption demand for non-agricultural goods and services. However, the role of commodity price inflation in the performance of the Indian macro economy acquired much greater significance after the onset of the global economic crisis.

Given their relatively small exposure to US asset-backed securities (ABSS) and structured derivative products like collateralized debt obligations (CDOS), Indian banks have not been seriously rocked by the global financial turmoil. However, apart from the heightened uncertainty and darkening prospects making domestic banks extremely wary of extending loans, there have been other routes through which the crisis has cast its long shadow on Indian financial markets and hence on the real sector of the economy. Then almost immediately after the crisis surfaced external commercial borrowings (ECB) and foreign institutional investment (FII) registering a steep fall between October and November 2007, from $3.6 billion and $5.7 billion to $2.2 billion and -$1.6 billion, respectively. Since then downward trend continued. We know that to the extent domestic producers relied upon ECBS for funding their projects partly or wholly, drying up of this source of long-term credit may have played a role in the significant dip in investment growth since the outbreak of the crisis. However, the importance of this factor for domestic demand can easily be exaggerated. When external borrowings are used entirely for buying machinery and equipment from abroad, the associated investment does not raise domestic income or employment.

Now, FII outflows might also have had a negative impact on domestic investment. We know that Indian share markets are relatively thin in terms of number of listed company's share trading in regular form. The sharp fall in FII followed by their withdrawal contributed to the bursting of the India's stock market bubble. Curiously enough, though IIP growth had started to decline since March 2007, the share market boom continued until early 2008; between March and December 2007, the Bombay Stock Exchange (BSE) index, fuelled in part by substantial FII inflows, went up from 12,858 to 19,827. The bullish sentiments prevailed for a short while even after the downward drift in FII began in November 2007. However, a whopping $3.2 billion FII (equity) outflow in January 2008 triggered a relentless bear run, making the BSE plunge by 52 per cent (to 9,350) between December 2007 and January 2009. For the Indian economy, it is true, there appears to be no direct, casual link between capital formation and either FII or share prices and between GDP growth and share market indices. Finally, despite the resilience of Indian banks, the global financial meltdown has had some adverse consequences for credit financed economic activities.

We have observed that for a little over a year after the outbreak of the financial crisis the world economy experienced, between September 2007 and October 2008, a pronounced stagflation phase (unabated deceleration of GDP growth with growing unemployment), with growth slowdown on the one hand and rising inflation on the other. The global inflation was driven mostly by commodity prices, especially prices of energy and agricultural goods. So far as the Indian economy is concerned, since practically all petroleum products are administered and trade in agricultural goods is far from free, transmission of global inflation to domestic prices occurred with a time lag, from November rather than September 2007. However, with the wholesale price index (WPI) inflation rising from 3.3 per cent in October 2007 to 12.8 per cent in August 2008, and staying in double-digit figures during the succeeding two months, the prices pressure in India was significantly greater than that in advanced countries. This is particularly so for consumer price index (CPI) inflation which turned double digit in August 2008 and did not show any sign of deceleration even by August 2009. The food price inflation is already around 10 per cent.

Though the worldwide commodity price-led inflation did not owe its origin to the global financial crisis, it reinforced the decelerating tendencies in the Indian economy in a number of ways. First, since the demand for food and fuel are income as well as price inelastic, the sharp rise in their prices relative to those of other goods led to a fall in demand for industrial products and services and strengthened the recessionary forces already at work in the domestic economy.

Besides, the surge in prices of crude oil in the international market affected the country's trade balance and hence the scale of domestic economic activity both directly and through the multiplier mechanism. However, since the global financial meltdown and recessionary tendencies have also affected domestic output and employment through exports and imports, it is useful to consider simultaneously the transmission of the main external impulses via the trade balance. The significance of the impact on external trade for the domestic economy arises on three counts. First, with the spectacular increase in both merchandise and services exports lasting for more than a decade, massive investment has been undertaken in export-oriented sectors (SEZs). A sharp drop in export growth has affected Indian economy through the multiplier process, but has also likely caused debt default, bankruptcies, and severe cutbacks in investment in the pipeline with all their adverse implications encompassing both the financial and the real sectors. The OECD countries account for around 42 per cent of India's merchandise exports and practically the entire export of services, especially the high-growth ones. With services accounting for 37 per cent of export earnings in recent years, the precipitous fall in GDP growth and emergence of strong recessionary tendencies in advanced countries, have constituted a major contractionary factor for the Indian economy. This is not to deny the importance of exports that jumped from 30.9 per cent in 2001-02 to 42.3 per cent in 2007-08.

We may identify two types of policy failures that contributed towards the per-crisis slowdown and magnified the negative impact of the global downturn: (i) structural policy, and the other is (ii) macroeconomic policy management.

We argue that the deceleration of GDP and industrial output significantly ahead of the global financial storm was, as we have seen, driven by the slowdown in private investment and exports; for both the government's structural policies were largely to blame. However, despite tardy execution in some instances, programmes like the Golden Quadrilateral and other highway projects, rural-*cum*-urban reconstruction, and the employment guarantee scheme have provided both are "demand-side" and "supply-side" boost to the economy. But, the initiative for roping in the private sector, through what is called the Public-Private Partnership (PPP) for closing the country's huge infrastructure gap is also well intentioned. The sharp downturn in private sector capital formation since 2004-05 attested to a serious deficiency in this policy of stimulating private investment, especially in sectors with large positive externalities. The basic weakness of the government policy relating to PPP lies in reliance on private funding of infrastructural project (through upfront grants). The government went in for large scale liberalization on FIIs, which led to inflating the sock market bubble as well as strengthen the value of rupee against foreign currencies (especially $) and posed serious problem to the export sector.

Now, so far as ongoing economic crisis is concerned macroeconomic policy management has had greater role to play to stabilize the economy. In 2008-09 budgets, union government proposed to reduce revenue budget by 0.4 and fiscal deficit by 0.7 per centage points in order to obey Fiscal Responsibility and Budget Management Act. This act may lead to upset income generation in the economy through the reduction of capital expenditure (via public investment) and to some extent revenue expenditure. However, the Reserve Bank of India (RBI) went in for a series of dear money measures over a period from January 2007 to late October 2008. These sort of measures were cotractionary monetary policy in economic sense usually used to control inflation at higher level (say, double digit); the repo rate and cash reserve ratio (CRR) were raised to 9 per cent from 7.5 per cent and 5.5 per cent respectively. The business lobby is angry about increase rate of interest (bank rate) and reduced volume of liquidity at hands of commercial banks. As a result they claim that GDP will decline as cost of investment would be higher. At this juncture, we are now going to explain the relationship between the rate of inflation, the real interest rate and GDP growth rate by focusing on statistical relationship. This will give us some idea on what to expect of our growth rate if the RBI keeps on raising the nominal interest in the face of sustained rise in inflation. However, unfortunately RBI and government policy-makers agreed to lower interest rate, CRR and repo rate at the end of October 2008 to satisfy business lobby (with a plea to move of US and European Central Banks cut in policy rate) and this led to high growth of liquidity in the economy and ignored sustained rise in commodity prices (as well as without banning future trading of food articles when CPI inflation is stand by with double digit). We know that current episode of CPI inflation (or sustained rise in food prices) is caused by enormous growth in money supply, liquidity, high level of petroleum oil prices (in spite of lower level of international prices), shortage of food supply due to lower level of public investment in agriculture sector (irrigation and infrastructure) and future trading in food items. The runaway CPI inflation threatens the real income of wage earners in unorganized and organized sectors as well as fixed income earners.

We have calculated in Table 1(a) the overall correlation between GDP growth and inflation that is -0.102, i.e. negative. In the post-reform period it is rather strongly negative (-0.347); while in the pre-reform period it is positive (0.352). So, for the past fifteen years they are negatively related. This is a relationship exactly opposite to what is predicted by the Phillips curve that higher inflation implies lower growth and hence possibly a higher rate of unemployment. Again our Table 1(b) demonstrates the absence of a significant correlation between

TABLE 1(a)

Growth Rate of GDP

	Pre-reform	*Post-reform*	*All Years (1980-2009)*
Inflation rate-WPI	0.35	-0.35	-0.103

Source: Handbook of Statistics on Indian Economy; RBI Bulletin, 2009.

TABLE 1(b)

Growth Rate of GDP

	Pre-reform	*Post-reform*	*All Years (1980-2009)*
Real lending rate*	-0.352	0.147	-0.123

*Based on WPI.

real interest rate and GDP growth rate. Now, what is shocking when we have tried to plot the rate of inflation against the real prime lending rate between 1980 and 2009 (from where data of Table 1(a) and 1(b) have been taken), it demonstrates negative relationship. As the rate of inflation goes up, whatever be the response of RBI policies and private investor's strategies, eventually real lending rate actually goes down. It is well known that rising inflation is a blessing to borrowers as in real terms they have pay back less than the initially contracted amount. Therefore, in spite of providing several concessions through government policy measures to the private investors, required level of private investment did not materialize. So, we argue that it is an effective demand problem; an interest cut will not do much. This is simple Keynesian argument. But the fact is that even if interest rates are down, people will be cautious in spending. If income of those whose marginal propensity to consume is very high rises substantially along with the hope that such a rise at least partly will be sustained in the future, there will be a demand upsurge via "Life Cycle Hypothesis." This is also in fact is the hallmark of consumer behaviour model of Franco Modigliani (1986). So the marked deterioration in the condition of both developed and emerging economy like India (where crisis started much earlier), what came to be called the "Decoupling Hypothesis" has proved to be wrong.

CONCLUSION

We argue that the financial system may be stable and flush with liquidity through injection, but in the absence of sufficient demand for liquidity from the real economy, the depressive economic conditions may continue. This is the real danger of the policies being pursued so far, because most of the governments of the world economy still refuse to go in for Keynesian strategy of direct massive public investment in physical as well as social infrastructure and agricultural sector for employment, income generation and controlling CPI inflation.

REFERENCES

Fama, Eugene (1970). "Efficient Capital Markets; A Review of Theory and Empirical Work", *Journal of Finance*, 25, pp. 383-417.

Government of India (2008). Central Statistical Organization (CSO), National Accounts Statistics.

IMF (2008). World Economic Outlook : Update, 28 January.

IMF (2008). World Economic Outlook : Update, 6 November.

Kalecki, M. (1976). Essays on Developing Economies, Harvester Press, London.

Keynes, John Maynard (1919). The Economic Consequences of the Peace, London, Macmillan & Co. Ltd.

Keynes, John Maynard (1924). A Tract on Monetary Reform, London, Macmillan & Co. Ltd.

Keynes, John Maynard (1930). A Treatise on Money, London, Macmillan & Co. Ltd.

Keynes, John Maynard (1936). The General Theory of Employment, Interest and Money, London, Macmillan & Co. Ltd.

Marx, K. (1981). Capital, Volumes 1 and 3 (translated by David Fernbach), London, Penguin Books.

Nayak, Pulin B. (2009). "Anatomy of the Financial Crisis : Between Keynes and Schumpeter", *EPW*, Vol. XVIV, No. 13, March, pp. 158-63.

Rakshit, M. (1982). "The Subprime Crisis : A Primer", *Money and Finance*, 3(3), 75-124.

Rakshit, M. (2009). "India Amidst the Global Crisis", *EPW*, Vol. XLIV, No. 13, March 28, pp. 94-106.

Rakshit, Mihir (2009). "Global Economic Crisis – Stagflationary Phase", Money & Finance, March, pp. 61-94.

Taylor, L. (1983). Structuralist Macroeconomics, New York, Basic Books.

Vakulabharanam, Vamsi (2009). "The Recent Crisis in Global Capitalism : Towards a Marxian Understanding", *EPW*, Vol. XLIV, No. 13, March, pp. 144-50.

APPENDIX TABLE I

Macro-Economic Indicators of World Economy: 2001-09

Country	Subject	Units	2001	2002	2003	2004	2005	2006	2007	2008	2009
World			2.2	2.8	3.6	4.9	4.5	5.1	5.0	3.9 (3.7)	3.0 (2.2)
Advanced economies			1.2	1.6	1.9	3.2	2.6	3.0	2.6	1.5 (1.4)	0.5 (-0.3)
Euro area	GDP, at constant prices	(Y-0-Y)	1.9	0.9	0.8	2.1	1.6	2.8	2.6	1.3 (1.2)	0.2 (-0.5)
Emerging and developing economics			3.8	4.8	6.3	7.5	7.1	7.9	8.0	6.9 (6.6)	6.1 (5.1)
Developing Asia			5.8	6.9	8.2	8.6	9.0	9.9	10.0	8.4 (8.3)	7.7 (7.1)
World			4.2	3.5	3.7	3.6	3.7	3.6	4.0	6.2	4.6
Advanced economies			2.1	1.5	1.8	2.0	2.3	2.4	2.2	3.6	2.0 (1.4)
Euro area	Inflation, average consumer prices	(Y-0-Y)	2.4	2.3	2.1	2.1	2.2	2.2	2.1	3.5	1.9
Emerging and developing economics			7.7	6.8	6.6	5.9	5.7	5.4	6.4	9.4 (9.2)	7.8 (7.1)
Developing Asia			2.8	2.1	2.6	4.1	3.8	4.2	5.4	7.8	6.2
World	Commodity price index includes both fuel and non-fuel price indices	Index, 2005 = 100	58.3	58.3	65.0	80.5	100.0	120.7	135.0	185.3	176.2
	Growth rate	(Y-0-Y)	-7.9	0.0	11.6	23.7	24.3	20.7	11.8	32.3	-4.9

(Contd.)

World	Commodity food and beverage price index includes food and beverage price indices	Index, 2005 = 100	79.0	83.2	88.3	99.4	100.0	110.3	129.9	164.5	154.7
	Growth rate	(Y-0-Y)	-3.0	5.2	6.1	12.6	0.6	10.3	15.1	29.6	-5.9
World			21.5	20.9	21.1	22.0	22.5	23.2	23.5	23.5	23.6
Advanced economies			20.8	19.9	19.9	20.5	21.0	21.4	21.2	20.7	20.2
Euro area	Real investment	Percent of GDP	21.0	20.0	20.1	20.4	20.8	21.6	22.1	22.2	21.8
Emerging and developing economics			24.5	25.0	26.0	27.3	27.3	28.2	29.3	29.7	30.4
Developing Asia			30.1	31.2	33.8	35.9	37.3	37.9	38.1	39.2	39.7
World	Trade volume of goods and services	Y-0-Y growth	0.3	3.5	5.4	10.7	7.6	9.3	7.2	4.9 (4.6)	4.1 (2.1)
Advanced economies			-0.8	-0.8	-0.7	-0.6	-1.1	-1.3	-0.9	-1.0	-0.6
Euro area			0.1	0.7	0.6	1.2	0.5	0.3	0.2	-0.5	-0.4
Emerging and developing economics	Current account balance	Percent of GDP	0.6	1.1	1.9	2.4	4.1	4.9	4.1	4.1	2.9
Developing Asia			1.5	2.4	2.7	2.6	4.0	5.9	7.0	5.4	5.2

Y - O - Y implies year to year

* Gross capital formation at market prices; Source : National Statistical Office, Euro Stat, Primary domestic curr

**IMF's World Economic Outlook (WEO) Oct. 2008 Projection; and the figures in bracket are the revised projec

Source: International Monetary Fund (IMF), World Economic Outlook Database, October 2008.

8

Financial Crisis: Indian Economic Growth and External Sector

D.K. Nauriyal and Bimal Sahoo

INTRODUCTION

In the backdrop of surging world economy prior to 2007, generating euphoric optimism about future with the prediction of BRIC countries led economic growth in coming times, the onset of protracted recession, greatest ever after 1930s, through financial meltdown in US and elsewhere in early 2007, has knock on effect on such projections. International financial and trade flows have contracted at unprecedented rates for the first time in the past fifty years, with all advanced countries in deepest post-World War II recession, with a job crisis intensifying across the board. The worst affected countries are the developing economies where a sharp fall in the export earnings and further pressure on current account and balance of payments were recorded, besides decline in workers' remittances, liquidity crunch and loss of confidence of consumers and investors. The most worrying offshoots of the crisis were the lower investment and growth rates and significant loss of employment. Much of the Asia, which was the engine of recent world economic growth, has also started manifesting the signs of a slowdown, cutting into the considerable economic progress accomplished in recent years. The growth forecasts for the fast emerging Asian economies such as India and China have also been downgraded by Asian Development Bank. The IMF growth forecasts have been revised significantly, for India -1.1 per centage points down to 6.9% real GDP growth, and China and Africa both down by -0.5 per centage points to 9.3% and 6.3% respectively (Dirk, 2008). In view of this backdrop, this paper attempts to explore the impact of recession, in particular financial crisis, on Indian Economy. The paper has been organized in four sections. Section I deals with the general discussion on the impact of current recession on the world and Indian economy. Section II discusses data sources and methodology. Section III captures the impact of on-going recession on Indian economy through regression analysis, while Section IV sums up conclusions and policy inferences.

Section I

THE CRISIS AND THE WORLD AND THE INDIAN ECONOMY

The Impact on the World Economy

First time after the Second World War, the world output and trade forecast by IMF has gone negative due to the present recession. Figure 1 suggest that the world output is projected to contract by 1.3 per cent in 2009-10 with newly industrialised Asian Economies projected to be the worst hit with shrinking of their output by 5.6 per cent. This is probably due to the fact that exports continue to act as the engine of growth for these countries. Advanced Economies' (G-7 Countries) GDP is predicted to go down by 3.7 per cent, while for European countries it is forecasted that GDP will decline by about 4 per cent. Other important projections have come from the WTO, which has predicted that world trade, which has virtually collapsed in the second half of 2008, is likely to decline by as much as nine per cent in 2009-10. These projections have gained strength from the fact that exports from world's major exporters, like Germany, Japan and China, have plummeted by more than 35 per cent in the last quarter of 2008 (Kumar 2009).

FIGURE 1

Annual Per cent Change of GDP

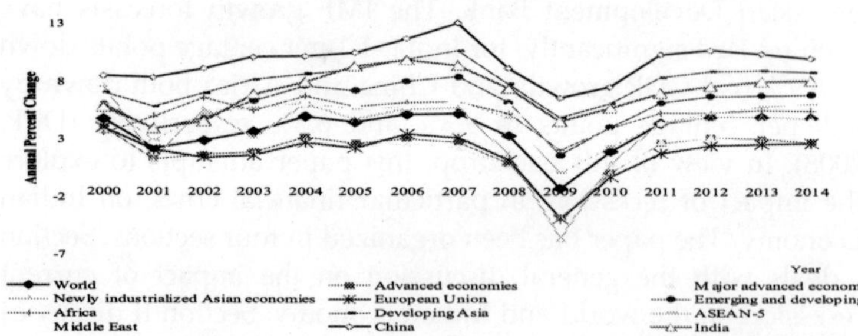

Source: International Monetary Fund, World Economic Outlook Database, April 2009.

It is evident from Figure 2 that world's total trade comprising exports and imports has been projected to decline by about 11 per cent in the financial year 2009-10.

FIGURE 2

Annual Per cent Change of World Trade

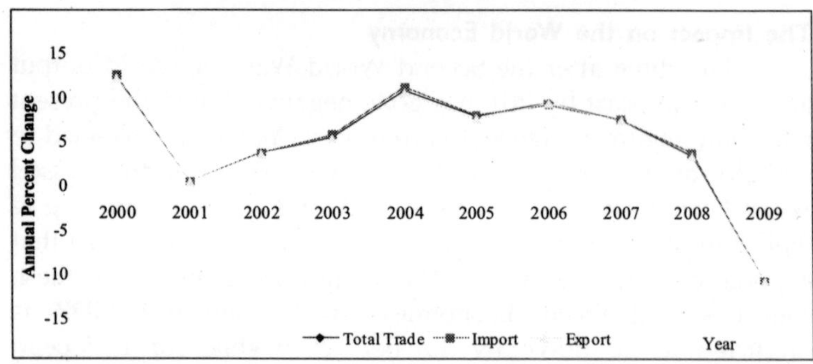

Source: International Monetary Fund, World Economic Outlook Database, April 2009.

The sharp decline in the world trade despite the staggering 11.9 trillion dollars stimulus put in place by the world economies did not seem to have helped so far. Any further decline in aggregate demand in US for foreign goods may lead to further decline in the world exports as she is the single largest importer of merchandize items and commercial services in the world. Besides, it might affect widespread unemployment and social stress in major exporting economies.

Impact on the Indian Economy

India's growth performance, since 2000, is highlighted in Table 1 based on RBI and Ministry of Finance Databases. The data suggest that economic growth in 2007–08 was high at 9 per cent despite the fact that the sub-prime crisis had already begun impacting the US and some other major economies. However, in the following quarters, the situation started looking grim with Government of India lowering its own projections of growth rate down to 6.7 per cent during 2008–09. Further, Table 1 indicates that agriculture and allied activities were projected to grow at 1.6 per cent in 2008-09, while the figure for the previous year was 4.5 per cent. Industrial sector growth rate was also projected to drop from 8.1 per cent in 2007-08 to 3.9 per cent in 2008-09. Service sector was projected to follow the same pattern.

Figure 3 illustrates India's growth performance in the new millennium as reported by IMF. It is evident that India's growth rate which was about 10 per cent in 2006 has been declining since 2007 and has touched as low as 4.5 per cent by end of year

TABLE I

India Growth Rates of Real GDP 2000-09 (%)

Sector	*2000–01 to 2007–08 (average)*	*2005–06*	*2006–07*	*2007–08*	*2008–09 (Revised estimates)**
1. Agriculture & Allied Activities	2.9	5.9	3.8	4.5	1.6
2. Industry	7.1	8.0	10.6	8.1	3.9
2.1 Mining & Quarrying	4.9	4.9	5.7	4.7	3.6
2.2 Manufacturing	7.8	9.0	12.0	8.8	2.4
2.3 Electricity, Gas & Water Supply	4.8	4.7	6.0	6.3	3.4
3. Services	9.0	11.0	11.2	10.7	9.7
3.1 Trade, Hotels, Restaurants, Transport, Storage & Communication	10.3	11.5	11.8	12.0	9.0
3.2 Financing, Insurance, Real Estate & Business Services	8.8	11.4	13.9	11.8	7.8
3.3 Community, Social & Personal services	5.8	7.2	6.9	7.3	13.1
3.4 Construction	10.6	16.2	11.8	10.1	7.2
Real GDP at factor cost	7.3	9.4	9.6	9.0	6.7

Source: RBI and *Ministry of Finance, Govt. of India.

Quarterly growth rate of India's GDP and its different components is reported in Table 2. Agriculture growth rate, as suggested by data in Table 2, in the 3rd quarter of 2008-09 is estimated to be negative at -0.8 per cent, whereas the figure for

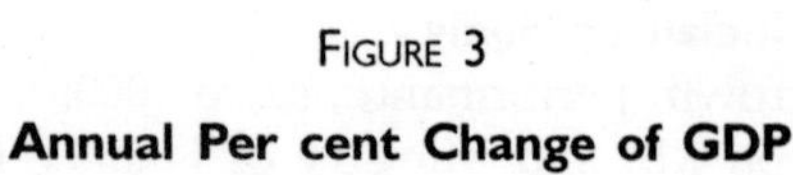

FIGURE 3

Annual Per cent Change of GDP

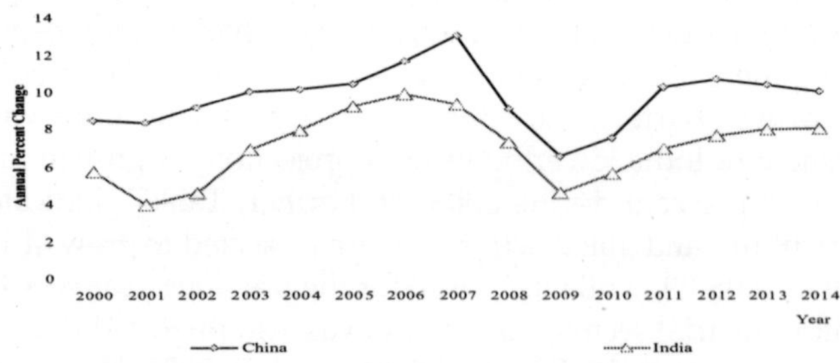

Source: International Monetary Fund, World Economic Outlook Database, April 2009.

the same period in the previous year stood at 8.1 per cent. It may be mentioned that industrial growth during first quarter of 2007-08 was 9.2 per cent, and it is projected to grow at 1.4 per cent by the last quarter of 2008-09. Among all the components of the industrial sector, manufacturing is the worst affected and it is predicted to shrink by 1.4 per cent at the end of fourth quarter of 2008-09. Service sector which was growing at 11 per cent in the first quarter of 2007-08 is estimated to grow at 4.2 per cent in the third quarter and may slightly improve to 6.8 per cent by the fourth quarter of 2008-09. Among the service sector, construction sector is predicted to grow faster than the previous year. This is because of the fact that India is experiencing demographic and urbanization pressure leading to acute shortage of urban housing which, in turn, has pushed up real estate prices, thus making it an attractive option for investment.

In regard of the Indian financial sector, it may be mentioned that though it is not overly exposed to the international financial arena, yet it has affected the domestic economy by three ways: lowering domestic liquidity, causing stock prices to fall and reducing Indian companies' access to

TABLE 2

Quarterly Estimates of GDP 2007-08 and 2008-09 (% Change over Previous Year)

Sectors	2007-08				2008-09			
	Q1	Q2	Q3	Q4	Q1	Q2	Q3	Q4
1. Agriculture & Allied Activities	4.3	3.9	8.1	2.2	3.0	2.7	-0.8	2.7
2. Industry	9.2	9.1	8.2	6.2	6	6.1	2.3	1.4
2.1 Mining & Quarrying	0.1	3.8	4.2	4.7	4.6	3.7	4.9	1.6
2.2 Manufacturig	10	8.2	8.6	6.3	5.5	5.1	0.9	-1.4
2.3 Electricity, Gas & Water Supply	6.9	5.9	3.8	4.6	2.7	3.8	3.5	3.6
3. Services	11	13.4	9.7	6.9	8.4	9.6	4.2	6.8
3.1 Trade, Hotels, Restaurants, Transport, Storage & Communication	10.8	10.3	10.3	11.8	10.2	9.8	10.2	8.6
3.2 Financing, Insurance, Real Estate & Business Services	13.1	10.9	11.7	13.8	13	12.1	5.9	6.3
3.3 Community, Social & Personal Services	12.6	12.4	11.9	10.3	6.9	6.4	8.3	9.5
3.4 Construction	4.5	7.1	5.5	9.5	8.2	9	22.5	12.5
Real GDP at factor cost	9.2	9	9.3	8.6	7.8	7.7	5.8	5.8

overseas finance. With the drying up of overseas finances, there was increasing pressure on Indian money and credit markets (Subbarao, 2008). This is primarily due to the withdrawal of about USD12 billion from the market by foreign portfolio investors between September and December 2008. Commercial credit, both for trade finance and medium-term advances from foreign banks has dried-up which has had to be replaced with credit lines from domestic banks but at higher interest costs. Some of the funds borrowed internally were converted in dollars to meet the overseas debt servicing obligations of the corporate sector. However, fall in the market capitalisation of the companies, due to fall in stock market indices, constrained their capacity to have access to the domestic and foreign markets. This is also corroborated by the fact that the total value of deals (M&A and PE) announced in the first half of 2009 was US$7.81 billion as against US$ 23.02 billion and $50.75 billion in 2008 and 2007 respectively. Cross-border M&A deal values have fallen from US$42 billion in the first half of 2007 and US$12 billion in the first half of 2008 to just US$1.4 billion in the first half of 2009 registering a fall of more than 85% over the same period last year. Reserve Bank's intervention in the forex market to manage the volatility in the rupee further added to liquidity tightening.

Domestic deals, however, have continued to remain buoyant with deal values clocking US$3.5 billion in the first half of 2009 compared to US$4.3 billion in the first half of 2008 (*Economic Times,* July 31, 2009). The banking sector by and large, remained unaffected except for ICICI, which was partly affected but managed to prevent a crisis because of its strong balance sheet and timely action by the government, which virtually guaranteed its deposits. However, given the fact that the banks and other financial institutions wanted to minimize the possibility of losses, they started cutting back on credit due to uncertainty as is evident from the fact that there was a fall in the rate of growth of loans for the purchase of auto and consumer durables by 30 and 66% respectively over the year ending June 30, 2008. Direct housing loans, which had increased by 25 per cent during 2006-07, decelerated to 11 per cent growth in 2007-08 and 12 per cent over the year ending June 2008. Although low volume of loans during the crisis could be partly attributed to low demand, yet, it is the supply side which has played a major role in this regard. The losses suffered by non-banking financial institutions (especially mutual funds) and corporates, as a result of their exposure to domestic stock and currency markets, is another noticeable issue. Such losses are expected to be large, as indicated by the decision of the RBI to allow banks to provide loans to mutual funds against certificates of deposit (CDs) or buy-back their own CDs before maturity (Chandrasekhar and Ghosh, 2008).

Impact on External Sector

As demand declines in the importing countries, exports from trading partners are adversely affected. The IMF has estimated that imports of goods and services in advanced economies may decline by 12 per cent in 2009 (*World Economic Outlook,* April 2009) which implies a significant decline in exports from developing economies. The Indian external sector may face the consequence of this development: first, there could be economic slowdown via multiplier process due to a sharp drop in export growth for the lack of external demand, as massive investment has already been undertaken in export-oriented sector with the rising trends in both merchandised and service exports before 2007-08. Secondly, given the share of exports at around 27% of GDP in 2nd quarter of 2008, the slowdown in exports may result in the disposal of exportable surplus in the domestic market which might affect the domestic economy. Third, changes in international oil price will have major impact on the Indian economy as it accounts for one-third of India's import with demand for petroleum products as price inelastic at least in the short-run (Rakshit, M., 2009).

FIGURE 3

Trade Intensity

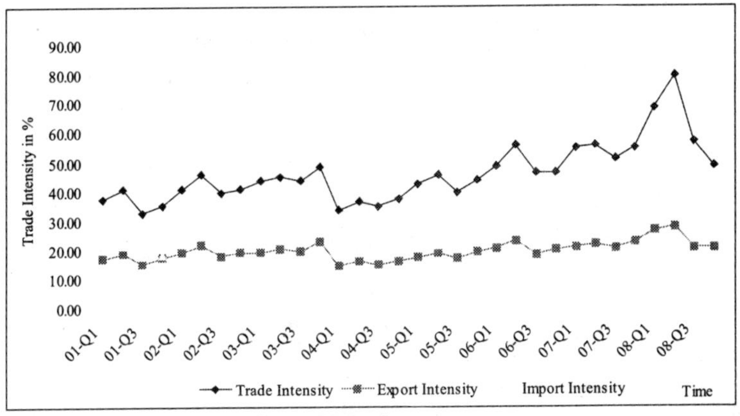

Source: Complied by authors from RBI Database.

Figure 4 highlights India's trade intensity on quarterly basis since 2001. It elucidates that the trade intensity which was about 37% in the first quarter of 2001 has gone up to 78% by the second quarter of 2008. This is primarily because of the increase in import intensity attributable to sharp rise in international oil prices. International oil prices have almost doubled during this period. However, after the cooling down of world oil prices, import intensity had come down to about 28% by last quarter of 2008 and so had the total trade intensity. On export front, export intensity which was about 16% at the beginning of the financial year 2001-02, had gone up to about 27% by the second quarter of 2008. However, due to demand constraints in the world economy, as an offshoot of financial crisis, export intensity declined to 19.7% by fourth quarter of 2008. Quarterly growth rate of India's trade intensity is reported in Figure 4. It is evident from Figure 5 that growth rate followed a cyclical pattern for total trade, export intensity and import intensity. All three growth rates followed almost same pattern. This is probably for the fact that India's external sectors depends heavily on the world economic scenario. It is evident from the Figure 4 that, India's export intensity which was growing at 17% at the end of last quarter of 2007 started registering negative growth of -26.3% by the second quarter of 2008.

FIGURE 5

Growth Rate of Trade Intensity

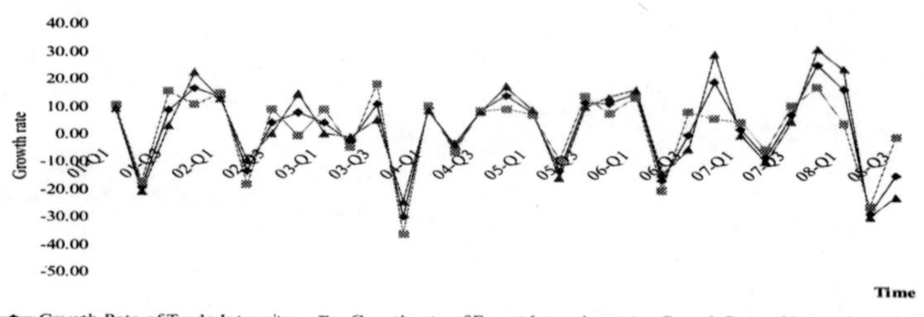

Source: Complied by authors from RBI Database.

In absolute terms (US $) India's exports and imports have been growing (See Figure 6). The value of imports has always been greater than that of exports for each year especially after 2002-03. It is also evident that India's exports and imports went up significantly only after financial year 2002-03. The increase in exports and imports may be due to the dismantling of quantitative restrictions on 715 items from April 1, 2001 (*Economic Survey*, 2002) and India's increasing integration to the world economy especially after WTO agreements. Figure 6 also brings to the fore that after 2008, the exports have stagnated while imports have been on rise though at declining rate. Further, annual growth rates of India's exports and imports have registered a decline after 2007.

In terms of growth rates of exports and imports, there has been a continued decline after the quantum jump in 2003-4 except for a brief recovery during 2006-08 as is highlighted by

FIGURE 6

India's Export and Import in US$ (Million)

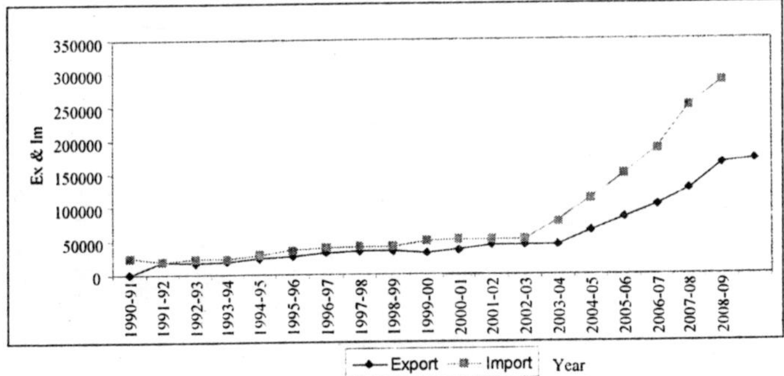

Source: Complied by authors from RBI Database.

Figure 7. The decline in growth rate of exports appears to be far steeper than that of imports after 2008-09.

FIGURE 7

Growth Rate of India's Export and Import (US$)

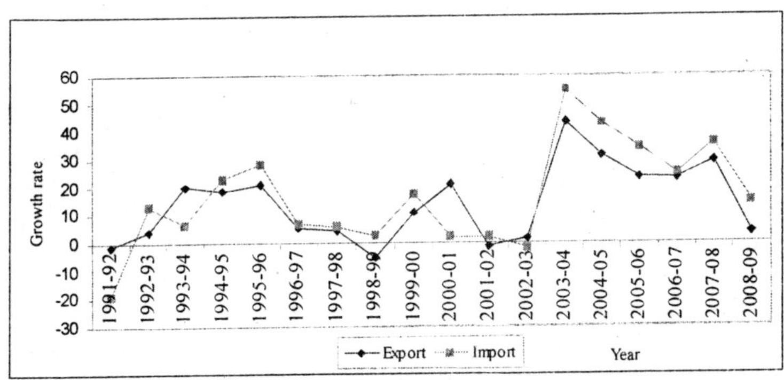

Source: Complied by authors from RBI Database.

India's exports (month-wise), since 2005-06 are reported in Figure 8. It can be observed from the Figure 8 during June to November 2007-08 that exports were only marginally higher than what they were during 2006-07. However, after November, an improvement in the same is noticeable.

FIGURE 8

Month-wise India's Export (US$ Million)

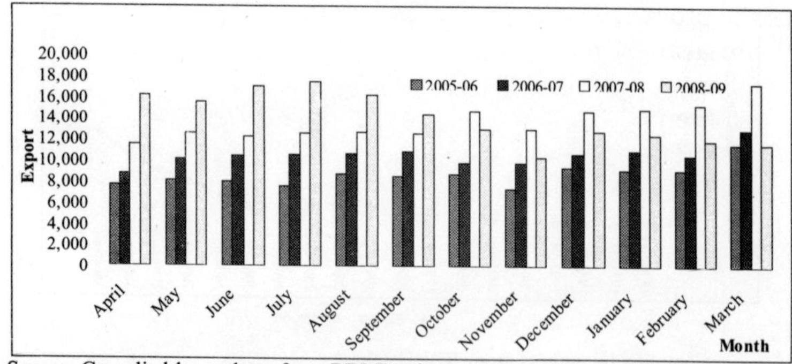

Source: Complied by authors from RBI Database.

Since October 2008-09, export is lower as compared to the previous year, and the gap has increased continuously. In February 2007-08, India's exports were US$ 15221 million, where as for 2008-09 they stood at US$ 11913 million. Till the month of September in the financial year 2008-09 export was higher than that of previous year. However, afterwards it has been declining and less than the figures of 2007-08. The impact of the recession on India's external sector is expected for the fact that OECD countries, which account for almost 39% of the India's goods and services export are hit by the current crisis. Same is true of Asia which accounts for 42.26% of India's exports. Looking at the data for balance of payments since 2000, there appears to be a visible impact of the current world-wide recession on India's foreign trade. India's foreign trade which had been steadily growing with imports moving up faster, started recording decline since the fourth quarter of 2007 with exports showing perceptible decline. The decline for imports, nevertheless, was found to be far more visible, albeit with a time lag, i.e., impact more evident from the second quarter of 2008 to the extent that it fell even below the growth rate of exports. As could be seen from the data in Table 1 in Appendix I, the increasing trend in India's exports got reversed in 2007-08, as was happening world over. The decline in the export of primary products was found to be much more pronounced as compared to manufactured products. In the second half of 2008, this decline led to the growth rate of Indian exports going negative for all items with much more visible decline in the export of primary products. Among the manufactured products, the worst affected were the textile and textile products, although the deceleration in the growth rates of chemical and related products, engineering goods and gems and jewellery was also discernible after 2007-08. So far as invisibles are concerned, there was a noticeable decline in the export of services since 2007-08, however, decline in the transfers were found to be far more rapid. The inflows, in the form of incomes, (investment income and compensation of employees) were, nevertheless, found to be maintaining, by and large, a steady growth. In regard of the services, while there has been decline in the growth rate of all types of exportable services, the decline in the export of software services were found to be the much faster since 2007-08. They, in fact, had started recording negative growth after the second quarter of 2007-08. The exports of transportation, and to some extent, travel services were found to be not much affected by the current world-wide meltdown.

In regard of FII, it is evident from the RBI data that during 2007-08, net FII inflows into India amounted to $20.3 billion out of which US$11.1 billion were pulled out during the first nine and half months of calendar year 2008, of which $8.3 billion occurred over the first six and a half months of financial year 2008-09 (April 1 to October 16). The trend continued till January-March 2009. As a result, the Sensex fell by approx. 60% from its closing peak of 20,873 on January 8, 2008 by October 2008 and there was a further fall in the following months. In addition, this withdrawal by the FIIs led to a sharp depreciation of the rupee. Between January 1 and October 16, 2008, the RBI reference rate for the rupee fell by nearly 25 per cent, even relative to a weak currency like the dollar, from Rs. 39.20 to the dollar to Rs. 48.86. This was despite the sale of dollars by the RBI, which was reflected in a decline of US$ 25.8 billion in its foreign currency assets between the end of March 2008 and October 3, 2008. The increasing current account deficit, rapidly decreasing remittances from overseas Indians along with FII withdrawal and RBI's manoeuvring in foreign exchange market to manage the volatility in the rupee led to decline in foreign exchange reserves from US$ 286 billion in September 2008 to US$ 247.7 billion in November 2008, though by July 10 2009, these reserves started registering increase to become worth US$ 264 billion (*Macroeconomic Review*, August 2009, RBI). There was, however, not much of the impact of recession on the FDI.

SECTION II

DATA SOURCES AND METHODOLOGY

For the purpose of this study, data on Gross Domestic Product, quarterly and annually, (GDP) have been taken from Central Statistical Organization's (CSO) monthly abstract. For obtaining a consistent series of GDP, the data belonging to different base years were converted to single base year, using price correction factor. Data on export, import, foreign direct investment (FDI) and foreign institutional investment (FII) were compiled from Reserve bank of India's (RBI) monthly statistical abstract. Data for other countries and world as a whole were taken from the databases of International Monetary Fund, World Economic Outlook Database, April 2009. To find out whether the present financial crisis trigged in the west has significantly impacted the Indian economy, the present paper has applied regression technique. Since the crisis can probably affect India's GDP most likely via external sector, only the external sector variables are taken in this study. Although GDP is not solely determined by the external factors as internal factors such as labour, capital, domestic government policy also play significant roles in shaping it, yet the external sector is the focus of this paper. Therefore, only variables relating to this sector have been accounted for. The functional form of the model is given as:

$$GDP = f(Export, Import, FDI, FII, GDP_{t-1}) \qquad ....(1)$$

The estimable regression equation is given as:

$$LnY_t = \alpha + \beta_1 LnX_t + \beta_2 LnI + \beta_3 FDI + \beta_4 FII + LnY_{t-1} + \lambda D + \mu_t \qquad ....(2)$$

where Y_t is the GDP at time period 't', X stands for exports, I stands for imports, FDI and FII stand for foreign direct investment and foreign institutional investment respectively. D is the dummy variable and it takes value of 1 for time period

January 2007 onwards, i.e. the fourth quarter of financial year 2006-07, otherwise zero. The main reason for taking this threshold period is that since the beginning of 2007, the financial crisis had started manifesting itself. The μ_2 is the error term and represents the variables which are not included in the model. Further details of the regression analysis and results are given in the 3rd section of the paper.

SECTION III

REGRESSION ANALYSIS: DISCUSSION AND INTERPRETATION

Prior to regression analysis, all the variables were tested for stationarity, applying Augmented Dickey-Fuller (ADF) test. The test revealed that log of GDP and Log Export follows I(3), whereas FDI follows I(2) and FII follows I(0). This implied that GDP's and exports' third difference is stationary, FDI's second difference is stationary, and FDI is stationary at its level (Appendix-II). Since different variables are stationary at different level, it is difficult to apply usual time series regression. Besides, a variable, stationary at third difference, will lose significant level of information. The problem of different variables being stationary at different levels may probably be attributed to seasonality in the data. Therefore, the data set were tested for seasonality by applying auxiliary regression. The details of the seasonality test are given in the proceeding section.

Seasonality Test

For seasonality test, all variables were transformed to their natural logarithm, except for FII for the fact that data for some quarters were negative. The auxiliary regression equation is given as

$$\nabla Z_t = \alpha + \sum_{i=1}^{3} \beta_i S_{it} + \mu_t$$

where Z_t is the variable under consideration, $\nabla Z_t = Z_t - Z_{t-1}$ is the first difference of Z_t, alpha is the constant term and S_{it} is the ith seasonal dummy variable that takes the value of one for i^{th} quarter otherwise zero. μ_t is the error term assumed to be stationary. The dependent variable is the first difference of Z_t is considered rather than the levels, in order to separate the stochastic trend in the series. The regression is performed for each of the variables for their full sample as well as two subset samples each with an equal number of observations. The regression results are reported in Table 3.

TABLE 3

Auxiliary Regression Result for Seasonality Test

Variable	*Sample*					R^2	*Adj* R^2	*F value*
Ln GDP	Full	0.012*	-0.035**	-0.036	0.138*	0.479	0.423	8.30*
	1st half	0.084	-0.031	-0.032	0.157***	0.358	0.320	2.29***
	2nd half	0.026*	-0.105*	-0.039*	0.118*	0.991	0.989	439.48*
Ln Export	Full	0.112*	-0.131*	-0.042	-0.110*	0.417	0.356	6.42*
	1st half	0.123***	-0.167**	-0.048	-0.090***	0.642	0.568	7.17**
	2nd half	0.101**	-0.085	-0.045	-0.130**	0.356	0.301	2.03
Ln Import	Full	0.013	0.089***	0.056	-0.006	0.176	0.078	1.84
	1st half	0.043	0.033	-0.002	0.020	0.092	0.042	0.40
	2nd half	-0.017	0.153	0.114	-0.034	0.364	0.310	2.10
Ln FDI	Full	0.361	0.071	-0.043	0.068	0.093	0.047	1.032
	1st half	0.143	-0.085	0.062**	-0.378*	0.424	0.369	0.478
	2nd half	-0.061	0.405	-0.149	0.516	0.235	0.169	1.127
FII	Full	977.23	-5246***	605.52	-243.32	0.195	0.157	2.295***
	1st half	-174	-1400**	332	1872***	0.474	0.342	3.605**
	2nd half	2128.25	-9991.2**	879.25	-2359.2*	0.309	0.251	2.644***

Note: * 1% level of significance, ** 5% level of significance, *** 10% level of significance.

The results of the auxiliary regression suggested that, the series GDP, export and FII exhibit substantial seasonal fluctuations while Imports and FDI witnessed mild seasonal fluctuations. The R^2 value provides information of the extent to which variation around the mean values of the three seasonal dummy variables affect movements of Z_t around its mean. The regression result for the GDP indicated that seasonality accounted for about 48% of variation in the whole sample, 35% in the first half and 99% in the second half; and for exports it accounted for 42%, 64% and 36% for full sample size, first half and second half, respectively. Based on the above, all the variables were de-seasonalised and then regression for equation-2 was performed. In order to avoid any possible autocorrelation problem, a time variable (T) was also introduced in the regression, which took the value of 1 to 31. Prior to regression analysis, multicolinearity test was conducted by applying correlation and the result suggested the existence of high degree of colinearity between exports and imports, exports and FDI, and imports and FDI. In order to overcome the problem of multicolinearity, three models were estimated and the results are reported in Table 4. Cochrane-Orcutt (C-O) procedure has also been applied in order to take care of probable autocorrelation. The regression results, based on equation-2, are presented in Table 4.

REGRESSION RESULTS AND DISCUSSION

The statistically significant F-value, reasonable high R^2 and close to two D-W statistics suggest that the model is good fit. The statistically significant coefficient of dummy variable with the value -0.141 in Model 1, as shown in Table 4 suggests that financial crisis has had negative impact on GDP. Similarly, for all the models, the coefficient of dummy variable was found to be negative and statistically significant. This suggested that, financial crisis, trigged in the west, has adversely impacted India's GDP. In Model-1, the coefficient of exports enters positively and found to be statistically significant. This suggested that export have contributed positively to the growth of India's GDP. Exports appear to have exercised stimulating influence over the economy probably through technological spillovers and other externalities (Bhagwati, 1988). Existing empirical studies also suggest that expanded international trade increases the number of specialized inputs, driving growth rates as economies opens to international trade (Helpman, 1991, Rivera-Batiz and Romer, 1991, Romer, 1990). Besides, there are other empirical studies that also support export led growth hypothesis (Love and Chadra, 2005, László Kónya, 2006, Dong and Zhang, 2009, Awokuse, 2007, Michaely, 1977, Feder, 1982, Marin, 1992, Thornton, 1996).

In Model-2, the coefficient of imports was found to be positive and statistically significant, implying that imports too have positively impacted India's growth. This is probably because India primarily imports machinery and oil which are used in the production process. In addition, imports are

TABLE 4

Alternative Specifications with Dependent Variable: ln GDP

Variable	Model-1	Model-2	Model-2
Intercept	0.850	0.733	7.820**
Log Export	1.139*	—	—
Log Import	—	1.098*	—
FDI	—	—	0.978*
FII	0.0001	0.0001	0.0001***
Ln GDP_{t-1}	0.003	0.008	0.126
D	-0.141***	-0.185**	-1.353*
T	-0.011**	-0.023*	0.0123
R^2	0.784	0.720	0.720
Adj. R^2	0.653	0.639	0.664
F value	385.65*	369.02*	12.87*
D-W	2.03	1.92	1.89

* 1% level of significance, ** 5% level of significance, *** 10% level of significance

important vehicles for the transfer of technology and knowledge products which, in turn, promote economic growth (Frankel and Romer, 1999, Romer and Cyrus, 1996, Grossman and Helpman, 1997). However, this proposition needs further investigation.

In Model-3, coefficients of FDI and FII suggested that both of them have exercised positive and statistically significant impact on Indian economy, although the value of the coefficient of FII is weak suggesting a weaker link. While FDI's contribution to growth could be explored through capital formation and technology transfer (Blomstrom and Kokko, 1998, Borensztein *et al.*, 1995) along with accumulation of knowledge due to labour training and skill acquisitions (De Mello, 1999), the role of FII to promote growth could be attributed to the availability of funds for further expansion and fresh investments both in the domestic sector and abroad. The most frequently cited benefits of FDI are probably productivity spillovers to the host economy, resulting in higher growth. There are empirical studies that support this contention (De Mello, 1999, Bende-Nebende *et al.*, 2000, Durham, 2004, Nair-Reichert and Weinhold, 2001, Xu 2000, Caves, 1974, Lipsey, 1999, Globerman, 1979), though the impact was found to vary across countries (UNTAD 1999, 2003; Borensztein *et al.*, 1998, Bende-Nabende, *et al.* 2001).

SECTION IV

CONCLUSION

1. As a result of recession, India's growth rate which was about 10 per cent in 2006 has been declining since 2007. Consequently, the growth projection for 2008-9 has been lowered down to 6.7 per cent. A perceptible decline in the growth rates of all the sectors was found. Among all the components of the industrial sector, manufacturing was found to be the worst affected and predicted to shrink by 1.4 per cent at the end of fourth quarter of 2008-09. Service sector which was growing at 11 per cent in the first quarter of 2007-08 is estimated to grow at 4.2 per cent in the third quarter and may slightly improve to 6.8 per cent by the fourth quarter of 2008-09. The recession has found to have affected the domestic economy by three ways: lowering domestic liquidity, causing stock prices to fall and reducing Indian companies' access to overseas finance. Fall in the market capitalisation of the companies due to fall in stock market indices was also found to have constrained their capacity to have access to the domestic and foreign markets.
2. India's foreign trade which had been steadily growing with imports moving up faster, started recording decline since the fourth quarter of 2007 with exports showing perceptible decline. The decline for imports, nevertheless, was found to be far more visible, albeit with a time lag, i.e., impact more evident from the second quarter of 2008 to the extent that it fell even below the growth rate of exports. In the second half of 2008, the growth rate of Indian

exports became negative for all items with much more visible decline in the export of primary products. Among the manufactured products, the worst affected were the textile and textile products, although the deceleration in the growth rates of chemical and related products, engineering goods and gems and jewellery was also discernible after 2007-08. In regard of the services, while there has been decline in the growth rate of all types of exportable services, the decline in the exports of software services were found to be the much faster since 2007-08. The exports of transportation, and to some extent, travel services were found to be not much affected by the current world-wide meltdown.

3. Although there was not much of the impact of recession on FDI, there was found to be reverse flow of FDI effected by heavy withdrawal triggering substantial plummeting of Sensex and depreciation of Rupee. The erosion in the external value of Rupee was also exacerbated by increasing current account deficit, rapidly decreasing remittances from overseas Indians, and RBI's manoeuvring in foreign exchange market to manage the volatility in the rupee.
4. The results pertaining to dummy variable in all the models suggest that financial crisis has exercised negative impact on India's GDP.
5. Both, the exports and imports, appear to have had stimulating influence over the economy probably through technological spillovers and other externalities.
6. FDI and FII were also found to have positively impacted the growth of India's economy, although the impact of FDI was found to be much stronger.

POLICY MEASURES

Given the increasing integration of Indian economy with rest of the world, the slowdown of Indian economy is expected to be reversed only with the recovery of global markets. Until then, the only policy option before government of India and RBI is to stimulate the domestic demand through fiscal and monetary measures. While government of India could put more disposable income in the hands of the tax payers, RBI could stimulate the demand for credit by facilitating monetary expansion and reduction in the cost of borrowing through infusion of additional liquidity by cutting the CRR, lowering the SLR and unwinding the Market Stabilisation Scheme (MSS). Both the policy measures, however, have their own limitations.

References

Awokuse, Titus O. (2007), "Causality between exports, imports, and economic growth: Evidence from transition economies", *Economics Letters*, Vol. 94, pp. 389–95.

Baltagi, Badi H. (2001), "Econometric analysis of Panel data", 2nd edition, John Wiley and Sons.

Bende-Nebende, A.A.., J.L. Ford, S. Sen, and J. Slater (2000), "Long-run Dynamics of FDI and Its Spillovers onto Output: Evidence from the Asia-Pacific Economic Cooperation Region", University of Birmingham, Department of Economics, Discussion Paper.

Bhagwati, J. (1988), "Protectionism, Cambridge", MA, MIT Press.

Blomström, M and A Kokko (1998), "Multinational Corporations and Spillovers," *Journal of Economic Surveys*, Vol. 12, pp. 247-77.

Borensztein, E.J., D. Gregorio and J.W. Lee (1995), "How Does Foreign Direct Investment Affect Economic Growth?" NBER Working Paper No. 3, 5057.

Caves, R.E. (1974), "Multinational Firms, Competition and Productivity in Host Country Market," *Economics*, Vol. 41, pp. 176-93.

Chandrasekhar, C.P. and Jayati Ghosh (2008), 'India and the Global Financial Crisis.

De Mello Jr., L.R. (1997), "Foreign Direct Investment in Developing Countries and Growth: A Selective Survey," *The Journal of Development Studies*, 34(1): 1-34.

De Mello Jr., L.R. (1999), "Foreign Direct Investment-led Growth: Evidence from Time Series and Panel Data," *Oxford Economic Papers*, Vol. 51, pp. 133-54.

Dicky, D.A and W.A Fuller (1981). "Likelihood ratio statistics for autoregressive time series with a unit root", *Econometrica*, 49: 1057-72, July.

Dirk Willem te Velde, 2008, The global financial crisis and developing countries, Background Note, Overseas Development Institute, Oct. London.

Durham, J. (2004), "Absorptive Capacity and the Effects of Foreign Direct Investment and Equity foreign portfolio investment of economic growth", *European Economic Review*, 48(2): 285-306.

Feder, G. (1982), "On exports and economic growth", *Journal of Development Economics*, Vol. 12, pp. 59-73.

Frankel, J.A., and Romer, D. (1999), "Does trade cause growth?", *American Economic Review*, Vol. 89, pp. 379-99.

Frankel, J.A., Romer, D., and Cyrus, T. (1996), Trade and growth in East Asian countries: Cause and effects?, NBER Working Paper No. 5732.

Globerman, S. (1979), "Foreign Direct Investment and Spillover Efficiency Benefits in Canadian Manufacturing Industries," *Canadian Journal of Economics*, Vol. 12, pp. 42-56.

Grossman, G.M. and Helpman, E. (1997), "Innovation and growth in the global economy. Cambridge", MA: MIT Press.

He Dong, and Wenlang Zhang (2009), " How dependent is the Chinese economy on exports and in what sense has its growth been export-led?", *Journal of Asian Economics*, Paper in the press.

Helpman E. and Grossman, G. (1991), "Innovation and Growth in the Global Economy, Cambridge", MA: MIT Press, 1991.

Kónya László (2006), "Exports and growth: Granger causality analysis on OECD countries with a panel data approach", *Economic Modelling*, Vol. 23, pp. 978-92.

Lipsey, R.E. (1999), "The Location and Characteristics of U.S. Affiliates in Asia," NBER Working Papers 6876, National Bureau of Economic Research.

Love Jim, and Ramesh Chandra, (2005), "Testing export-led growth in Bangladesh in a multivariate VAR framework", *Journal of Asian Economics*, Vol. 15, pp. 1155–168

Marin, D. (1992), "Is the export-led growth hypothesis valid for industrialized countries?", *Review of Economic Statistics*, Vol. 74, pp. 678-88.

Michaely, M., (1977). "Exports and growth: an empirical investigation", *Journal of Development Economics*, Vol. 40, pp. 49-53.

Mohan, T.T. Ram (2009), "The Impact of the Crisis on the Indian Economy" *Economic and Political Weekly*, March 28, 2009, Vol. xliv, No. 13.

Nair Reichert, U. and D. Weinhold (2001), "Causality Tests for the Cross-country Panels: A New Look at the FDI and Economic Growth in Developing Countries," *Oxford Bulletin of Economics and Statistics*, Vol. 63, pp. 0305-9049.

Rakshit Mihir (2009), " India amidst the Global Crisis", *Economic and Political Weekly*, March 28, 2009, Vol. xliv, No 13.

Rivera-Batiz, L., Romer, P. (1991), "Economic integration and endogenous growth", *Quarterly Journal of Economics*, Vol. 106, pp. 531-56.

Romer, P. (1990), "Endogenous technological change", *Journal of Political Economy*, Vol. 98, pp. 71-102.

Subbarao, 2009, 'Impact of the Global Financial Crisis on India Collateral Damage and Response', Speech delivered at the Symposium on "The Global Economic Crisis and Challenges for the Asian Economy in a Changing World", organized by the Institute for International Monetary Affairs, Tokyo on February 18, 2009. Accessed on July 12, 2009

Thornton, John (1996), "Co-integration, causality and export-led growth in Mexico, 1895-1992", *Economics Letters*, Vol. 50, pp. 413-16

UNCTAD (1999), Trends in International Investment Agreements: An Overview, United Nations Publication, Sales No. E.99.11.D.23.

UNCTAD (2003), "Investment Policy Review of Nepal," New York.

Wooldridge Jearey, M. (2002), "Econometric Analysis of Cross Section and Panel Data", The MIT Press, Cambridge, Massachusetts London, England.

Xu, B. (2000), MNEs, Technology Diffusion and Host Country Productivity Growth, *Journal of Development Economics*, Vol. 16, pp. 477-93.

Appendix I

Table I

Sector-wise India's Export Performance (US $ Million)

Commodity / Year	*2000-01*	*2001-02*	*2002-03*	*2003-04*	*2004-05*	*2005-06*	*2006-07*	*2007-08*	*2008-09*
1. Primary products	7126.2	7163.6	8706.1	9901.8	13553.3	16377.4	19686	27500	23200
A. Agriculture and allied products	5973.2	5901.2	6710	7533.1	8474.7	10213.8	12683.5	18400	16000
B. Ores and minerals	1153	1262.4	1996	2368.7	5078.6	6163.6	7002.5	9100	7200
2. Manufactured Products	34835.2	33369.7	40244.5	48492.1	60730.7	72562.8	84920.6	102900	100900
A. Chemicals and Related products	5885.9	6051.8	7455.3	9445.9	12443.7	14769.5	17335.5	21200	20500
B. Engineering goods	6818.6	6957.8	9033	12405.4	17348.3	21718.8	29567.2	37400	40700
C. Textile and textile products	11285	10206.5	11617	12791.5	13555.3	16402.1	17373.2	19400	17700
D. Gems and jewellery	7384	7306.3	9029.9	10573.3	13761.8	15529.1	15977	19700	17200
3. Petroleum products	1869.7	2119.1	2576.5	3568.4	6989.3	11639.6	18678.7	28400	24900
4. Invisibles (a+b+c)	328.8333	371.104	417.2015	526.8431	687.4979	901.7234	1145.812	1486.04	729.7
(a) Services	165.8986	173.2283	206.6264	264.4273	427.4624	579.746	758.6059	900.77	514.06
(i) Travel	35.74536	31.73631	32.90377	49.49143	65.8877	79.07256	90.72299	113.49	94.32
(ii) Transportation	20.83662	21.88375	25.22876	31.58744	46.38708	63.54422	80.28236	100.14	127.77
(iii) Insurance	2.745877	2.911899	3.668777	4.126075	8.634824	10.64399	11.98699	16.39	11.31
(iv) G.n.i.e.	6.6444	5.228279	2.91568	2.372171	3.965443	3.165533	2.492693	3.3	7.91
(v) Miscellaneous of which	99.92635	111.4681	141.9095	176.8502	302.5874	423.3197	573.1208	667.45	272.75
Software services	64.55927	76.37483	95.52401	126.1888	175.2209	237.2608	311.8204	403	28.14
Business Services	NA	NA	NA	NA	NA	93.77778	191.7565	167.71	152.69
Financial Services	NA	NA	NA	NA	NA	12.14286	28.81376	32.17	29.61
Communication Services	NA	NA	NA	NA	NA	15.87302	20.9695	24.08	9.96
(b) Transfer	135.6205	163.7975	175.4943	223.9694	214.4936	257.5193	294.5569	442.59	27.46
(i) Official	2.572313	4.656072	4.473315	5.433453	6.09491	6.734694	6.34644	7.53	4.13
(ii) Private	133.0482	159.1414	171.021	218.536	208.3987	250.7846	288.2104	435.06	23.33
(c) Income	27.31414	34.07812	35.08075	38.44635	45.54191	64.45805	92.64876	142.68	188.18
Investment income	26.0124	32.82138	33.91818	37.16902	40.90784	62.65986	88.71781	138.08	174.99
Compensation of employees	1.301733	1.256737	1.162568	1.277323	4.634074	1.798186	3.930955	4.6	13.19

Appendix II

Augmented Dickey Fuller Test

$$\Delta X_t = \alpha_0 + \alpha_1 t + \beta X_{t-1} + \sum_{j-1}^{k} \gamma_j \Delta X_{t-j} + \varepsilon_t$$

The Augmented Dickey Fuller (ADF) test is (Dickey and Fuller, 1981) based on the following regression:

Where D is the difference operator and e_t is the stationary random error. The null hypothesis is that X_t is a non-stationary series and it is rejected when b is significantly negative. The constant and trend terms are retained only if they are significantly different from zero. There are three possible models according to whether, the estimation take into account constant term and trend. The possible outcomes are: (1) when there is no constant and no trend; (2) when there is constant but no trend; (3) when there is both trend and constant. Only the negative coefficients are reported here, because a positive coefficient implies the series is explosive. The optimal number of lags, *k*, is determined by minimizing the Akaike information criterion. The present study used JMulTi statistical software to calculate the

Table I

Unit Root Test at Levels

Variable	*Order of integration*	*ADF Statistics (Without C&T)*	*ADF Statistics (With C&T)*	*ADF Statistics (With C and Without T)*
Log of GDP	I (3)	-1.06	-2.21	-2.32
Log of Export	I (3)	-0.43	-2.34	@
Log of Export	I (2)	@	-1.14	-0.42
FDI	I (1)	-0.71	-1.19	-0.71
FII	I (0)	@	-3.01	-3.43**

Notes: The critical values for unit root tests are -3.43, -2.86 and -2.57 without trend with intercept, and -3.96, - 3.41 and -3.13 with trend and intercept, and -2.56, -1.94, -1.62 for without trend and intercept term constant at 1%, 5% and 10% level of significance respectively, (Davidson, R. and MacKinnon, J. 1993). 'C' stands for constant and 'T' stands for trend. *signifies statistically significant at 1% level, **signifies statistically significant at 5% level, ***signifies statistically significant at 10% level; @ $\beta > 0$.

ADF statistics and to find the critical values. The critical values for unit root tests are -3.43, -2.86 and -2.57 without trend with intercept, and -3.96, - 3.41 and -3.13 with trend and intercept, and -2.56, -1.94, -1.62 for without trend and intercept term constant at 1%, 5% and 10% level of significance respectively, (Davidson, R. and MacKinnon, J., 1993).

TABLE 2

Unit Root Test for First Difference

Variable	*Order of integration*	*ADF Statistics (Without C&T)*	*ADF Statistics (With C&T)*	*ADF Statistics (With C and Without T)*
Log of GDP	I (3)	-1.32	-3.01	-2.35
Log of Export	I (3)	-1.25	-3.10	-1.62
Log of Export	I (2)	-1.32	-2.24	-1.22
FDI	I (1)	-3.49*	-1.19	-1.01

TABLE 2

Unit Root Test for Second Difference

Variable	*Order of integration*	*ADF Statistics (Without C&T)*	*ADF Statistics (With C&T)*	*ADF Statistics (With C and Without T)*
Log of GDP	I (3)	-1.44	-3.11	-2.42
Log of Export	I (3)	-1.46	-3.11	-1.75
Log of Export	I (2)	-2.96*	-2.24	-1.21

TABLE 2

Unit Root Test for Third Difference

Variable	*Order of integration*	*ADF Statistics (Without C&T)*	*ADF Statistics (With C&T)*	*ADF Statistics (With C and Without T)*
Log of GDP	I (3)	-1.57	-3.87**	-2.54
Log of Export	I (3)	-2.56*	-3.14***	-1.[illegible]

9

A Study of Interrelation between London and Indian Stock Market and Impact of the Global Slowdown on the Indian Economy

SHRI PRAKASH AND RITISNIGDHA PANIGRAHI

This Paper focuses on the study of integration of Indian economy in International economic system and its impact on Indian economy under conditions of worldwide economic slowdown. The following hypotheses have been evaluated in this study:

(1) Indian economy has been integrated to a great extent in International Economic System. Close and direct relationship between equity prices of Bombay and International stock market have been considered as an indicator of international stock market; (2) Degree of integration has also been postulated to be represented by the slowdown of (a) Growth of GNP, and (b) Growth of export earnings under economic slowdown.

First hypothesis is supported by the evidence of:

(i) positive and significant rank and Pearson's correlation coefficients, and (ii) positive and significant slope and elasticity coefficients.

INTRODUCTION

Globalization has resulted in the integration of various national markets into international markets. This has made national economies closely interdependent where change in one economy affects the entire world economy. Naturally, economic slowdown since September 2008 has adversely affected the world economy. World-wide repercussion of slowdown of US economy reflects the degree and direction of integration of national systems of production of goods and services, financial services and investment into world economic system of the day. This study examines the impact of US slowdown on Indian economy with reference to growth and exports. These two facets have been linked to international demand for Indian goods and interrelation between Indian and foreign stock markets. We have considered only London Market in this study. As international representatives we could have taken up Wall Street, Paris, Bonn, Tokyo, but time and data constraints did not allow us to examine markets other than London. We have taken London Stock Market FTSE100 as the representative of stock market of developed countries. It is linked closely to Wall Street on the one hand, and other national markets on the other.

OBJECTIVES

To examine the impact of US slowdown on Indian economy with reference to growth and exports and international demand for Indian goods and interrelation between Indian and foreign stock markets.

HYPOTHESES

The following hypotheses have been evaluated in this Study :

1. Indian economy has been integrated to a great extent

in International Economic System. Close and direct relationship between equity prices of Bombay and International stock market have been considered as an indicator of international stock market; and

2. Degree of integration has also been postulated to be represented by the slowdown of: (a) Growth of GNP, and (b) Growth of export earnings under economic slowdown.

First hypothesis is supported by the evidence of: (i) positive and significant rank and Pearson's correlation coefficients, and (ii) positive and significant slope and elasticity coefficients.

IMPACT ON THE INDIAN ECONOMY

We examine the impact of slowdown on Indian economy in historical comparative perspective. But we focus only on growth of: (i) GDP, (ii) exports, and (iii) exports as proportion of GDP. Besides, we have also evaluated interrelation between London Stock Market FTSE 100 and Bombay Stock Market BSE SENSEX for having an idea about the degree of integration of these two markets.

First we examine the growth of GNP at factor cost and exports. Study covers a period of 17 years from 1990-91 to 2007-08. This provides the back-drop for a comparison of two scenarios before and after the onslaught of slowdown.

STOCK MARKET—A BAROMETER OF ECONOMY

Stock market is considered to be a barometer of economic health of a country. It is an index of macro-fundamentals of an economy. Higher the development stage of an economy, healthier and more vibrant will be its stock market. Stage of growth reflects greater purchasing power income, and hence, greater tend to be the savings and investment, a substantial part of which is likely to be parked in equity capital. Besides, population and income together determine market size, where the size of market is an indicator of capital absorption capacity of an economy. Size and role of stock market increases within increase in market size of the economy. Market size to a great extent moves up with the growth of an economy. Then, New Economic Policy of 1991 has opened up the Indian economy. It has facilitated entry of foreign investors. FDI and FII enter the economy through stock market. In and outflows of foreign investment directly affect the stock prices. This imparts a substantive volatility to stock prices, since FII is foot loose. Thus, stock market also indicates the degree and direction of integration of national capital market into international financial system. In and outflows of foreign investment directly affect the stock market. As New York and London markets are Apex Markets, these markets have the strongest linkages with markets of other counties, including Indian market. Therefore, we have considered the relation of BSE SENSEX with London market FTSE 100 in order to furnish an idea about the integration of Indian market into world financial system. This integration directly shows the economic interdependence of countries.

CONCEPT OF VOLATILITY

The concept of volatility is intricate and complex. Conventionally, the term instability has been used and contrasted with stability. But, volatility goes a step beyond instability. Volatility may be associated with extreme changes in stock prices in a highly short period such as a day or even an hour. Unlike instability, volatility may not necessarily be associated with dis-equilibrium. (Sri Prakash and Ritisnigdha Panigrahi, 2008)

Volatility may be in two directions; positive and negative; which leads to a reduction in equity prices is negative volatility. A fall in price brings about a reduction in returns which acts as transformation of investors' behaviour. Under the negative volatility either the market is dominated by the bearish sentiment which may turn bulls into bears. As against this positive volatility represents domination of bullish sentiment which transforms bears into bulls. We define it as psychologically driven consequence which represents switching behaviour (cf. K.N. Badhani and L.S. Bisht, 2007).

EXPORTS AS REPRESENTATIVE OF TRADE

Exports represent the purchasing power in international markets. Imports are proportional to exports. The coefficient of proportionality will be one in case of balance of trade. It shall be greater than one if trade balance is adverse. Favourable trade balance will make the coefficient less than one.

$$M \propto E$$

$$M = \lambda E$$

$$\lambda \begin{matrix} < \\ = \\ > \end{matrix} 1$$

No country can afford to be perpetually in adverse trade balance. If that is so, the country will have to earn foreign exchange through other means such as Invisibles, Capital, etc. or alternatively the country has to receive exchange from grant or investment and NRI remittances.

SOURCES OF DATA

We have downloaded one year five months' daywise data of index of BSE Sensex from Prowess. Data thus cover the period from 1st April, 2008 to 8th September, 2009. London FTSE 100 data have been taken from Yahoo Finance. Data pertaining to exports and GNP have been taken from Economic Survey, 2008-09.

METHODS OF DATA ANALYSIS

Data have been analyzed by different methods. Methods for data analysis have been selected on the basis of objectives of the study and nature of the data. For the evaluation of inter-relation between variables, rank correlation and regression function have been used. ANOVA has been employed to examine the degree and direction of variation.

Results of ANOVA enable us to evaluate the degree of variation between days and four different prices of two stock markets. ANOVA furnishes results for entire data set, covering all days and prices together. Results will thus embody an aggregation/averaging effect of all days and different prices of BSE SENSEX and London Stock market FTSE 100.

For disentangling effect of aggregation of different prices from day effect, we have used regression analysis for which we take 1 year 5 months data of two stock exchanges. We have examined interrelation between 4 different prices of BSE SENSEX and London FTSE 100, that is, opening price, highest price, lowest price, and closing price. Following linear regression equation has been used.

$$Y_i = a + b X_i \qquad \text{....(1)}$$

where Y_i denotes price of Bombay Stock Exchange and X_i expresses i[th] price of London FTSE 100, I = 1, 2, 3, 4.

EMPIRICAL RESULTS

Empirical results have been organized and presented in different sections.

Both these markets report following 4 prices of stocks: opening, lowest, highest and closing. All prices have been analyzed jointly as well as separately. ANOVA takes all four prices of all days together for BSE SENSEX and London FTSE 100 separately. Regression model examines interrelation between each pair of prices of two markets.

SECTION I

NATURE OF PRICE MOVEMENTS

For having an overview of variation and nature of price movements in two markets, we have plotted the same in three sets of graph. But the data have been periodized in order to detect change in trend, if any. Periods covered are from April 1, 2008 to June 30, 2008; July 1, 2008 to December 31, 2008, January 1, 2009 to June 30, 2009; and July 1, 2009 to September 8, 2009. Thus, we have 16 period-wise graphs for 4 prices of both the markets.

A perusal of these graphs highlights the following main facets of price movements:

(i) Prices of Indian equity capital have all along been much higher than those of U.K. market;

(ii) In all periods, there is coherence in price movements in two markets;

(iii) Bombay stock market depicts higher degree of volatility in almost all periods, while London market does not show volatility. Though London stock market does fluctuate but fluctuations are in a narrow band;

(iv) Price movements of London market lend empirical support to Prakash-Subramanian thesis that movements of prices of scripts are generally contained in a narrow band, while big bang changes occur only occasionally due to external shocks. Indian market also supports the thesis but in a weaker way. The weak support may be accounted by international slowdown; and

(v) Troughs and peaks of two markets, by and large, coincide with each other. This suggests direct relation between two markets.

The reason behind volatility is that the Indian stock market is much more subject to external shocks, especially those related to Foreign Institutional Investment than the stock markets of developed countries. Stock market of developed countries moves mainly along with macro-fundamentals of the economy, while Indian stock market may register volatility, despite macro-fundamentals being sound. The Foreign Institutional Investment mostly goes in search of greener pastures and it takes advantage of instability created by its own in and out movements of portfolio investment. In October 2008, there was more volatility than before in Indian stock market due to US financial crisis.

SECTION II

BSE SENSEX VARIATION

This section deals with the variation of 4 equity prices of BSE over 17 months. Following tables report the results ANOVA of BSE Index of Four Prices:

As critical values of F are lower than the calculated values both for rows and columns, between price and between days variation is significant. Thus, prices vary significantly from each other and prices also vary significantly between the days. Between days significant variation of prices highlights the volatile nature of prices.

Stock Price Variation in London Market

The significant variation between prices suggests that each price of BSE should be related to the corresponding price of London market. But the question is whether prices of London market also vary in a fashion similar to that of Bombay market. For this, we examine the results of ANOVA for London market.

Critical values of F are less than actual values both for rows and columns; so both row and column variation is significant. Significant variation of prices is captured by columns and significant intertemporal variation between days for London Stock Exchange is captured by rows. Following table reports the results of ANOVA for one year five month's data of FTSE 100 London for all four prices.

Aggregating London FTSE 100 over 1 Year 5 Months

ANOVA						
Source of Variation	*SS*	*Df*	*MS*	*F*	*P-value*	*F crit*
Rows	1.0559E+10	344	30694083	1687.59	0	1.1525039
Columns	23362174.7	3	7787392	428.1581	1.2E-180	2.6135273
Error	18770141	1032	18188.12			
Total	1.0601E+10	1379				

SECTION III

INTER-RELATION BETWEEN PRICES OF BSE AND FTSE 100

This section deals with interrelations between each pair of prices of BSE Sensex and London FTSE 100 Index. Opening price of BSE has been related to opening price and closing price to closing price of London FTSE 100, and so on. Results will be discussed later. First we discuss results of rank correlation analysis.

Rank-Correlation Coefficients between Prices of London and Indian Stock Markets

Results	*Opening Price*	*Highest Price*	*Lowest Price*	*Closing Price*
Rho	0.806803	0.800446	0.822994	0.810753
t value	42.7435	41.2006	47.16684	43.75368

The table shows that all 4 Spearman's rank correlation coefficients are high and statistically significant. It may be inferred that all prices of London and Bombay Stock Exchange markets move together in the same direction. It highlights a high degree of relation between these two markets. It is observed that foot loose FII moves back and forth among the markets. This makes stock crises (i) depend a great deal on FII. As institutional investment is substantial in quantum, in an outflow directly affect the prices; (ii) tendency of these foot loose investors to exploit both falling and rising prices in and outflows of FII make stock prices more volatile than what these price generally are. Two facets of relations may, however, be distinguished: Complimentary and competitive. Complementary makes two markets to move together, while competition may lead to opposite directional movement. FII moves from one market to park it in another market to take advantage of relative state of the markets. In such cases, price in two markets will move in opposite direction. During upward phase of the cycle, both markets may move upwards together. Recently, when 56 billion worth of FII was withdrawn from Indian markets to park it in Chinese market, two markets moved in opposite directions. After a couple of days, reverse direction flow of FII into Indian market pushed its index up.

SECTION IV

This section deals with results of regression analysis of interrelation between the growth of different prices of BSE SENSEX Index and London FTSE 100 Index. Table on nwxt page shows these results.

Regression of BSE SENSEX

All four correlation and slope coefficients are statistically significant. Corresponding to unit change in prices of London

TEACHERS	INTERCEPT	SLOPE	t^1	t^2	R^2	F
Open price of BSE SENSEX and FTSE 100	-1016.86	2.91	-1.64984	22.79489	0.60376797	519.6068
High price of BSE SENSEX and FTSE 100	-995.14	2.90	-1.56611	22.33887	0.59405965	499 0249
Low price of BSE SENSEX and FTSE 100	-1163.198	2.94	-1.99204	23.98561	0.62785505	575.3096
Close price of BSE SENSEX and FTSE 100	-1074.058	2.92	-1.75472	23.03255	0.60871986	530.4984

Stock Market, change in Bombay Stock prices is 2.91, 2.90, 2.94, and 2.92 respectively for the opening, lowest, highest and closing prices. Thus, changes in prices of Bombay Stock Market are explained by prices of London FTSE markets. This is an indicator of integration of Indian into international financial market.

In order to estimate elasticity of Indian stock prices with respect to prices of London stock market FTSE 100, we have estimated log linear equation also:

$$\log Y_i = \beta_0 + \beta_1 \log X_i$$

Table below contains OLS estimates of these equations. The slope coefficients of the constant elasticity function furnish direct estimates of price elasticity.

SECTION V

EFFECT OF SLOWDOWN

Now we examine the growth effect of slowdown on growth of Indian Economy and Exports.

Explosive growth of exports has been one of the propellers of growth of Indian economy in the post-reforms period, especially after 2003. Naturally, downturn in the world economy has adversely affected export sectors of the economy severely. The growth effect is reflected by the slackening of growth of the economy during second half of the financial year, 2008-09. Growth rate declined from near 9 per cent to a much lower figure during this period. First quarter of the current financial year has, however, recorded a growth of 6.1 per cent, which is an improvement over growth of 5.3 and 5.1 per cent during previous two quarters.

Increasing export dependence of Indian economy and consequent rise in its vulnerability to external shocks may be gauged from the following.

Export earnings in 1950-51 were only 5.01 per cent of GNP, it rose to 9.71% in 2003-04 and 17.84% in 2007-08. Export sectors of the economy have been decisively affected adversely by international slowdown. Export earnings have declined nearly by 21 per cent in July 2009, decline has touched 30% in August 2009. As the developed economies like US, Japan, UK Germany and other West European economies experienced the pangs of recession since September 2008, their consumption fell sharply down that greatly affected Indian exports. These countries account for major proportion of Indian exports. During 11 months from September 2008 to August 2009, Indian exports continued to decline month after month. From Jan. 2009 to August 2009, exports of India registered a decline of 33 per cent (Prabhakar Sinha, p. 19). This was bound to affect the production and plan for future development. We subject the thesis for further evaluation.

Exports will however, partially represent the impact of slowdown on Indian economy. Extent of adverse effect of slowdown depends only partly upon export dependence of growth of the economy. The export dependence of Indian economy has, however, been increasing over the years. The decade-wise change in proportion of exports in GNP is shown by the following table:

Year	1951	1961	1971	1981	1991	2001	2008
Export Earnings as % of GDP	6.26	3.91	3.95	5.05	5.57	9.79	17.85

Despite decrease in export earnings relative to GNP from 1951 to 1961, there is a definite trend of rise in export dependence of Indian economy. Export dependence of GNP has increased from slightly more than one-twentieth of GNP in 1951 to about one sixth in 2008. This opening up of the economy highlights the increasing dependence of Indian upon world economy on the one hand, and increasing degree of integration of Indian into world economy, making it more vulnerable to international shocks. It may be inferred that relatively lower degree of openness and integration of Indian and Chinese economy into global economy restricted the damage to their systems during the global economic stress. The thesis is also supported by the fact that Indian public sector banks continued to transact normal business. Government regulation and no international linkage of these banks made investors, depositors and fellow banks to continue to repose confidence in public sector commercial banks, though depositors withdrew money heavily from private banks. As against this, financial crisis started building up in 2007 with great increase in default by sub-prime borrowers in the US housing sector. In less than a year, it acquired gigantic weight, resulting in global slowdown. Immediate effect was that both borrowers and banks lost faith in banking system of the country. This pushed the financial market into a state of ill-liquidity. Export and IT sectors' loss of business also lend support to our thesis of integration.

This section discusses Growth of Exports and GNP. A perusal of Table 1 shows that (i) both exports and GNP have grown consistently together from 1990-91 to 2007-08; (ii) exports seem to have grown ahead of income; (iii) pace of growth has not been uniform; (iv) trend has, however, been positive and the pace of growth of GNP and exports appear to accelerate or decelerate together.

Above results highlight that growth of the economy has now come to be linked with the growth of exports, indicating a greater degree of integration of national system of production and commodity markets into international economic system. This also highlights increasing nature of openness of the economy. Besides, earlier strategy of import substitution-based growth has been replaced by export-led growth to a great extent. We examine Table 2 in order to assess the validity of above inferences.

A comparison of column 1 with column 2 of second table reveals that year on year growth of GNP and exports has moved in opposite direction in 8 out of 17 years. This does not provide conclusive evidence to support the thesis that growth of GNP and exports has accelerated or decelerated together. It also renders the hypothesis of growth strategy being export led suspect. This inference is further supported by change in direction of GNP, accounted by exports, being in consonance with the opposite directional change in growth of exports and GNP (Column 4, Table 2). For further examination of the thesis,

TABLE I

Year	*Exports*	*GNP at factor cost*
1990 -91	32553	507487
1991 -92	44041	584099
1992 -93	53688	669872
1993 -94	69781	780070
1994 -95	82674	912956
1995 -96	106353	1069805
1996 -97	118817	1247628
1997 -98	130100	1388729
1998 -99	139752	1601114
1999 -00	159561	1771094
2000 -01	203571	1902284
2001 -02	209018	2077654
2002 -03	255137	2244725
2003 -04	293367	2517462
2004 -05	375340	2855326
2005 -06	456418	3256269
2006 -07	571779	3749607
2007 -08	655864	4297047

we have used Spearman's rank correlation coefficient between growth rates of (a) exports and GNP; (b) exports and GNP and GNP and share of exports in GNP. Results are shown on next page.

First two coefficients are negative but not statistically significant. This highlights the fact that Indian economy is far too big for its growth to be driven mainly by exports. The growth of Indian economy is still inward looking, though exports do contribute to it. Third coefficient is, however, not only positive and high; it is statistically significant also. It may suggest that the bi-directional relationship between the growth of GNP and exports depends substantially upon the exportable surpluses. Thus, export sectors are lagging rather than leading sectors of the economy if this thesis is accepted. Then, shrinking growth of

TABLE 2

Growth (Exports)	*Growth (GNP)*	*Exp GNP*
35.29014223	15.0963473	7.53998894
21.90458891	14.68466818	8.014665488
29.97504098	16.45060549	8.945479252
18.47637609	17.03513787	9.055639045
28.64141084	17.18034604	9.941344451
11.71946254	16.62200121	9.523431664
9.496115876	11.30954098	9.368278476
7.418908532	15.29348059	8.728422836
14.17439464	10.61635836	9.009177379
27.58192791	7.407286118	10.70139895
2.675724931	9.21891789	10.06028915
22.06460688	8.041329307	11.36606934
14.98410658	12.15012975	11.65328414
27.94213391	13.42081827	13.14525907
21.6012149	14.04193427	14.01659384
25.27529589	15.1504068	15.2490381
14.70585663	14.59993007	15.26313303

P (12)	*P* (13)	*P* (23)
-0.02	-0.221	0.92

exports will relate to exportable surpluses rather than demand recession in markets. It implies that there exists sufficient demand in international market to sustain consistent growth of Indian exports. Then, any decline in growth of exports may be attributed to competitive prices, standards of quality and adherence to supply schedules. Alternatively, if demand is really deficient, continuing growth of exports shall be accounted by fulfilment of past orders.

But this needs evidence. We go to diagrams representation of data. Following diagrams map the three variables of Table 2.

Diagrams in Appendix highlight the volatile nature of export growth. Each successive peak moves higher up, while each successive trough slumps deeper. As against this, fluctuations of GNP growth are relatively milder. Peaks and troughs of GNP and Exports in several cases do not coincide. But each successive peak and trough is higher than the preceding one. It reveals long-run trend of consistent growth of both GNP and Exports. This also suggests that export fluctuations are influenced more by the state of demand in foreign markets than by availability of exportable surpluses. But the curve, depicting exports as a proportion of GNP, shows much lower degree of fluctuations. The long-run trend, suggested by this discussion, is that India needs to diversify its export basket and broaden and widen the direction to reduce export dependence on demand in markets of developed countries. Asian and Africa markets need more attention. We are not suggesting trade creation rather than diversion. Results do suggest that Indian economy is being increasingly integrated into World economy.

Results of Regression Analysis

In view of the above results, we have examined the trend of change in three variables: exports, GNP and exports as a proportion of GNP. OLS estimates of linear regression are reported below.

$$Y_1 = 23.196 - 0.3948X,\ R^2 = 0.0492$$
$$t = (5.05)\ (-0.88)$$
$$Y_2 = 15.442 - 0.2234X,\ R^2 = 0.1306$$
$$t = 10.12 - 1.50$$

$$Y_3 = 6.7320 + 0.4388X,\ R^2 = 0.9156$$
$$t = 13.21\ 8.82$$

where Y_1, Y_2, Y_3 and X denote exports, GNP, exports as proportion of GNP and time respectively. First two equations do not show any definite trend which is explained by year on year fluctuations. This lends empirical support to our hypothesis of volatility of exports which may be explained by the changing state of the market, including changing intensity of competition offered by other countries. This is supported by results of third equation. Exports as a proportion of GNP not only depict positive trend but the regression coefficient is also statistically significant. As has already been explained, Y_3 is, by and large, free from volatile oscillations of exports. We may now infer that (i) globalization policy in 1990-91 has forged greater links between World and Indian Economy through increasing degree of openness; (ii) exported growth strategy has moved quite far, though the journey is not complete; and (iii) slowing down of growth of export and GNP may be attributed to worldwide slowdown.

SECTION VI

ELASTICITY ESTIMATES

All elasticity coefficients are statistically significant. Corresponding to 1 per cent change in prices of London Market, prices of Indian stocks change as highly as by 116.83, 116.70, 118.37 and 117.72 per cent respectively. Interestingly, per centage change in all four prices of Bombay market in response to change in London prices are almost the same, low differences notwithstanding. These results lend further support to the thesis that equity prices in India not only respond to changes in domestic environment but these prices are highly sensitive to international influences.

TEACHERS	*INTERCEPT*	*SLOPE*	t_1	t_2	R^2	*F*
Open price of BSE SENSEX and FTSE 100	-0.1929	1.1683	-1.0249	22.80435	0.60396657	520.0384
High price of BSE SENSEX and FTSE 100	-0.1881243	1.16700298	-0.97966	22.35903	0.59449477	499.9263
Low price of BSE SENSEX and FTSE 100	-0.2492017	1.18369114	-1.38572	24.14322	0.63091047	0.6309
Close price of BSE SENSEX and FTSE 100	-0.2257095	1.1772163	-1.22471	23.46667	0.61619562	550.6844

CONCLUSION

- Stock market of developed countries moves mainly along with macro fundamentals of the economy, while Indian stock market may register volatility, despite macro fundamentals being sound.

- Bombay stock market depicts higher degree of volatility in almost all periods, while London market does not show volatility. Though London stock market does fluctuate but fluctuations are in a narrow band;
- Troughs and peaks of two markets, by and large, coincide with each other. This suggests direct relation between two markets.
- Prices vary significantly from each other and also prices vary significantly between the days of both BSE SENSEX and London FTSE 100.
- The significant variation between prices suggests that each price of BSE should be related to the corresponding price of London market.
- Rank Correlation highlights a high degree of relation between these two markets.
- India not only responds to changes in domestic environment but these prices are highly sensitive to international influences.

References

CMIE, Prowess, New Delhi.

Investment and Growth of Indian Economy—A study in Input-Output Framework, Proceedings of IIOA's 17th International Conference of Input-Output Economics.

K.N. Badhani and L.S. Bisht (2007), Regime-Switching in Stock Returns and Volatility: Evidence and Implications, *NICE Journal of Business*, Vol. 2, No. 1, January-June, 2007.

Ministry of Finance (2009), *Economic Survey*, New Delhi.

Prabhakar, Sinha (2009), *Economic Times of India*, p. 19, September 16th, 2009.

Prakash, Shri (1981), Cost Based Prices in Indian Economy, *Malyalan Economic Review*, Vol. XXVI, No. 1.

Prakash, Shri and Panigrahi, Ritisnigdha (2008), Impact of Volatility of Stock Market on Foreign.

Prakash, Shri and Subramainan, R. (2006), Modeling of Share Price Movements in NSE: An Empirical Study of Selected Cases, *Finance India*, Vol. XX, No. 4, December.

Yahoo Finance (2008-09).

APPENDIX

Opening Prices of BSE Sensex and London FTSE 100 from 1ST April 2008 to 30th June 2008

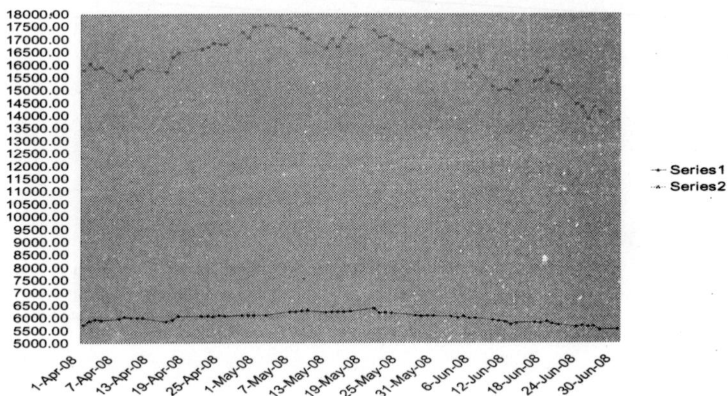

Opening Prices of BSE Sensex and London FTSE 100 from 1ST July 2008 to 30th December 2008

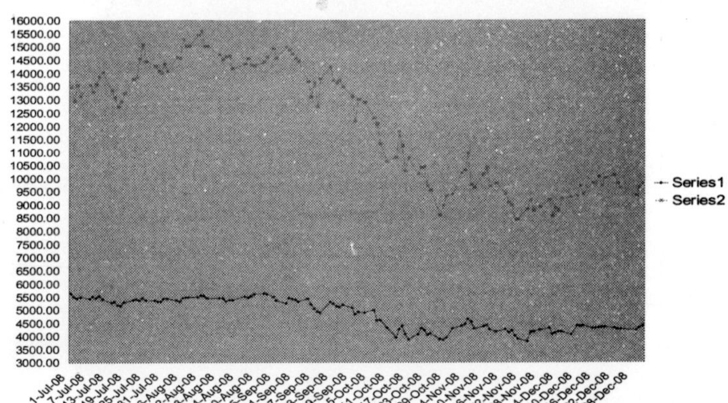

Opening Prices of BSE Sensex and London FTSE 100 from 1ST January 2009 to 30th June 2009

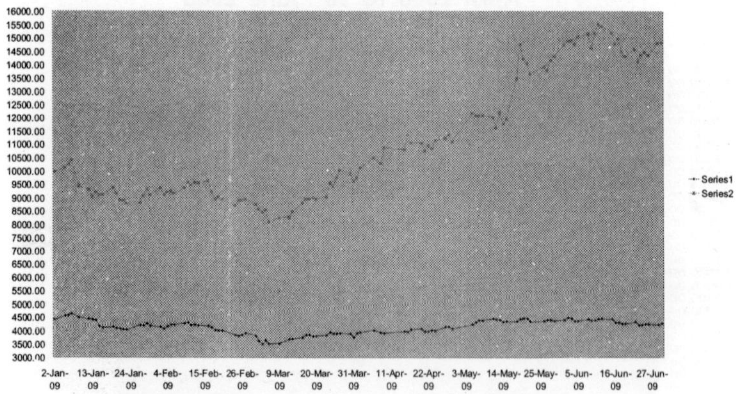

Opening Prices of BSE Sensex and London FTSE 100 from 1ST July 2009 to 8th September 2009

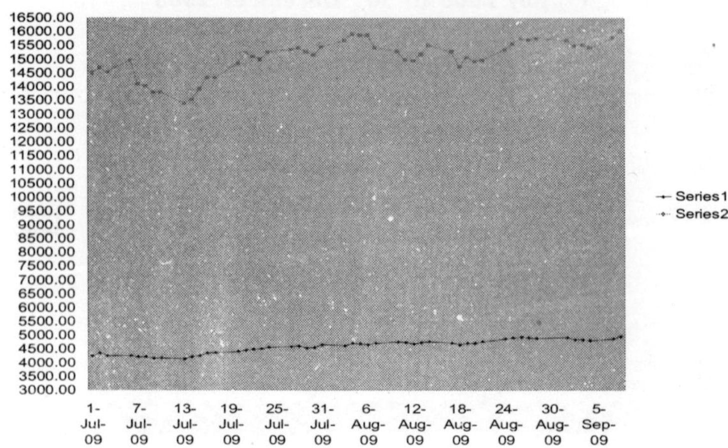

Highest Prices of BSE Sensex and London FTSE 100 from 1st April 2008 to 30th June 2008

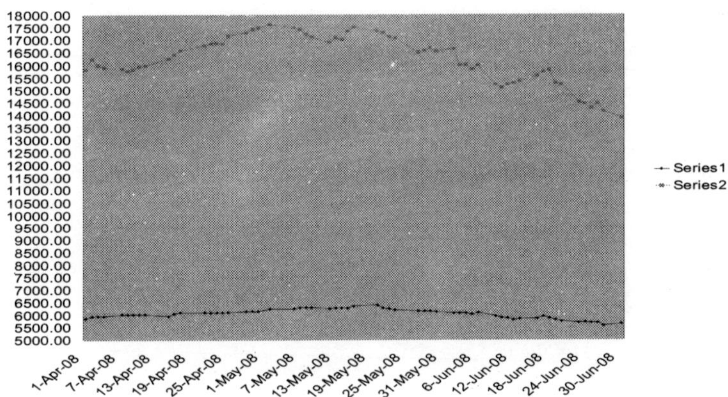

Highest Prices of BSE Sensex and London FTSE 100 from 30th June 2008 to 31st December 2008

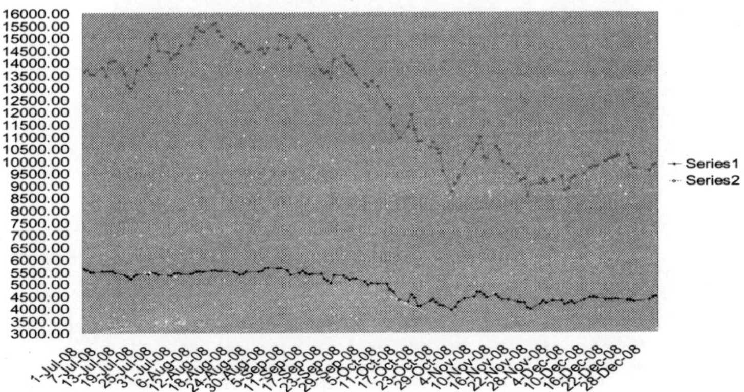

Highest Prices of BSE Sensex and London FTSE 100 from 1st January 2009 to 30th June 2009

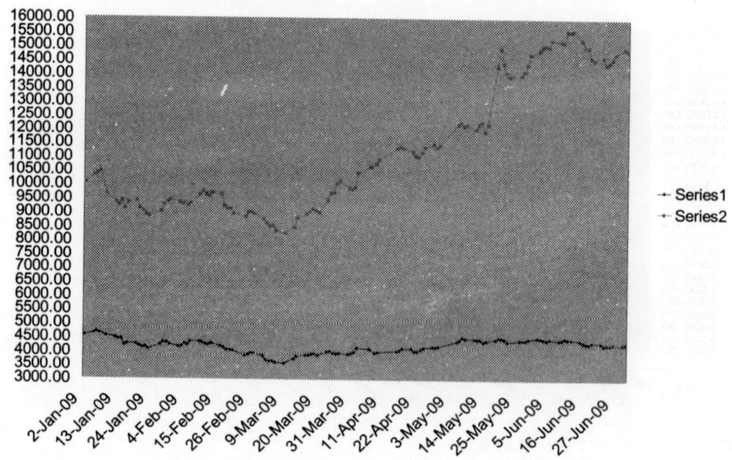

Highest Prices of BSE Sensex and London FTSE 100 from 30th June 2009 to 8th September 2009

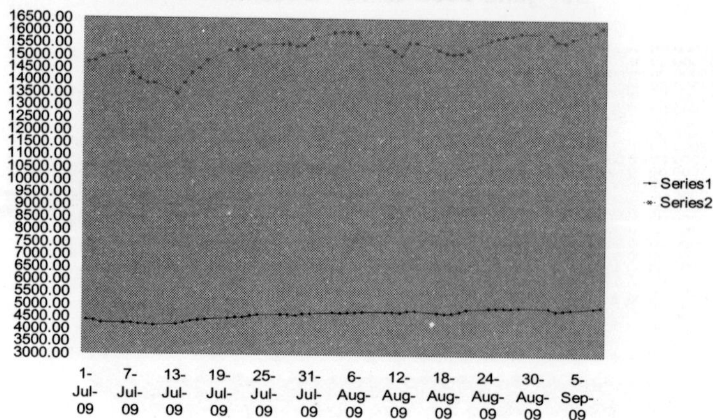

Low Prices of BSE Sensex and London FTSE 100 from 1st April 2008 to 30th June 2008

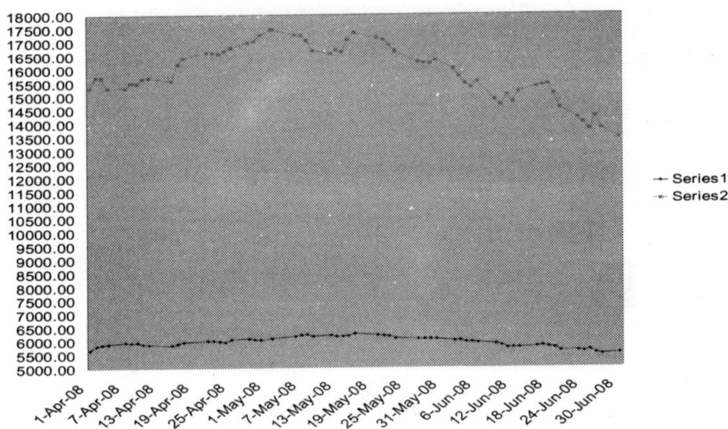

Lowest Prices of BSE Sensex and London FTSE 100 from 30th June 2008 to 31st December 2008

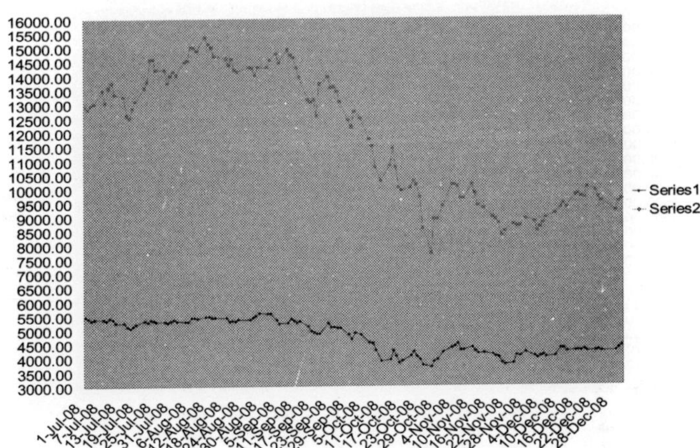

Low Prices of BSE Sensex and London FTSE 100 from 1st January 2009 to 30th June 2009

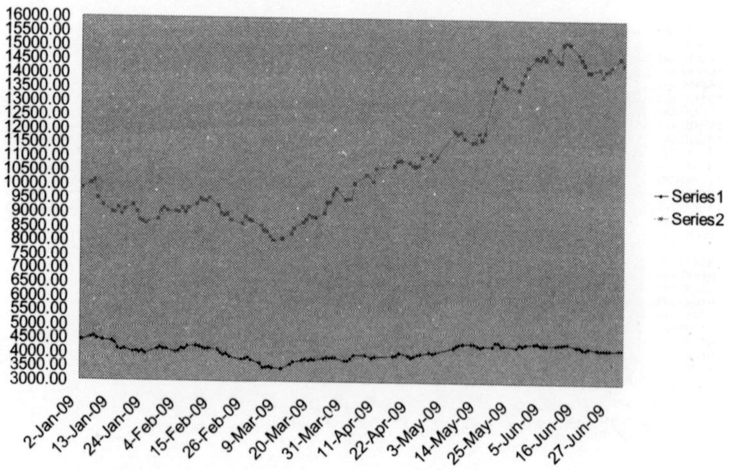

Low Prices of BSE Sensex and London FTSE 100 from 30th June 2009 to 8th September 2009

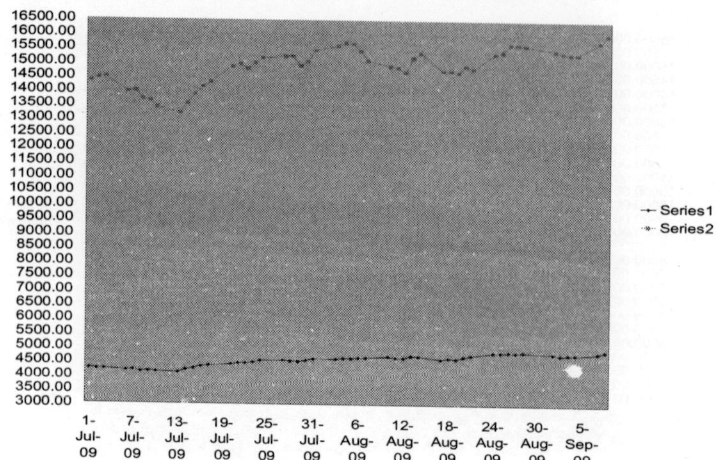

Prices of BSE Sensex and London FTSE 100 from 1st April 2008 to 30th June 2008

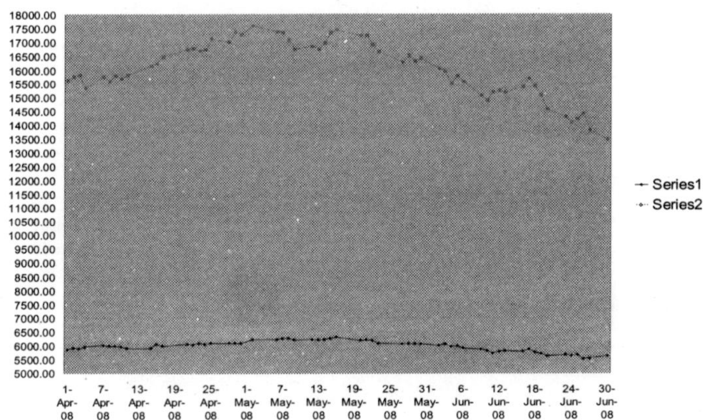

Close Prices of BSE Sensex and London FTSE 100 from 30st June 2008 to 31st December 2008

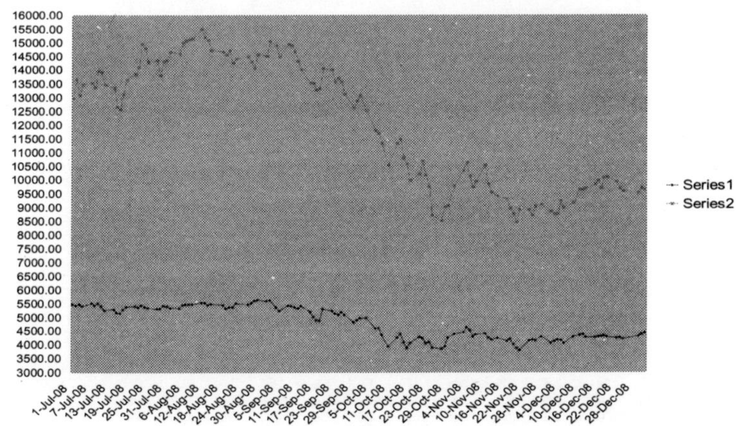

Close Prices of BSE Sensex and London FTSE 100 from 1st January 2009 to 30th June 2009

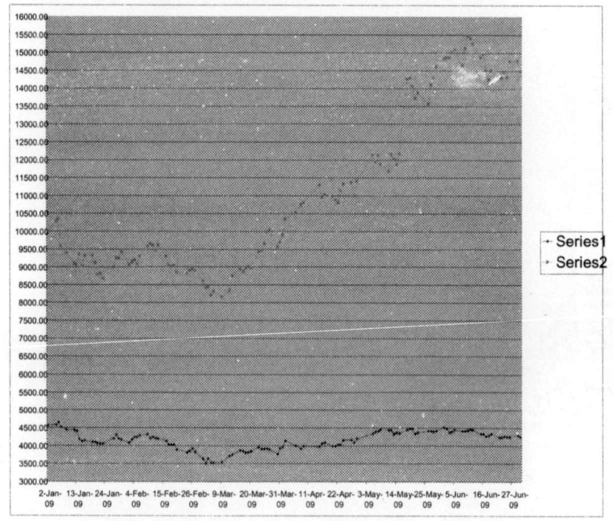

Close Prices of BSE Sensex and London FTSE 100 from 30st June 2009 to 8th September 2009

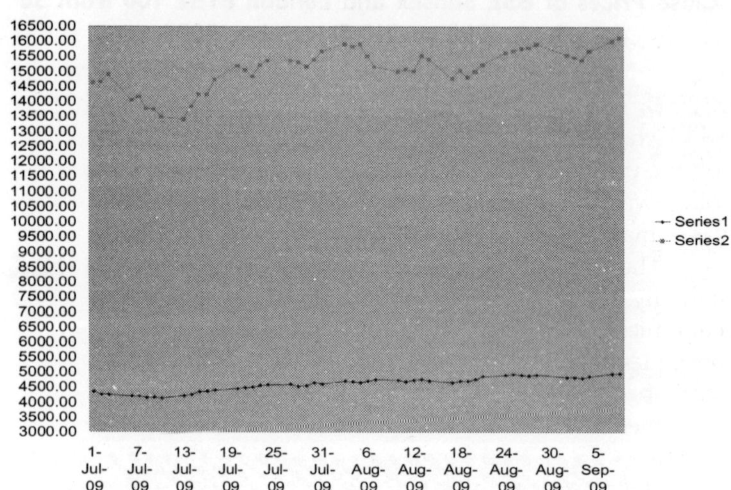

10

Global Financial Meltdown and its Impact on the Indian Economy

Abhishek Kumar

Global economic crises, an offshoot of US financial meltdown, has taken into its grip almost all the economies of the world. The first 'great recession' of the new millennium was triggered by the US housing bubble that burst during the mid of 2007-08. For the loose monetary policies of the Federal Reserve of US, adopted in the aftermath of the bursting of the tech bubble in 2000, encouraged financial institutions to adopt innovative debt schemes and derivatives to maximize their short-term volume-driven gains. One of the outcomes of this easy money policy was inflating the housing mania, an implosion of which was a matter of time.

The impact of global financial meltdown on Indian economy has not been so severe as in the case of developed economies. However, the global financial meltdown and consequent economic recession in developed countries has clearly been a major factor in India's slowdown. Given the origin and dimensions of the crisis in the advanced countries, the worst since the 'great depression' of 1930s, every developing and under-developed country has suffered to a varying degree. No country, including India, remained immune to the global economic shock (GOI, 2009: 1).

In the light of the global economic crises, the present paper analyses the impact of this great upheaval on economic front on Indian Economy.

ORIGIN OF GLOBAL FINANCIAL MELTDOWN

The global financial crisis is a direct result of the collapse of global housing bubble, which had its roots in US. It was at its peak in US in 2006, when the values of securities tied to housing prices decreased considerably. This damaged financial institutions globally (Glass, 2009). High default rates on 'sub-prime' and 'adjustable rate mortgages' began to increase quickly. An increase in loan incentives, such as easy initial terms and a long-term trend of rising prices of housing properties had encouraged borrowers to assume difficult mortgages in the expectations that they would be able to quickly refinance at more favourable terms. However, with the sudden increase in interest rates and drop in housing property prices in 2006-07 in many parts of the US, refinancing became more difficult. Excessively accommodative monetary policy for an extended period in the major advanced economies in the post-dot com crash period sowed the seeds of the current global economic crisis. Too low policy interest rates, especially in US, during the period 2002-04 boosted consumption and asset prices, and resulted in aggregate demand exceeding output, which was manifested in growing global imbalances. Too low short-term rates also encouraged aggressive search for yield, both domestically and globally, encouraged by financial engineering, heavy recourse to securitization and tax regulation and supervision. The great moderation over the preceding two decades led to under-pricing of risks and the new financial and economic regime was considered as sustainable (Mohan, 2009). The net outcome of these developments was high indebtedness of households, credit booms, asset price booms and excessive leverage in the major advanced economies, as well as in emerging market economies. Some, like American Enterprise Institute fellow Peter J. Wallison (2008) believe the roots of the crisis can be traced directly to sub-prime landing by Fannie and Freddie Mae, which are government sponsored entities.

What first appeared merely a sub-prime mortgage crack in US housing market during the summer of 2007 began widening during 2008 into deeper fissures across the global landscape and ended with the collapse of major banking institutions (Northern Rock, Lehman Brothers, Merrill Lynch Freddie Mae and AIG, Fannie Mae), precipitous falls on stock markets, across the world and a credit freeze (UN, 2009). Economist Paul Krugman and US Treasury Secretary Timothy Geithner explain the credit crisis via the implosion of shadow banking system, which had grown to nearly equal the importance of the traditional commercial banking sector without the ability to obtain investors funds in exchange for most types of mortgage-backed securities or asset-backed commercial paper, investment banks and other entities in the shadow banking system could not provide funds to mortgage firms and other corporations. The crisis quickly developed and spread into a global economic shock, resulting in number of European Banks failures, decline in various stock indices, large reductions in the market values of equities and commodities.

IMPACT OF RECESSION ON GLOBAL ECONOMY

The immediate fallout of US financial crisis was the steep fall in the stock prices in almost all the leading stock markets of the world. The world economy decelerated quickly-buffeted by an extraordinary financial shock and by high energy and commodity prices, many advanced economies moved into recession. On an annual basis, global growth moderated from 5.0 per cent in 2007 to 1.9 per cent in 2008 and is expected to come down to (-)1.7 per cent in 2009. In 2010 the growth rate is most likely to remain around 2.3 per cent. Developed economies are leading the global down-turn, but the weakness has rapidly spread to developing countries and the economies in transition, causing a synchronized global downturn. Following outcomes are expected in 2009 in this regard.

- Among the economies in transition, growth of the CIS countries is on course for a marked slowdown in 2009, dragged largely by the impact of a global recession and falling commodity prices in the

TABLE I

Growth Rates of World Output

(Annual Per centage change)

Area	2003	2004	2005	2006	2007	2008	2009		
							Baseline scenario	*Pessimistic* scenario	*Optimistic* scenario
World ou tput	2.7	4.0	3.5	4.0	3.8	2.5	1.0	-0.4	1.6
Of which developed economies	1.8	3.0	2.9	2.8	2.0	1.2	-0.5	-1.5	0.2
US	2.5	3.6	2.9	2.8	2.0	1.2	-1.0	-1.9	-0.5
Euro zone	0.8	2.1	1.8	2. 7	2.6	1.1	-0.7	-.15	0.3
Japan	1.4	2.7	1.9	2.4	2.1	0.4	-0.3	-0.6	0.5
Economi es in transition	7.4	7.7	6.5	7.8	8.3	6.9	4.8	2.7	6.1
Developing economies	5.2	7.1	6.8	7.1	7.2	5.9	4.6	2.7	5.1
China	10.0	10.1	10.4	11.6	11.9	9.1	8.4	7.0	8.9
India	7.3	7.1	11.5	7.3	8.9	7.5	7.0	4.7	7.5
Brazile	1.1	5.7	3.2	3.8	5.4	5.1	2.9	0.5	3.0
Mexico	1.4	4.0	3.1	4.9	3.2	2.0	0.7	-1.2	1.5
Least developed countries	5.2	7.2	7.9	7.7	7.8	6.4	5.1	2.0	6.1

economies of Kazakhistan, The Russian Federation and Ukrain.

- Growth in Africa is expected to decelerate in 2009, because of contagion effects of the global economic slowdown spread throughout the region, leading to weakened export demand, low commodity prices and a decline in investment.
- Growth in East Asia is expected to decline in 2009 because of sharp decrease in exports and sizeable financial losses as a result of their relatively high exposure to global financial institutions.
- Growth in South Asia and China is likely to remain at lower level because of sharp decline in export earnings.
- Western Asia and Latin America and the Caribbean is also expected to have a moderate growth.

Thus, it is clear that the developed economies are leading the global meltdown, the majority of them have experienced a recession in second half of 2008, which continued in the first quarter of 2009. Meanwhile, through trade and financial channels, the weakness has spread rapidly to developing economies and economies in transition, causing a synchronized global downturn in outlook for 2009.

IMPACT OF GLOBAL RECESSION ON THE INDIAN ECONOMY

Initial impact of financial meltdown in US economy on Indian economy was rather muted. The reduction in the US Fed Funds rate in August 2007, in the wake of sub-prime crises, resulted into massive increase in net-capital inflow into India (Table 2). The RBI had to sterilize the liquidity impact of large foreign exchange purchases through a series of increases in CRR, from 6.00 per cent on March 3, 2007 to 9.00 per cent on August 30, 2008, and issuance under the market stabilization scheme. Thus, direct effect of the sub-prime crises on Indian Banks/ financial sector was almost negligible because the Indian banking system has had no direct exposure to the sub-prime assets or to failed institutions (Subbarao, 2009). It has very limited off-balance sheet activities as securitized assets. Indian banks continue to remain sound and healthy. Secondly, Indian financial sector's limited exposure to complex derivatives and other prudential policies put in place by the RBI, kept the system rather unaffected (Mohan, 2009). Thirdly, there is relatively lower presence of foreign banks in India.

Banking sector also minimized the direct impact on the domestic economy. However, following the failure of investiment banks in US, there was panic in capital markets in India and elsewhere. There was a sell-off in domestic equity markets by portfolio investors reflecting deleveraging. As a result there was a net outflow of US$ 1403 million in September 2008 and US$ 5243 million in Oct. 2008. Outflow of capital continued in November 2008, January, February and March 2009. It caused pressure in foreign exchange market despite resilience exhibited by FDI inflow during the same period. It is another thing that the quantum of FDI decreased to US $ 1497 million in October 2008, US$ 1083 million in November 08 and US$ 1362 million in Dec. 2008 from US $ 3932 million in May 2008. Moreover, access to external commercial borrowings and trade credits was rendered difficult (Table 3). On the whole, net

TABLE 2

Foreign Capital Inflow into India

(US $ million)

Month	*Foreign direct* investment	*Portfolio* Investment	*Total inflow*
April 2007	1643	1974	3617
May 2007	2120	1852	3972
June 2007	1298	3664	4902
July 2007	705	6713	7418
Aug. 2007	831	(-)2875	(-) 2044
Sept.2007	713	7081	7794
Oct. 2007	2027	9564	11594
Nov. 2007	1864	(-) 107	1757
Dec. 2007	1558	5294	6852
Jan. 2008	1767	6739	8506
Feb. 2008	8670	(-) 8904	(-) 5234
March 2008	4438	(-) 1600	28238
2007-2008	**34362**	**29395**	**63757**
April 2008	3740	(-) 880	2869
May 2008	3932	(-) 288	3644
June 2008	2392	(-) 3010	(-) 618
July 2008	2247	(-) 492	1755
Aug. 2008	2328	593	2921
Sept. 2008	2562	(-) 1403	1159
Oct. 2008	1497	(-) 5243	(-) 3746
Nov. 2008	1083	(-) 574	509
Dec. 2008	1362	30	1392
Jan. 2008	2733	(-) 614	2119
Feb. 2008	1488	(-) 1085	403
March 2008	1956	(-) 889	1067
2008-2009	**35168**	**(-) 13855**	**21313**

Source: *Monthly Bulletin*, RBI, April 2009, Sept. 2009.

capital inflows during 2008-09 were significantly lower than in 2007-08. Large outflows of capital along with the sharp decrease in export earnings resulted into depletion of foreign exchange reserves. Out of total loss of foreign exchange reserve during April-December 2009, 61.11 per cent was due to valuation losses.

TABLE 3

Trends in Capital Flows in India

(US $ billion)

Component	*Period*	*2007-08*	*2008-09*
FDI to India	April-Feb	27.6	51.7
FII (net)	April-March	20.3	(-) 15.0
ECB (net)	April-Dec.	17.5	6.0
Short-term Trade Credit (n et)	April-Dec.	10.7	0.5
Total Capital Flows (net)	April-Dec.	82.0	15.3
Foreign Exchange Reserves	April-Dec	+9.0	(-) 33.4
Foreign Exchange Reserves (Variation)	April-Dec.	76.1	(-) 59.8
Foreign Exchange Reserves (Variation)	April-March	110.5	(-) 57.7

Source: RBI Bulletin, May 2009.

IMPACT ON CAPITAL MARKET

Indian Capital market felt the punch of global financial meltdown in a big way. Indian stock market crashed from the high of 21000 in Jan. 2008 to a low of 8509.54 in October 2008. The movement in equity prices in Indian Capital market was in tandem with trends in major international equity markets. The Indian equity market weakened considerably during September 08 and March 2009, following sharp decline in stock markets across the globe and perceptible change in investors preferences.

After recording strong growth during 2006 and 2007, the primary capital market received a knee jerk response in 2008. The number of new issues and capital raised there of declined sharply. Total amount of capital raised through equity issues during 2008 was Rs. 49,485 crore, recording a decline of 15.7 per cent as compared to the level in 2007. The total number of initial public offerings (IPOs) were only 37 in 2008 as compared to 100 in 2007. The amount mobilized by IPOs in 2008 was Rs. 18,393 crore which was lower by 45.8 per cent as compared to 2007. Reflecting volatile capital market conditions, the net-inflow of savings into mutual funds, which had recorded a steady rise during 2007-08, turned negative in later part of 2008 and recorded a net outflow of Rs. 12506 crore.

The worst sufferer was secondary market segment. BSE sensex and S&PCNX Nifty were at their peaks on January 8, 2008 at 20873 and 6287 respectively. However, their momentum could not be sustained and indices received recorded severe set back during the month of November 2008 in line with the fall in all major stock markets of the world.

IMPACT ON FOREIGN TRADE

Another sector that was hit badly by global financial meltdown is foreign Trade sector. For the first time in the last five years, India's export-growth turned negative in October 2008, when export contracted by 15 per cent on a year-on-year basis. With the US and EU already falling into recession, India's export growth had to fall sharply. It must be noted that this growth contraction came after a robust 25 per cent plus average growth since 2003.

India's exports declined a record 33.3% in March 2009, as the continued global economic recession affected demand for goods shipped from India. Exports contracted for the sixth consecutive month to US $11.5 bn in March 2009, more than a third lower than the corresponding number in the previous year. Experts said the dip in exports was to be expected, as advanced economies like the US and Europe, which account for more than 35% of India's exports, are experiencing a slump in demand. Imports declined by 34% to $15.6 bn in the month under consideration, in part due to the fall in commodity prices.

A deceleration in export growth has implication for India, even though Indian economy is far more domestically driven than those of east Asia. Sill, the contribution of merchandise export to GDP has risen steadily over the past six years—from about 10 per cent of GDP in 2002-03 to nearly 17 per cent by 2007-08. If one includes service exports, the ratio goes further. Therefore, any meltdown in the global economic environment will definitely hurt India. A positive correlation between the growth of exports and growth of GDP shows that any decline in export would result in decline in GDP growth rate. Export growth declined from 26.7 per cent in 2007-08 to 3.4 per cent in 2008-09, having a direct bearing on GDP growth rate which declined to 6.7 per cent in 2008-09 from 9.0 per cent in 2007-08.

TABLE 4

Trends in India's Foreign Trade

(US $ million)

Year Month	*Export*	*Import*	*Balance*
2003-04	63,843	78,149	-14,307
2004-05	83,536	1,11,517	-27,981
2005-06	1,03,091	1,49,166	-46,075
2006-07	1,26,414	1,85,735	-59,321
2007-08	1,62,904	2,51,439	-88,535
2008-09	1,82,631	2,91,475	-1,08,844
2007-08			
April	11,327	18,371	-7,044
May	12,456	21,150	-8,694
June	12,101	20,016	-7,915
July	12,513	21,129	-8,615
August	12,641	20,366	-7,725
September	12,521	18,271	-5,696
October	14,675	21,833	-7,158
November	12,909	22,104	-9,195
December	14,625	20,117	-5,491
January	14,889	22,844	-7,955
February	15,116	20,804	-5,688
March	17,254	23,574	-6,320
2008-09 R			
April	16,076	24,823	-8,747
May	15,550	26,684	-11,133
June	17,732	26,855	-9,123
July	19,036	31,189	-12,153
August	17,724	33,512	-15,787
September	14,298	29,722	-15,424
October	12,861	24,501	-11,640
November	10,308	22,461	-12,154
December	12,690	18,419	-5.729
January	12,381	18,455	-6,075
February	11,433	13,141	-1,708
March	12,902	16,043	-3,142
2009-10 P			
April	10,743	15,747	-5004
May	11,010	16,212	-5202
June	12,815	18,977	-6,163
July	13,623	19,621	-5,998
August	14,289	22,661	-8,372

Source: *RBI Bulletin* September 2009.

A slowdown in export growth also has other implications for the economy. Close to 50 per cent of India's exports-textiles, garments, gems and jewellery, leather and so on originate from the labour-intensive small and medium enterprises. A sharp fall in export from these sectors has resulted in job loss of higher order.

IMPACT ON THE REAL ECONOMY

Reflecting the slowdown in external demand, and the consequences of reversal of capital flows. growth in industrial production decelerated to 2.8 per cent in 2008-09 (April-February) from 8.8 per cent in the corresponding period of 2007-08. On the other hand, services sector activity has held up relatively well in 2008-09 so far (April-December) with growth of 9.7 per cent (10.5 per cent in the corresponding period of 2007-08). Service sector activity was buoyed up by acceleration in "community, social and personal services" on the back of higher government expenditure. Overall, real GDP growth had slowed to 6.9 per cent in the first three quarters of 2008-09 from 9.0 per cent in the corresponding period of 2007-08. On the expenditure side, growth of private final consumption expenditure decelerated to 6.6 per cent form 8.3 per cent. On the other hand. reflecting the fiscal stimuli and other expenditure measures, growth in government final consumption expenditure accelerated to 13.3 per cent from 2.7 per cent.

India's industrial output posted a record contraction of 1.2% in February 2009, against 9.5% growth seen in the same month last year, due to a combination of factors including falling exports and weak domestic demand in some sectors. All major categories—manufacturing, mining, consumer non-durables, basic goods and intermediate items—registered negative growth in February.

Production growth in the six core infrastructure industries during March 2009 stood at 2.9%, the highest since September 2008, indicating some recovery. Compared to the previous months, core sector growth in March was better due to higher output of cement and electricity, which was supported by the coal and petroleum products sectors. However, crude and finished carbon steel output contracted, compared to the same

TABLE 5

Growth in Core Industrial Sector

Sector	*Weight in IIP (%)*	*March 2008*	*March 2009*	*April-March 2007-08*	*April-March 2008-09*
Crude Oil	4.2	-0.3	-2.3	0.4	-1.8
Petroleum refinery products	2	0.1	3.3	6.5	3
Coal	3.2	9.3	5.2	6	8.1
Electricity	10.2	3.6	5.9	6.3	2.7
Cement	2	9.3	10.1	8.1	7.5
Finished steel (carbon)	5.1	-0.9	-2.6	6.2	0.4
Overall	26.7	2.9	2.9	5.9	2.7

Source: Ministry of Commerce and Industry.

month the previous year, pulling down overall growth in the core sector.

Growth scenario of Indian economy changed during 2008-09, under the black shadow of global recession. Higher GDP growth rate, registered during 2005-06 (9.5%), 2006-07 (9.7%) and 2007-08 (9.0%) decelerated to 6.7% during 2008-09 (Table 5). Slowdown trend continued in 2009-10. The RBI annual policy statement 2009 presented on July 28, 2009 projected GDP growth at 6 per cent in 2009-10. Manufacturing sector has shown extremely poor performance in third and fourth quarters of 2008-09 and registered 0.9% and (-)1.4% growth rates respectively due to deepening impact of economic crises.

IMPACT ON FISCAL SECTOR

Government finance, which had shown a noteworthy correction during 2002-03 to 2007-08, came under renewed pressure in 2008-09 on account of higher expenditure outgoes due to:

(i) Higher international crude oil prices and incomplete pass-through to domestic prices,
(ii) Higher fertilizer subsidies,
(iii) Sixth pay commission award, and
(iv) Debt waiver scheme.

TABLE 6

Rate of Growth at Factor Cost (At 1999-2000 prices)

(%)

S. No.	Sector	2003-04	2004-05	2005-06	2006-07	2007-08	2008-09
1.	Agriculture, forestry and fishing	10.0	0.0	5.8	4.0	4.9	1.6
2.	Mining and quarrying	3.1	8.2	4.9	8.8	3.3	3.6
3.	Manufacturing	6.6	8.7	9.1	11.8	8.2	2.4
4.	Electricity, gas & water supply	4.8	7.9	5.1	5.3	5.3	3.4
5.	Construction	12.0	16.1	16.2	11.8	10.1	7.2
6.	Trade, hotels and restaurants	10.1	7.7	10.3	10.4	10.1	9.0
7.	Transport, storage and communication	15.3	15.6	14.9	16.3	15.5	9.0
8.	Financing, insurance real estate, business services	5.6	8.7	11.4	13.8	11.7	7.8
9.	Community, social and personal services	5.4	6.8	7.1	5.7	6.8	13.1
	Total GDP at Factor cost	8.5	7.5	9.5	9.7	9.0	6.7

Source: CSO.

On revenue side tax cuts in the form of stimulus packages have put further stress on the fiscal deficit. Reflecting these factors, the Central Government's fiscal deficit more than doubled from 2.7 per cent of GDP in 2007-08 to 6.0 per cent in 2008-09, reaching again the levels seen around the end of the 1990s. The revenue deficit at 4.4 per cent of GDP will be at its previous peak touched during 2001-02 and 2002-03. Primary balance again turned into deficit in 2008-09, after recording surpluses during the preceding two years. Net market borrowings during 2008-09 almost trebled from the budgeted Rs. 1,13,000 crore to Rs. 3,29,649 in the revised estimates (actual borrowings were Rs. 2,98,536 crores as per Reserve Bank records) and are budgeted at Rs. 3,08,647 crore (gross borrowings at Rs. 3,98,552 crore) in 2009-10 (RBI, 2009).

CONCLUSION

If global financial crisis had a minimal effect on India economy, then credit must go to India's approach to financial globalization. There was a gradual opening up of current account convertibility and a more calibrated approach towards full convertibility on capital account with all possible safeguards. As far as capital account is concerned, whereas foreign investment flows, especially FDI inflows are encouraged, debt flows in the form of ECBs are generally subject to caps and some end-use restrictions. Macro-caps have also been stipulated for portfolio investment in government securities and corporate bonds. Banking sector in India is adhering to prudential norms stipulated by RBI. Moreover, key regularoty bodies—RBI and SEBI—keep a strong vigil on the activities of financial intermediaries. It helped in past and current situations to minimize the impact of financial meltdown. The current economic crisis has been blessing in disguise for India. It forced the authorities and policy-makers to visualize regulatory mechanism in more effective manner.

Global economic slump is not over. While many major economies, including the US, Germany and Japan, have come out of recession, recovery has so far been aided by vast emergency infusions of tax payer's cash. Indian economy has also felt the brunt of global recession, but with a little pain because of her strong macroeconomic indicators and limited capital account convertibility RBI, the SEBI and ministry of Finance have emerged as watchful regulators which did not allow the free play by financial institutions. Three consecutive stimulus packages, announced by government of India, significantly arrested the downfall of the economy. However, no one is sure what will happen when those life support measures are removed next year and RBI begins to shut off low-cost lifelines to banks and raise interest rates.

References

Geiltner, Tinwlty (2009): "Reducing Systemic Risk in a Dynamic Financial System", Federal Reserve, US. Speech on June 9 at the Economic Club, New York.

Glass, Ira (2009): "This American Life: Giant Pool of Money Wins Peabody", PRI Public Radio International, April 05, 2009.

GOI (2009): Economic Survey 2008-09, Ministry of Finance, New Delhi, p. 1.

IMF (2008): Global Economic Outlook-2008, New York.

IMF (2009): Global Economic Outlook-2008, New York.

Krugman, Paul (2009): "The Return of Depression Economics and the Crisis of 2008", WW Norton Comnay Ltd., p. 6.

Mohan, Rakesh (2009): "Global Financial Crisis, Impact, Policy Responses and Lessions", *RBI Monthly Bulletin*, May, Mumbai, p. 887.

RBI (2009): *Monthly Bulletin*, September.

Subbarao, D. (2009): "Indian-Managing the Impact of the Global Financial Crisis", *RBI Bulletin*, Mumbai, April, p. 529.

United Nations (2009): "World Economic Situation and Prospects 2009", New York, p. 1.

Wallison, Peter J. (2008): "What got us there?" American Enterprise Institute for Public Policy Research, Hudson, New York.

11

Contagion Effect of Global Financial Crisis on Stock Market in India

MAHENDRA RANAWAT AND VEENU YADAV

INTRODUCTION

The housing burst in the US has led to a sequence of economic repercussions in the US and then it has got transmitted to other economies, engulfing many developed and emerging economies. The shock originated from the housing sector affected the financial sector severely as many of the insurance and investment companies dealing with the real assets and debts suffered financial losses on account of falling housing prices and loan defaults. The losses dragged them to go bankrupt and have closure of the business. The attention of the policy-makers got diverted from averting overheating of the world economies in the beginning of the 2007 to averting slowdown in the economies.

The stock market activity is one of the principal activities in the corporate world among the chain of activities, which got affected due to the financial crisis. The stock market indices are one of the principal indicators of the economic activities. The movement of stock market indices presents the future economic outlook. A falling stock index reflects the dampening of the investment climate while a rising stock index indicates more confidence and soundness of the economy. The latter attracts more investment demand on stocks. Rising investment on stocks raises sock prices and generates profits.

When crisis affects the real activities, it affects the stock market, as profit expectation on financial investments would be lower. If financial investment would be affected, its impact would be felt on the real investment, as real investment would not increase. Once the real sector activity lessens, that would affect the entire economy. Thus, it is mainly the expectation of the investors that affects both the financial and real investment in the economy.

In India the stock market has undergone significant transformations with the liberalization measures. The Bombay Stock Exchange (BSE) of India has emerged as one of the largest stock exchange in the world in terms of the number of listed companies, comprising many large, medium-sized and small firms. As regards transaction cost, the Indian stock market compares with some of the developed and regional economies (Raj and Dhal, 2008). The inflow of foreign capital has made a crucial contribution to the growth of the stock market. India has become a major destination, representing about a fourth of total portfolio capital inflows to the emerging market economies (EMEs) group. India has also become engaged in various bilateral trade and economic cooperation agreements with several countries and regional groups across Asia, Europe and the Western hemisphere. In this context, the concerns regarding its exposure to risk in case of the global crisis are compelling. The analysis contained in the IMF's Global Financial Stability Report (October 2008) (IMF, 2008a), finds that correlation of equity markets in EMEs with those in the advanced economies has risen, suggesting a growing transmission channel for equity price movements. Amongst the three groups of EMEs (Latin America, Asia and Emerging Europe), the spillover from global factors is found to be strongest in Latin American EMEs followed by Emerging Europe and Asia. One of the Central bankers in India, Rakesh Mohan (2008) sometimes remarked that one of the key features of the current financial turmoil has been the lack of perceived contagion being felt by banking systems in EMEs, particularly in Asia. The Indian banking system also has not experienced any contagion, similar to its peers in the rest of Asia. But this needs to be empirically verified whether it is true that India's stock market has not been affected during the crisis period.

The aim of this study is to test whether there exists a contagion effect of the recent crisis on Indian stock market. In order to recognize the contagion effect, the study estimates the time-varying correlation coefficients by employing the dynamic conditional correlation (DCC) Bi-variate GARCH model of Engle (2002).

REVIEW OF THE LITRETURE

A large body of literature exists on the equity market integration. Since the seminal work of Grubel (1968), which explained the benefits of international portfolio diversification, the relationship among national stock markets has been analyzed in a series of studies such as by Granger and Morgenstern (1970), Ripley (1973), Lessard (1974,1976) and Panton, Lessig and Joy (1976) among others. Following the seminal works of Engle and Granger (1987), Johansen (1988) and Johansen and Juselius (1990), numerous studies beginning with Taylor and Tonks (1989), Kasa (1992) and, subsequently, Masih and Masih (1997, 2002), Chowdhry (1994) and Chowdhry *et. al.* (2007), among several others, have used the co-integration hypothesis to assess the international integration of financial markets. When analyzing linkages among international stock markets, it is of interest to determine if there are any common forces driving the long-run movement of the data series or if each individual stock index is driven solely by its own fundamentals; this relationship can be captured by co-integration analysis. When markets are said to share a single common stochastic trend, it indicates that these markets are perfectly correlated over long horizons and gains to international diversification will diminish or disappear over the long-term. Kasa (1992) was the first to apply multivariate co-integration method to five well-established financial markets in order to examine the existence of a single common stochastic trend as a driver of the co-integrated system. Using Johansen's test (Johansen and Juselius, 1990), for co-integration he found a single common trend driving stock markets of US, Japan, England, Germany, and Canada, particularly when using quarterly data. According to Kasa (1992) in case of co-integration between equity indices it is possible that gains from diversification occur in the short-term but not in the long-term. Phylaktis and Ravazzolo (2002) apply Kasa's (1992) methodology and examined the potential inter-relationships among the trend behaviour of the stock price indices of a group of Pacific-Basin countries, Japan and US, for the period 1980 to 1998. The paper shows that international investors have opportunities for portfolio diversification by investing in most of the Pacific Basin countries since short-run benefits exist due to substantial transitory fluctuations. Moreover, the estimated common trends showed that though US markets were definitely found to play a role, but were small in magnitude, while Japan played a more significant role. Neither Japan, nor the US had any unique influence in the Pacific Rim stock markets.

There are varied views on the after effect of the Asian financial crisis on the integration of the Asian markets. Ghosh, Saidi, and Johnson (1999) consider whether nine Asia-Pacific markets are separately co-integrated with either the US or Japanese stock market. Their results suggest that while some markets are co integrated with the US, some are co integrated with Japan, and others are not co-integrated with either. However, they consider daily data covering only a nine month period in 1997. Sheng and Tu (2000) discovered that the co-integration relation among 12 Pacific nations, including Taiwan and the US, did not exist in the stock markets until the 1997 Asian financial crisis occurred. The variance decomposition further showed that none of nations, during the financial crisis, had the exogenous characteristic, which verified the existence of the contagion effect. At the same time, causality tests pointed out that the US indices were the leading factors affecting the stock performance of other nations. Applying vector auto-regression (VAR) to test for causal relationship and to analyze the shock response, Nagayasu (2001) discovered the contagion effect of Thailand's currency crisis that affected the industrial indices in Philippine's stock market via foreign exchange rate.

Yang and Lim (2002) in an empirical study of nine East Asian stock markets for the period January 1990 to October 2000 find some evidence of short-term linkages. Their results indicate that there was a significant difference between sub-periods pre- and (during) post-Asian crisis, with an overall improvement of correlation coefficients for each pair from the pre-crisis to the post-crisis period, except for Malaysia and Taiwan. Unlike results from short-run tests, there is no long-run co-movement among East Asian stock markets, as the absence of co-integration in the post-crisis period rules out the existence of a long-term equilibrium trending relationship among East Asian stock markets.

METHODOLOGY

In order to examine the impact of USA stock market on India's stock market, the paper estimates Dynamic Conditional Correlation under Bivariate GARCH model and compares the mean of correlation in two sub-periods namely, crisis and pre-crisis. We find the break points in the sample by using the Bai-Perron structural break test and use the most recent break in the series as the break that occurred as a result of the US sub-prime crisis (see Bai and Perron, 1998, 2003).

DCC Bi-variate GARCH is estimated by applying log likelihood estimation procedures. The details are as follows.

With the information of the pervious period, the conditional correlation between two random variables r_1 and r_2 that have mean zero can be written as:

$$P_{12,t} = \frac{E_{t-1}\left(r_1, tr_2, t\right)}{\sqrt{Et_{-1}\left(r_1, t^2\right) Et_{-1}\left(r_2, t^2\right)}} \quad (1)$$

And letting

$hi,t = Et_{-1}\left(r_{it}^{2}\right)$ for i=1, 2 where *ei, t* is the standardized disturbance that has zero mean and a variance of one.

Substituting the above into equation (1) we get :

$$P_{12,t} = \frac{E_{t-1}\left(\varepsilon_1, {}_t\varepsilon_2, t\right)}{\sqrt{Et-1\left(\varepsilon_1, t_2\right) E_{t-1}\left(\varepsilon_2, t^2\right)}} = E_{t-1}\left(\varepsilon_1, {}_t\varepsilon_2, t\right) \quad (2)$$

Thus, conditional correlation is the covariance of standardized disturbances. In the progress of time, the stock return variance is constant and undisputable. Hence, the correlation coefficients between stock returns also vary along with time. The estimation of Engel's (2002) DCC model comprises two steps: one is the estimation of the univariate GARCH model, and the other is the estimation of the correlation coefficient. It is generally agreed that GARCH (1, 1) is enough to capture the characteristics of heteroscedasticity of stock and financial variables (Bollerslev, Chou, and Kroner, 1992).

Utilizing the conditional correlation coefficients and variances of two stock returns to parameterize the stock return covariance matrix Ht, we have:

$$Ht = Dt\ Rt\ Dt \tag{3}$$

where *Dt* is a 2×2 diagonal matrix of the time varying standard deviations from univariate GARCH models with $\sqrt{hi,t}$ on the ith diagonal. *Rt* is a 2×2 time varying conditional correlation matrix. As indicated, the elements in *Dt* follow the univariate GRACH process of the following,

$$hi,\ t = wi + \acute{a}i\mathring{a}^2i,\ t\text{-}l\ +\ \hat{a}ihi,\ t\text{-}l \tag{4}$$

Using GARCH (1, 1) specification, the covariance between the random variables can be written as

$$q\ l2 = p\ l2 + \acute{a}\ (\mathring{a}l,\ t\text{-}l\ \mathring{a}2,\ t\text{-}l\ \text{-}\ p\ l2) + \hat{a}\ (ql2,\ t\text{-}l\ \text{-}\ p\ l2) \tag{5}$$

The unconditional expectation of the cross product is $P12$, while for the variances

$$\bar{P}12 = 1$$

The correlation estimator is:

$$P^{12,t}\ \frac{q^{12,t}}{\sqrt{q^{11,t}\ q^{22,t}}} \tag{6}$$

This model is mean reverting if *á* + â < 1. The matrix version of this model is written as:

$$Q_t = S(1-\alpha-\beta)+\alpha(\varepsilon_{t-1}\varepsilon'_{t-1})+\beta Q_{t-1} \tag{7}$$

where S is the unconditional correlation matrix of the disturbance terms and Qt = $|q_{1,2,t}|$

If *á* + *â* =1, the model is simplified as the constant conditional correlation model of Bollerslev (1990). The log likelihood for this estimator can be written as:

$$L=-\tfrac{1}{2}\sum_{t=1}^{T}(n\log(2\pi)+2\log D_t+\log R_t+\varepsilon' R_t\varepsilon_t) \tag{8}$$

where D_t = $diag\left\{\sqrt{h_{it}}\right\}$ and R_t is the time varying correlation matrix.

DATA AND RESULTS

We use stock price indices of US and India to compute the stock reruns and find the correlation between the two series. BSE Sensex and NASDAQ 100 are taken as representative of Indian and US stock markets respectively. The sample period is from January 2, 2002 till June 1, 2009 and excludes holidays.

Table 1 contains the summary statistics of the market returns. For the entire sample India has mean returns of 0.099, minimum returns of -11.14%, and maximum returns of 15.99% with a variance of 3.11 during the period. US has mean return of 0.007%, minimum return of -10.52%, and maximum return of 12.58% with a variance of 3.18. As should be the case, during the crisis period mean return has become negative in US market and in India it has come down drastically. Variances have increased significantly compared to the pre-crisis period. The skewness coefficients are positive depicting right-skewed distributions except the value corresponding to the pre-crisis period for India. All the stock returns are in a leptokurtic distribution as explained by the kurtosis figures, which is a common characteristic of financial variables.

TABLE I

Summary Statistics of the Returns Data

Market	*Sample*	*Obs.*	*Mean*	*Skewness*
India	Entire	1786	0.099	0.115
	Pre-Crisis	1597	0.105	-0.336
	Crisis	189	0.056	0.522
US	Entire	1786	0.007	0.285
	Pre-Crisis	1597	0.018	0.315
	Crisis	189	-0.089	0.248

Market	*Sample*	*Kurtosis*	*Variance*
India	Entire	10.22	3.11
	Pre-Crisis	7.308	2.28
	Crisis	6.01	10.16
US	Entire	7.75	3.18
	Pre-Crisis	5.75	2.46
	Crisis	5.26	9.28

The results in Tables 2 and 3 suggest that GARCH (1, 1) coefficients are found to be significant and positive, thus implying that volatility is captured by GARCH (1, 1) model. Most of the estimated parameters are statistically significant at the 1% level. The significance of coefficients in the model indicates the tendency of the shocks to persist. The sum of the coefficients of lagged squared disturbance and that of past variance [GARCH (-1)] is less than one indicating shocks die with time. The sums of the shocks are very close to 1, imply a highly persistent volatility, this phenomenon is commonly observed in practice.

The standardized residuals from GARCH (1, 1) estimation and maximum likelihood method are used to estimate the mean reverting dynamic conditional correlation coefficients.

Variances of Table 1 increase with time (variances in the post-crisis period are significantly higher than those in the pre-crisis period). The increasing variances get the unconditional correlation coefficients biased. It is clearly seen, in the entire sample period, that the unconditional correlation coefficients

TABLE 2

Estimation of GARCH (1, 1) Process for NASDAQ Returns

Dependent Variable: NASDAQ Return
Method: ML - ARCH
GARCH = C(0) + C(1)*RESID(-1)^2 + C(2)*GARCH(-1)

	Coefficient	*Std. Error*	*z-Statistic*	*Prob.*
C	0.052750	0.030472	1.731087	0.0834
		Variance Equation		
C	0.010005	0.005437	1.840257	0.0657
RESID(-1)^2	0.052892	0.013902	3.804537	0.0001
GARCH(-1)	0.943687	0.012702	74.29226	0.0000
Log likelihood	-3200.842	Durbin-Watson stat	2.163865	

TABLE 3

Estimation of GARCH (1, 1) Process for BSE Returns

Dependent Variable: NASDAQ Return
Method: ML - ARCH
GARCH = C(0) + C(1)*RESID(-1)^2 + C(2)*GARCH(-1)

	Coefficient	*Std. Error*	*z-Statistic*	*Prob.*
C	0.153404	0.029652	5.173517	0.0000
		Variance Equation		
C	0.056845	0.020991	2.708052	0.0068
RESID(-1)^2	0.137523	0.024979	5.505445	0.0000
GARCH(-1)	0.849002	0.023464	36.18386	0.0000
Log likelihood	-3198.511	Durbin-Watson stat	1.877271	

without consideration of variance variations are higher than the correlation coefficients estimated by the DCC model (see Table 4). We use the t-statistic to test whether the correlation coefficients between the markets are consistent in the pre-crisis and post-crisis periods. If the correlation coefficients between the two markets are significant and the null hypothesis is rejected,

TABLE 4

Comparison of Unconditional Correlation and DCC

Unconditional Correlation			*Mean of DCC coefficients*		
Pre	*Crisis*	*Entire*	*Pre*	*Crisis*	*Entire*
0.048	0.395	0.162	0.096	0.157	0.102

Note: all coefficients are significant at 5% level.

TABLE 5

t-Test for Difference in Mean of DCC in Two Samples

Sample	*Pre-Sub-Prime Crisis*	*Crisis*
Mean	0.095714871	0.157132543
Variance	0.000339718	0.00496785
Observations	1596	188
Hypothesized Mean Difference	0	
Degrees of freedom	195	
t Stat	-18.793	
t Critical one-tail (5% level of signf.)	1.652	
t Critical two-tail (5% level of signf.)	1.972	

there is a contagion effect. If the correlation coefficients are significant and the null hypothesis is not rejected, there is an interdependence relationship.

Table 4 reports the dynamic correlation coefficients and unconditional correlation coefficients in pre-crisis and crisis periods. This is intended to compare the difference between conventional unconditional and conditional correlation coefficients where dividing standards may affect the conclusions about the contagion effect. The crisis period increase of the unconditional correlation coefficients stated corresponds to the increase of the post-crisis conditional correlation coefficient. But the rise in unconditional correlation is more than hat in the conditional correlation. This result is consistent with the conclusions by Forbes and Rigobon (2002) that unconditional correlation coefficients are likely to support the contagion effect. The t-test for difference in mean of dynamic conditional correlation coefficients in the pre-crisis and crisis period reveals that the correlation in crisis period is significantly different from the pre-crisis period. Thus, it is evident that there is a contagion effect of US sub-prime crisis on India's sock market apart from the interdependence relationship.

CONCLUSION

In this paper we have examined whether during current US sub-prime there was any contagion from the US economy to India. Following Engle (2002), we estimated the Dynamic Conditional Correlation under Bi-variate GARCH. The empirical finding shows that the conditional correlation coefficients of stock returns are positive, and co-movement exists between US and Indian markets. The conditional correlation coefficient mean in the crisis period increased at a significant level, providing the evidence of the contagion effect. This result is in line with the other studies of similar nature [e.g., Wang *et al.*, (2006), Kenourgios *et. al.* (2007)]. As Kenourgios *et. al.*, (2007) put-forth—when bad news hit stock markets, conditional equity correlations increase dramatically. And, policy responses to a crisis are unlikely to prevent the spread among countries since cross-market correlation dynamics are driven by behavioural reasons.

As per the 'decoupling theory' it was putforth that even if advanced countries went into a downturn, emerging economies will at worst be affected only marginally, and can largely steam ahead on their own. In a rapidly globalizing world where India's integration with other economies has been increasing, the decoupling theory was never totally persuasive; given the evidence recently—capital flow reversals, sharp widening of spreads on sovereign and corporate debt, and abrupt currency depreciations—the decoupling theory has almost completely lost credibility (Subbarao, 2008). Subbarao views that, in the advanced countries the contagion spread from the financial to the real sector but, in India, the slowdown in the real sector is affecting the financial sector, which in turn, has a second-order impact on the real sector. This needs to be examined as an extension of this paper, i.e. there is need to examine further the channels of contagion effect of the crisis on the financial market and the impact of such effect on the real sector variables.

REFERENCES

Agarwal, R.N. (2000): "Capital Market Development, Corporate Financing Pattern and Economic Growth in India," Institute of Economic Growth Discussion Paper No. 20.

Bai, Jushan and Pierre Perron (1998): "Estimating and Testing Linear Models with Multiple Structural Changes", *Econometrica*, Vol. 66, No. 1, pp. 47-78

Bai, Jushan and Pierre Perron (2003): "Computation and Analysis of Multiple Structural Change Models", *Journal of Applied Econometrics*, Vol. 18, No. 1, pp. 1-22

Bollerslev, T. (1990): "Modelling the coherence in short-run nominal exchange rates: A multivariate Generalized ARCH model", *Review of Economics and Statistics*, 72, 498-505.

Bollerslev, T., Chou, R.Y. and Kroner, K.F. (1992): "ARCH modeling in finance: A review of the theory and empirical evidence", *Journal of Econometrics*, 52, 5-59.

Bollerslev, T., Chou, R.Y., and Kroner, K.F. (1992): "ARCH modeling in finance: A review of the theory and empirical evidence", *Journal of Econometrics*, 52, 5-59.

Cappiello, L., R.F. Engle and K. Sheppard (2003): "Asymmetric Dynamics in the Correlations of Global Equity and Bond Returns", ECB Working Paper No. 204.

Chiang, T.C., Jeon, B.N. and Li, H. (2007): "Dynamic correlation analysis of financial contagion:evidence from the Asian Markets", *Journal of International Money and Finance*, Vol. 26, pp. 1206-28.

Chowdhry, A.R. (1994): "Stock market interdependencies: evidence from the Asian NIEs", *Journal of Macroeconomics*, Vol. 16, No 4.

Chowdhry, T, Lin Lu and Ke Peng (2007): "Common stochastic trends among Far Eastern stock prices: effects of Asian financial crisis", *International Review of Financial Analysis*, Vol. 16.

Edwards, S., and Susmel, R. (2001): "Volatility dependence and contagion inemerging equity markets", Working paper, IASE Seminar, Buenos Aires, Argentina.

Égert, Balázs and Evžen Kocenda (2007): "Time-Varying Comovements in Developed and EmergingEuropean Stock Markets:Evidence from Intraday Data", William Davidson Institute Working Paper, Number 861

Engle, R.F. and C.W.J. Granger (1987): "Cointegration and error correction: representation, estimation, and testing", *Econometrica*, Vol. 55, No. 2, pp. 251–76.

Engle, R. (2002): "Dynamic conditional correlation: A simple class of multivariate generalized autoregressive conditional heteroskedasticity models", *Journal of Business and Economic Statistics*, 20(3), 339-50.

Engle, R.F. and Sheppard, K. (2001): "Theoretical and empirical properties of dynamic conditional correlation MVGARCH", Working Paper No. 15, University of California, San Diego.

Engle, R.F. and K. Sheppard (2001): "Theoretical and Empirical Properties of Dynamic Conditional Correlation Multivariate GARCH", NBER Working Paper, 8554.

Forbes, K. and Rigobon, R. (2000): "Contagion in Latin America: definitions, measurement, and policy Implications", *Economatrica,* Volume 1, Number 2, 2001, pgs 1-46.

Forbes, K. and Rigobon, R. (2002): "No contagion, only interdependence: Measuring stock market comovements", *The Journal of Finance,* 5, 2223-2261.

Ghosh, A., Saidi, R. and Johnson, K. (1999): "Who moves the Asia-Pacific stock markets—U.S. or Japan?, Empirical evidence based on the theory of cointegration", *Financial Review,* 34, 159-70.

Granger, C.W.J. and O. Morgenstern (1970): "The Predictability of Stock Market Prices", Heath Lexington Books, Heath & Co, Lexington.

Grubel, H.G. (1968): "Internationally Diversified Portfolios: Welfare Gains and Capital Flows," *American Economic Review;* 58(5), 1299-1314.

Hamao, Y., Masulis, R. and Ng., V. (1990): "Correlations in price changes and volatility across international stock markets", *The Review of Financial Studies,* 3, 281-307.

International Monetary Fund (2008): "Global Financial Stability Report", October.

Ignatius, R. (1992): "The Bombay Stock Exchange: Seasonality's and Investment Opportunities", *Indian Economic Review,* 27(2), 223-27.

Johansen, S. (1988): "Statistical analysis of co integrating vectors", *Journal of Economic Dynamics and Control,* Vol. 12, pp. 231–54.

Johansen, S. and K. Juselius (1990): "Maximum likelihood estimation and inferences on cointegration—with applications to the demand for money", *Oxford Bulletin of economics and Statistics,* Vol. 52, No. 2, pp 169-210.

Kasa, K. (1992): "Common stochastic trends in international stock markets", *Journal of Monetary Economics,* Vol. 29, pp. 95–124.

Kenourgios Dimitris., Aristeidis Samitas and Nikos Paltalidis (2007): "Financial Crises and Contagion: Evidence for BRIC Stock Markets", paper presented at the European Financial Management Association Annual Conference, 27th-30th June 2007, Vienna, Austria,

King, M. and Wadhwani, S. (1990): "Transmission of volatility between stock markets", *Review of Financial Studies,* 3(1), 5-33.

Kumar, K. and C. Mukhopadhyay (2002): "Equity Market Interlinkages: Transmission of Volatility—A Case of US and India", NSE Working Paper No.16.

Lee, S.B. and Kim, K.J. (1993): "Does the October 1987 crash strengthen the co-movements among national stocks markets?", *Review of Financial Economics,* 3, 89-102.

Lessard, D.R. (1974): "World, National, and Industry Factors in Equity Returns", *Journal of Finance,* 29(2), 379-91.

Lessard, D.R. (1976): "International Diversification," *Financial Analysts Journal,* January/February, 32-38.

Masih, A.M.M. and R. Masih (1997): "Dynamic linkages and the propagation mechanism driving major international markets: an analysis of the pre- and post-crash areas", *Quarterly Review of Economics and Finance,* Vol. 37, No. 4.

Masih, A.M.M. and R. Masih (2002): "Propagative causal price transmission among international stock markets: evidence from pre- and post-globalisation period", *Global Finance Journal*, Vol. 13.

Mohan, Rakesh (2008): "Global Financial Crisis and Key Risks: Impact on India and Asia", Remarks prepared for IMF-FSF High-Level Meeting on the Recent Financial Turmoil and Policy Responses at Washington D.C. October 9, 2008.

Nagayasu, J. (2001): "Currency crisis and contagion: Evidence from exchange rates and sectoral stock indices of the Philippines and Thailand", *Journal of Asian Economics*, 12(4), 529-46.

Nath, G.C. and S. Verma (2003): "Study of Common Stochastic Trend and Cointegration in the Emerging Markets—A Case Study of India, Singapore and Taiwan", NSE Working Paper No. 25.

Panton, D., V.P. Lessig and O. Joy (1976): "Co-movement of international equity markets: A taxonomic approach", *Journal of Financial and Quantitative Analysis*, 11(3), 415-32.

Phylaktis, K. and F. Ravazzolo (2005): "Stock market linkages in emerging markets: implications for international portfolio diversification", *Journal of International Financial Markets, Institutions and Money*, Vol. 15, pp. 91-106.

Phylaktis, Kate and F. Ravazzolo (2002): "Stock Market Linkages in Emerging Markets: Implications for International Portfolio Diversification", Working Paper 2/2002, Emerging Markets Group, Cass Business School.

Raj, Janak and Sarat Dhal (2008): "Integration of India's stock market with global and major regional markets", BIS Papers No. 42.

Ripley, D.M. (1973): "Systematic Elements in the Linkage of National Stock Market Indices", *Review of Economics and Statistics*, 55(3), 356-61.

Sheng, H.C., and Tu, A.H. (2000): "A study of cointegration and variance decomposition among equity indices before and during the period of the Asian financial crisis", *Journal of Multinational Financial Management*, 10, 345-65.

Subbarao, D. (2008): "The Global Financial Turmoil and Challenges for the Indian Economy", Speech, Reserve Bank of India at the Bankers' Club, Kolkata, December 10

Taylor, M.P. and I. Tonks (1989): "The internationalization of stock markets and abolition of UK exchange control", *Review of Economics and Statistics*, Vol. 71, pp. 332–36.

Wang, K.M. and T.-B.N. Thi (2006): "Does Contagion Effect Exist Between Stock Markets of Thailand and Chinese Economic Area (CEA) during the "Asian Flu?" Asian Journal of Management and Humanity Sciences, Vol. 1, No. 1, pp. 16-36, 2006.

Wong, W.K., A. Agarwal and J. Du (2005): "Financial Integration for India Stock Market, a Fractional Cointegration Approach", National University of Singapore Working Paper No. WP0501.

Yang, T. and Lim, J.J. (2002): "Crisis, Contagion, and East Asian Stock Markets", Working Paper on Economics and Finance No 1, February 2002, Institute of South East Asian Studies.

12

Impact of Global Financial Crisis on Indian Economy

RAJIV KUMAR BHATT

Financial crises seem to have been occurring with greater frequency in the era of globalization. The four major crises were in Latin America in the early 1980s and Mexico, Asia and Russia in the 1990s. The fifth one is the recent global financial crisis. Ten year ago, financial crisis of the East Asia was due to a real estate bubble in the Thailand that had burst, triggering the flight of international speculative capital; today, it is fallout of the real estate crisis in the USA which threatens the financial markets. The current crisis differs from the Asian crisis also because the search of its origins is not leading to some form of crony capitalism in emerging economies but to the centres of the world financial system with all modern financial innovations. Some analysts say that this is first crisis in the modern financial markets where new products created by debt and asset securitization are traded globally.

The current crunch shares certain qualities with prior financial crisis, such as the pattern of rising asset prices, expending lending activity, increasing speculation to excess and then declining prices, insolvency and finally panic in which the 'investors' try to save their gains as rapidly as possible.

The global financial crisis of 2008-09 emerged in September 2008 with the failure and merger of several large United States based financial firms and spread with the insolvency of additional companies, recession and declining stock market prices around the globe. But the financial crisis really started to show its effects in the middle of 2007 and into 2008. Around the world, stock markets have fallen, large financial institutions have collapsed or been bought out and governments in even the wealthiest nations have had to come up with rescue packages to bail out their financial systems.

The crisis has become one of the most radical factors reshaping the global banking sector, as governments and the private sector battle to save up the financial system following the disappearance of Lehman Brothers and Merrill as independent entities. Actually, the collapse of Lehman Brothers was a symbol of the global financial crisis. The real economy in many countries is already feeling the effects. Many industrialized nations are sliding into recession if they are not already there. The crisis became so sevêre that after the failure and buyouts of major institutions, the Bush administration offered a $700 billion bailout plan for the US financial system.

This bailout package was controversial because it was unpopular with public, seen as a bailout for the culprits while ordinary person would be left to pay for their folly. Nobel Prize winner for economics Joseph Stiglitz also argued that the plan "remains a very bad bill." He said that this bill is again based on "trickle down economics"—you throw enough money at Wall Street and some of it will trickle down to the rest of the economy. It does not do anything about the basic source of the problem.

Some of bailouts have also been accompanied with charges of hypocrisy due to the appearance of socializing the costs while privatizing the profits. The bailouts appear to help the financial institutions that got into trouble while smaller business and poorer people rarely have such options for bailout and rescue when they find themselves in crisis.

On the one hand many people are concerned that those responsible for the financial problems are the ones being bailed out, while on the other hand, a global financial meltdown will affect the livelihoods of almost every one in an increasingly inter-connected world.

A collapse of US sub-prime mortgage market and the reversal of the housing boom in other industrialized economies have had a ripple effect around the world. Further more, other weaknesses in the global financial system have surfaced. Some financial products and instruments have become so complex and twisted, that as things started to unravel, trust in the whole system started to fall.

The global economy is on the dangerous situation of recession. The downturn after four years of relatively fast growth is due to a number of factors: the global fallout from the financial crisis in the United States, the bursting of the housing bubbles in the US and in other large economies, increasingly restrictive monetary policies in a number of countries and stock market volatility.

There is the argument that when the larger banks show signs of crisis, it is not just the wealthy that will suffer, but potentially every one. With an increasingly interconnected world, things like a credit crunch can ripple through the entire economy.

Market liberalization and privatization in the commodity sector have not resulted in greater stability of international commodity prices. There is widespread dissatisfaction with the outcomes of unregulated financial and commodity markets, which fail to transmit reliable price signals for commodity producers.

The Bretton Woods system of international finance devised by 44 nations after the Second World War, mostly represented by the IMF and the World Bank was designed to help reconstruct and stabilize a post-war global economy. In the 1970s, the purpose of these international financial institutions (IFIs) shifted towards a neo-liberal economic agenda, championed by Washington (also known as the Washington Concensus). It was at this time that policies such as structural adjustment started to be pushed too much on the developing world, following a "one size fit for all" prescription of how economies should be structured, which had disastrous consequences for much of the world's population.

Although such institutions have rarely been held accountabe for such policies and their effects that last for many years, people have been calling for their reform, or even for their abolition. Lack of transparency in these institutions has not helped. However, these have been signed for discontent.

We may be at a new "Bretton Woods" moment. The old institutions have recognized the need for reform, but they have been moving at glacial speed. They did nothing to prevent the current crisis and there is concern about their effectiveness in responding to it now that it has hit.

It took the world fifteen years and a world war to come together to address the weakness in the global financial system that contributed to the Great Depression. It is to be hoped that it will not take us that long this time; given the level of global interdependence the costs would simply be too high.

For the developing countries like India, the rise in food prices as well as the knock on effects from the financial instability and uncertainty in the industrialized nations are having compounding effect. High fuel costs, soaring commodity prices together with fears of global recession are warning many analysts.

Section II

IMPACT OF THE CRISIS ON THE INDIAN ECONOMY

The Indian economy has shown negative impact of the present global financial crisis. Though the public sector in India, including nationalized banks, could some how insulate themselves from the injurious effects of globalization but as we are also part of the globalization strategy of neo-liberalization, there is a limit of our ability to resist global recession, which may change into a great depression.

The impact of the crisis will be significantly different for the Indian economy as opposed to the western developed nations.

After a long spell of growth, the Indian economy is experiencing a down turn. Table 1 shows that in 2006-07 the GDP growth rate was 9.9% which became 9.0% in 2007-08 and due to the impact of recent global financial crisis and global recession, the growth rate of Indian economy is now declining. In 2008-09, it reduced to 7.1%. The International Monetary Fund (IMF) has also projected the growth prospects for Indian economy at 5.1% in next year. This declining trend has affected

TABLE I

Trends in GDP at Factor Cost

(in Rs. Crore)

Year	*GDP (at 1999-00 Price)*	*Growth in %*
1999-2000	1792292	-
2000-01	1864773	4.4
2001-02	1972606	5.8
2002-03	2048287	3.8
2003-04	2222758	8.5
2004-05	2388384	7.5
2005-06	2612847	9.4
2006-07	2871120	9.9
2007-08	3129717	9.0
2008-09	3351653	7.1

Source: Central Statistical Organization, Government of India.

the service sector adversely. Service export growth is also likely to slow as the recession deepens and financial services firms, traditionally large users of out sourcing services are restructured. The financial crisis in the advanced economies and likely slowdown in developing economies could have adverse impact on the IT sector. About 15 to 18 per cent of the business coming to India includes projects from banking, insurance and the financial services sector, which is now uncertain.

FIGURE I

Trends in GDP (Growth Rate in %)

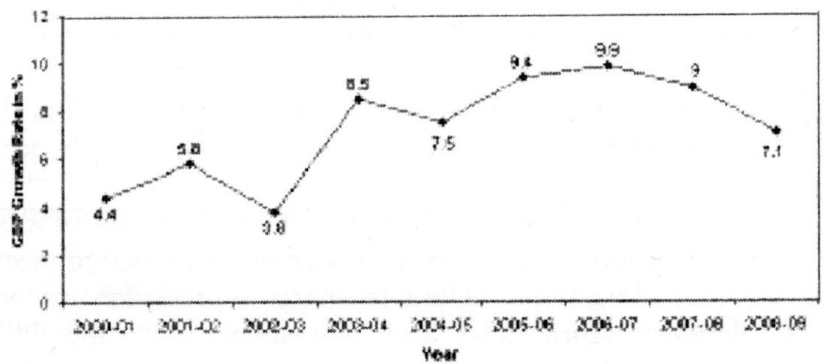

A financial crisis can cause workers' earnings to fall as jobs are lost in formal sector, demand for services provided by the informal sector declines and working hours and real wages are cut. When formal sector workers who have lost their jobs enter the informal sector, they put additional pressure on informal labour markets.

Industrial growth is faltering. India's industrial sector has suffered from the depressed demand conditions in its export markets as well as from suppressed domestic demand due to the slow generation of employment. As per the Index of Industrial Production (IIP) data released by CSO, the overall growth in April-November 2008 is estimated at 3.9 per cent compared to a growth of 9.2 per cent in April-November 2007.

The recent crash in the Sensex is not simply an indicator of the impact of international contagion. There have been warning signals and signs of fragility in Indian finance for some time now, and they are likely to be compounded by trends in real economy.

The most immediate effect of the crisis on India has been an outflow of foreign institutional investment from the equity market. Foreign Institutional Investments (FIIs), which need to retrench assets in order to cover losses in their home countries and are seeking havens of safety in an uncertain environment, have become major sellers in Indian markets. As FIIs pull out their money from the stock market, the large corporate will no doubt be affected. The worst affected are likely to be the exports and small and marginal enterprises that contribute significantly to employment generation.

As is seen in Table 2 and Figure 2 in 2007-08, net Foreign Institutional Investments (FIIs) inflows into India amounted to $16040 million. But in April-November 2008 it was negative to $8857 million. Due to this, there is a collapse in stock prices. As a result, the Sensex fell from its closing peak of 20873 on January 2008 to nearly 8000 in October-November 2008. Figure 3 depicts this.

In addition this withdrawal by the FIIs and corporates was converting the funds raised locally into foreign currency to meet their external obligations, leding to sharp depreciation of the rupee. Between April 2008 and November 2008, the RBI reference rate for the rupee fell by nearly 25 per cent; rupees per

TABLE 2

Net Investment of FIIs at Monthly Exchange Rate

(in US $ Million)

Year	*Amount*
1999-2000	2339
2000-01	2160
2001-02	1846
2002-03	562
2003-04	9949
2004-05	10272
2005-06	9332
2006-07	6707
2007-08	16040
2008-09*	-8857

*April-November, 2008-09.
Source: Security and Exchange Board of India (SEBI).

FIGURE 2

Net Investment of FIIs (At Monthly Exchange Rate)

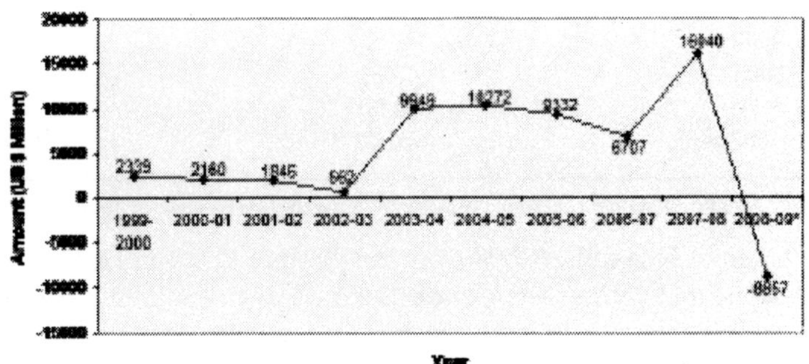

unit dollar went up from Rs. 40.02 in April 2008 to Rs. 49.00 in November 2008. (Table 3 and Figure 4)

The currency depreciation may also affect consumer prices and the higher cost of imported food hurt poor individuals and households that spend much of their income on food. Figure 5 shows that the rate of inflation has gone down to 8.98% in the

FIGURE 3

Daily movements of BSE Sensex in 2008-09

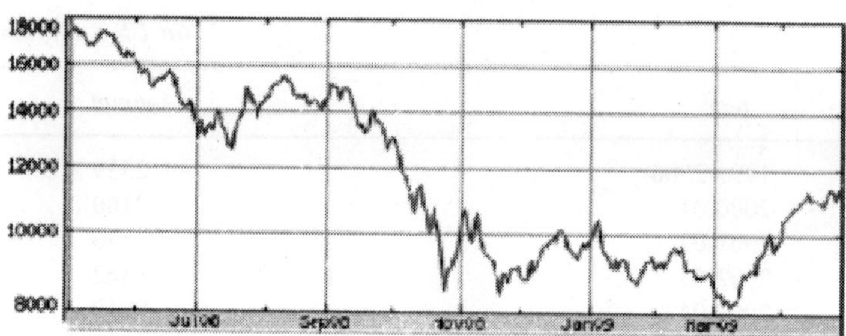

TABLE 3

Foreign Exchange Rate

Month	*Rupees per unit of Dollar*	*Appreciation*
Depreciation		
March 2008	40.36	-
April 2008	40.02	+0.85
May 2008	42.13	-4.2
June 2008	42.82	-5.74
July 2008	42.84	-5.79
Aug. 2008	42.91	-5.95
Sep. 2008	45.56	-11.42
Oct. 2008	48.66	-17.05
Nov. 2008	49.00	-17.64
Dec. 2008	48.63	-17.01

Source: Monthly Economic Report, Ministry of Finance, Government of India.

last week of November 2008 from the peak of 12.9% in first week of August and further sharply declined during recent few weeks. The recent trends suggest a faster than expected reduction in inflation. The decline in inflation should support consumption demand and reduce input costs for corporates. From the external sector perspective, it is projected that imports will shrink more than exports, keeping the current account deficit modest. But the current account deficit is widening.

The foreign exchange market came under pressure because of reversal of capital flows as part of the global

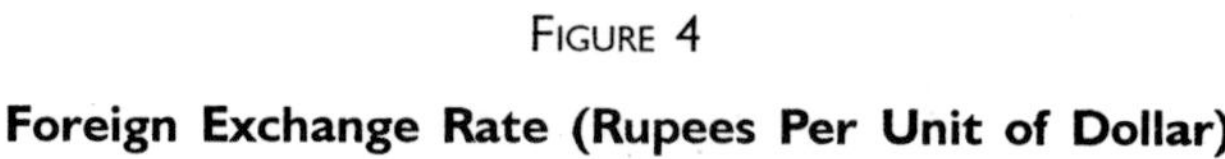

FIGURE 4

Foreign Exchange Rate (Rupees Per Unit of Dollar)

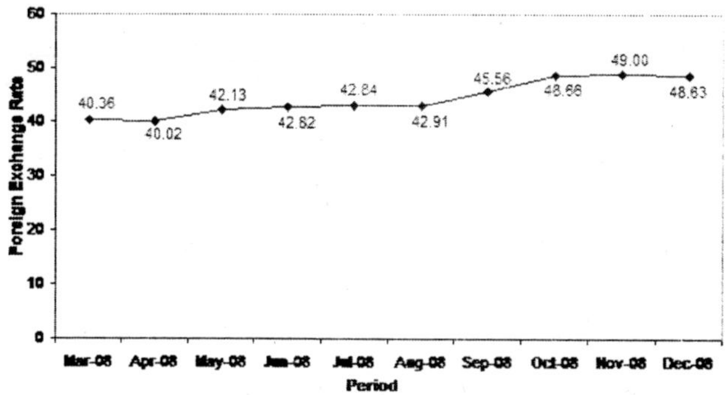

decelerating process. Foreign exchange reserves are depleting. It was $ 309161 million in 2007-08 and now in 2008-09 it is $247621 million, which shows the direct impact of the financial crisis on India's foreign exchange reserves. (Table 4 and Figure 6)

The shrinking of aggregate in the world market as a consequence of the crisis has hurt the exporting manufacturing industries in the country. Table 5 shows that in 2007-08, India's

FIGURE 5

Rate of Inflation (WPI) in India

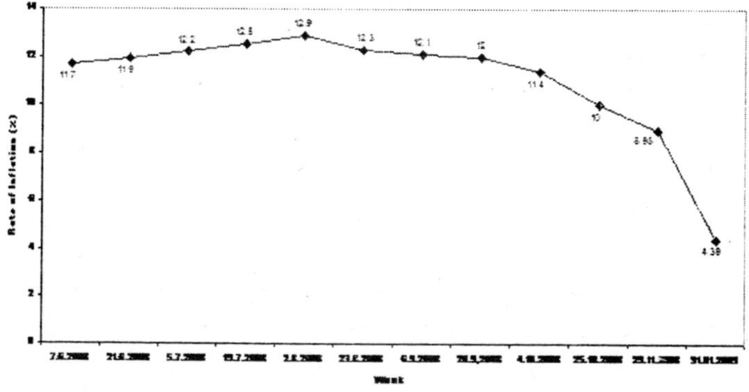

Source: Official of the Economic Advisor, Government of India.

TABLE 4

Foreign Exchange Reserves

(in US $ Million)

	2001-02	2002-03	2003-04	2004-05	2005-06	2006-07	2007-08	2008-09*
Foreign Exchange Reserves	54106	75428	112959	141514	151622	199179	309161	247621

*As on 23rd January 2009.

Source: RBI Weekly Statistical Supplement.

exports and imports were $155512 million and $235911 million respectively and balance of trade was $ -80398 million. And now exports and imports are $131990 million and $225809 million respectively. The balance of trade is $ -93819 million. This shows that India's exports are adversely affected by the slowdown in global markets. This is already evident in certain industries like the garments industries where there have been significant job losses with the on set of the crisis. This along with a squeeze in the high-income service sectors like financial services, hospitality, tourism, etc. will lead to a reduction in consumption spending and overall demand in the domestic economy. A direct consequence of this is a simultaneous loss of informal

FIGURE 6

Foreign Exchange Reserves (in US $ Mullion)

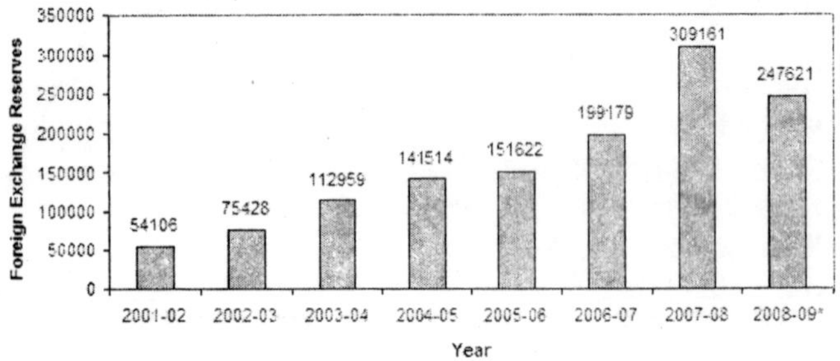

*As on 23rd January 2009.

TABLE 5

India's Foreign Trade

(in US $ Million)

	2002-03	*2003-04*	*2004-05*	*2005-06*	*2006-07*	*2007-08*	*2008-09**
Export	52719	63843	83536	103091	126414	155512	131990
Import	61412	78150	111517	149166	185735	235911	225809
Balance of Trade	-8693	-14307	-27981	-46075	-59321	-80398	-93819

*April-December, 2008-09.

Source: DGCI&S, Kolkata.

employment and lower generation of new non-farm employment in the economy. The depreciation of rupee could not positively affect the exports bill of India.

The other direct impact of the global financial crisis will occur in the area of credit availability to the small-scale agriculture and other rural livelihoods. The impact of the crisis on the rural sector will originate from the slowdown experienced by secondary and tertiary sectors. The fact that the present crisis will adversely affect the manufacturing and service sectors implies that occupational diversification will be more difficult to achieve. The financial crisis therefore threatens to intensify the income deflation that is already a feature of the rural economy and simultaneously aggravate the alarming levels of hunger and malnutrition that currently exist in India.

How has RBI Responded

In aftermath of the turmoil caused by bankruptcy, the Reserve Bank has announced a series of measures to facilitate orderly operation of financial markets and to ensure financial stability, which predominantly includes extension of additional liquidity support to banks. The RBI has been effectively able to manage domestic liquidity and monetary conditions consistent with its monetary policy.

This has been enabled by the appropriate use of a range of instruments available for liquidity management with the Reserve Bank such as the Cash Reserve Ratio (CRR) and Statutory Liquidity Ratio (SLR) stipulation and Open Market Operations

(OMO) including the Market Stabilization Scheme (MSS) and Liquidity Adjustment Facility (LAF). Furthermore, money market liquidity is also impacted by our operation in the foreign exchange market, which in turn, reflects the evolving capital flows. The existing set of monetary instruments has thus provided adequate flexibility to manage the evolving situation.

So the financial sector has emerged without much damage, thanks in part of our strong regulatory framework and in part on account of most of the nationalized banking sector.

SECTION III

CONCLUSION AND SUGGESTIONS

No doubt India has been hit by the global crisis, it is clearly due to India's rapid and growing integration into the global economy. The strategy to counter these effects of the global crisis on the Indian economy and prevent the latter from any further collapse would require an effective departure from the dominant economic philosophy of the neo-liberalism. The first such departure should be a return to Food-First doctrine, not only to ensure food security of the large population but also due to the fact that food production will be more profitable given the current signs of a shrinking market for export-oriented commercial crops. The other important initiative that needs to be adopted is the building of institutions based on the principle of cooperation that will provide an alternative framework of livelihood generation in the rural economy as opposed to the dominant logic of markets under capitalism. Institutions like cooperative markets and credit cooperatives can go a long way in addressing the lack of economically viable producer prices and loaning credit availability for economic activities in the primary sector. Such an alternative policy to tackle the consequences of the financial crisis will require effective Keynesian policies in the form of increased public expenditure at the rural and urban infrastructure. We see that government's engagement generally arrives very late to solve the financial crisis, by which time many financial firms are near insolvency. This generates larger cost for the economy and exchequer. Our key goal today should be to avoid these costs through rapid action.

The need of today is not just the pumping of liquidity in to the Indian economy but also the injection of demand. This can occur only through direct fiscal action by government. In India, larger government expenditure has to be oriented towards a substantial increase in agricultural, especially food grains output.

The new growth will have to come not from some new speculative bubble but from enlarged government expenditure that directly improves the livelihoods of the people and that is geared towards improving the production of foodgrains through a changing of peasant agriculture and not through corporate farming since that would reduce purchasing power in the hands of the peasantry and perpetuate its distress. In short, the new paradigm must entail infrastructure and foodgrain-led growth strategy on the basis of peasant agriculture sustained growth, through larger government spending towards the agriculture and rural sector, which can simultaneously remove both recession and food crisis in India.

REFERENCES:

Akyuz, Yilmaz (2008), "The Global Financial Crisis and Developing Countries", Resurgence, December, Penang, Third World Network.

Athukorala, P. and Sen, K. (2002), "Saving, Investment and Growth in India", Oxford University Press, New Delhi.

Central Statistical Organization, Government of India.

Chandrasekhar, C.P. and Ghosh, Jayati (2004), "The Market that Failed: Neoliberal Economic Reforms in India", Left World Books, New Delhi.

Chandrasekhar, C.P. and Pal, Parthapratim (2006), "Financial Liberalization in India: An Assessment of its Nature and Outcomes", *Economic and Political Weekly*, March 18.

International Monetary Fund (2008a), "Global Financial Stability Report", Washington D.C. October.

International Monetary Fund (2008b), "World Economic Outlook", Washington D.C. October.

Monthly Economic Report, Ministry of Finance, Government of India.

Monthly Statistics of Foreign Trade of India, Vols. I and II (Various issues), Director General of Commercial Intelligence and Statistics (DGCI & S), Ministry of Commerce, Government of India, Kolkata.

Panagariya, Arvind (2008), "India: The Emerging Giant", Oxford University Press, New York.

Patnaik, Prabhat (2007), "Financial Crisis, Reserve Accumulation and Capital Flows", *Economic and Political Weekly*, December 15.

Patnaik, Prabhat (2008), "The Value of Money", Tulika Books, New Delhi.

Reserve Bank of India (2008), "Annual Policy Statement for the Year 2008-09", April.

Reserve Bank of India, Mumbai.

Reserve Bank of India, "Weekly Statistical Supplement", Reserve Bank of India, Mumbai.

Security and Exchange Board of India (SEBI), Mumbai.

13

Global Financial Crisis and its Impact: Need for a Comprehensive and Swift Action

K.M. NAIDU, L.K. MOHAN RAO, P.V. MANJUSHREE AND K. MAHESH NAIDU

> *"We are moving in uncharted waters. No one can be sure what will work. But longstanding economic principles can help guide us. Incentives matter. The long-run fiscal position of the US matters."*
> —*Joseph Stiglitz (2009)*

Any crisis does not appear all of a sudden but starts its action unnoticed, slowly picks up speed, spreads its wings very wide which engulf, like tsunami, all parts of the globe un-noticed even by experts in the field, even surprising the government of its failure to act from the beginning and later it also shirking to take swift action expecting automatic correction by wise appropriate action by the people and stake-holders. All these expectations have proven futile. The situation appears to be slowly drifting to the level of 1929 that developed into great Economic Depression which had taken nearly four years for the governments in the world to bring their economies to normal position by perfecting their State level institutions to adopt world level quality regulations to boost up their economies overcoming all the negative tendencies and encouraging every positive tendency to grow to the highest growth position. The paper attempts to critically examine the impact of global financial meltdown which developed into financial crisis affecting almost all countries in the world since March 2007, requiring appropriate, remedial, rejuvenating, relevant, viable and vibrant as well as swift action for putting the world economy on elegant path of prosperity benefiting all countries.

The global financial crisis, which is in its third year, has been viewed by many as the worst financial crisis of the last century because it began in the US, spread to Europe and slowly affected the whole world, including Asia in a severe way than it was expected. Section I explains the causes for the occurrence of global financial crisis, followed by analysis of impact of the crisis on western developed countries in section II, the next section III delineates its impact on India and section IV provides some suggestions for overcoming the crisis in a practical way.

Section I

OCCURRENCE OF GLOBAL FINANCIAL CRISIS

A global financial crisis is a reality and impacted all countries linked with world trade. It has not occurred all of a sudden in one throw, but slowly developed into a crisis affecting governments all over the world. The search of crisis revealed the part played by six main characters in a play.

The seeds of the crisis were sown in the good times (post-9/11 recession of 2001) with a large monetary policy and a free macroeconomic environment. The world continues to discuss about the role of six suspects—Alan Greenspan, Bill Clinton, George Bush, the banks, the system of fair value accounting and the credit rating agencies.

Alan Greenspan, a prominent character is the former chairman of the USA Federal Reserve. He initiated low interest rates monetary policy in response to the collapse of new economic "Bubble" and the then post-9/11 recession of 2001. Heavy liquidity was pumped into the global monetary system during 2001-05 with short-term interest rates reduced to 1% (lowest level in 50 years). The artificially low rate of interest rates allowed excessive risk taking possible, thus resulting in the sub-prime crisis. Low interest rates led to carry trade through which money went into bonds, stocks, real estate, emerging markets and commodities and anywhere that it is likely to earn a higher return than the very low interest rates that were prevailing in USA and Japan. He accepted his mistake in being negligent of regulatory philosophy in the 24 October 2008 testimony to the US Congress.

President Bill Clinton (1993-2001) is fully involved in the National Home ownership strategy. The second character is former president Bill Clinton as he wanted to walk that way by directing Department of Housing and Urban Development (Secretary Henry Cisneros) to formulate a plan which was announced in August 1994. He helped banks to deviate from commercial considerations in the housing loan disbursements, after Mr. Clinton came to power on 20, January 1993. He, it is alleged, rewrote the rules of Fannie and Freddie and influenced the social case for larger home owing. Banks encouraged by government, fully supported the aggressive loan disbursements, poured billions of dollars of loans into poor households even without following commercial rules like incomplete documents.

The third character in the play of crisis is George Bush who, instead of changing the direction, followed the earlier scenario during his eight years of presidential period. On assuming office, he said on 30 January 2007, "as the economy is in good shape—inflation down, interest rates down, wages on increase, unemployment rate low, people are working hard and putting more money in their pocket—we do not need more government, we need more enterprise" (Speech at Caterpillar, Inc, East Peoria, Illinois, 30th January 2007). It is clearly proved that the heavy rise in housing prices in the US is not due to hike in construction costs or population pressure (Schiller, 2008). No doubt low interest rates and affirmative government action might have pushed houses prices to some extent, but, viewed in the present advantage position, the occurrence of the bubble in the housing market is obvious. Because, between 2001 and 2005, US homeowners experienced an average increase of more than 54% in their house values as calculated by the office of Federal Housing Enterprise Oversight. But the Bush administration has not recognized it; the bubble in the housing market went unnoticed by Bush administration, since the prices were rising they assured credit for the growing (Goldilock's) economy.

A combination of events like complete adjustable rate mortgage, added with a low degree of financial literacy of an average American sub-prime borrower, aided by the liberal government housing policy and low interest rates created a fertile ground for the sub-prime crisis which was about to take place.

BAD LOAN AND GLOBAL FINANCIAL CRISIS

In brief a bad loan taken by a lower middle class family in mid-west America led to an unprecedented global financial crisis. Simply, this is the way a great financial crisis happens. If a borrower is unable to repay a loan taken from a bank, then the bank has to provide for this bad loan; if a bank fails in this action; it is the duty of a bank inspector to identify this failure and set right the failure. Both the bank and bank inspector were lax. Further, all the loans taken from all the banks also scripted the same story. Hence the failures (sins) of bad loans got turned into global misfortune through three other persons in the drama. They are: (a) Government sponsored enterprises (GSES) and the investment bankers in search of a structural financial product; (b) the accountant; and (c) the credit rater. Thus all the six charters in the play (or drama) clearly articulated their role to the author of global financial crisis.

SECTION II

GLOBAL IMPACT ON WESTERN DEVELOPED COUNTRIES

The financial meltdown started in USA in 2007 and slowly showed its impact at the global level, more or les equal to or as serious as that experienced in Great Depression times of 1930 (1929). The prime cause for global financial crises (originated in USA) is the collapse of sub-prime mortgage industry in March 2007 with several prominent leaders applying for bankruptcy protection One can easily observe comparable fallout of great depression of 1929 and present financial crisis of 2007. For example, the Wall Street crash of 1929 rapidly grew upto the Great Depression which heavily crippled the economies of USA

(US), the United Kingdom (UK) and Western Europe. By 1933 the macro-unemployment rate in US had reached to nearly 25%, its manufacturing output fell to 54% (of its 1929 level). The UK and German Economies, being closely linked with US economy, were also severely hit.

World receives everyday adverse economic news. The US budget deficit in 2009, (the largest, so for) is likely to triple and reach to $1.75 trillion, compared to $450 billion in 2008. Toyota, big automobile corporation, announced its first ever losses. The once popular housing Mortgage companies, Freddie Mae and Fannie Mae; the biggest insurance company, AIG, and largest banks like City Bank, survive on Government dollars pumped in by US Government.. During the last quarter of 2008, the US economy fell by 6% per year, Euro Zone declined by1.5%, Japan fell by a high level of 12.1% per year, Britan, Russia and Canada experienced recession. While the Chinese, Brazilian, South Korean and Indian economies fell down rapidly, smaller economies such as Spain, Mexico, Ireland, Singapore, Greece, Hungary, Pakistan and Ukarine are in dire straights. This adverse situation is faced by these economies despite massive bailout packages by governments. For eg: USA has given higher package of $88 trillion and spent $2 trillion in 2009. Such bailouts (still being utilized) aggregate to more than $ 11 trillion.

Reputed economists (Noble Laureates) like Joseph Stiglitz and Paul Krugman strongly argued that the collapse was inevitable, based on the size of the financial bubble. Positive public intervention became inevitable to rescue the world economy and Dr. J. Stiglitz is correct when he observed that no one now can afford to not be Keynision as until 2007 (before crisis zoomed) no one could afford to be called to be a Keynesian.

U.S.A. followed a model of leveraged investment, credit consumption and finance-led growth. The financial crisis in US revealed the collapse of this model as it is linked with the unregulated derivatives market. Infact USA used world savings (due to supremacy of its dollar) particularly that of China as it implemented a model of high savings, over-investment in USA, to help it achieve export led growth. This model also did not succeed; not only it failed in China, but also led to world economic crisis and economic melt-down. The two giants—USA and China are responsible for more than half of the world's economic growth during six years, 2002-08. One half did the savings (China) and the other half did the spending (USA) as China's international reserves (estimated at $2 trillion) helped finance the US current account deficit and also allowed China's exports feasible. In other words USA's total debts (in 2008) exceeded the sum of their debts in the previous 40 years. (US savings fell from 5% to less than zero per cent of gross national income and that of China rose from 30% to 45%). This relationship was also extended to the rest of Asia (export driven) which increased trade deficits and have house hold indebtedness in USA and also spread to Europe. The crisis was rapidly creeping up, willingly supported by government deregulation and loose liberalism, which forced them to offer substantial bail out programme with strong fiscal implications. The crisis led to exceptional bail out plans in US and Europe; such assistance represented 12% of GDP in USA, 8% in U.K. during 2009.

Global economic crisis needs a new dealing combining both free market and regulated market mechanism (M.P. Bezbaruah, 2009). The IMF admitted that "our warning systems within and outside the Fund were insufficiently specific, detailed or dire to gain traction with the policy-markers. Financial overheating was the major problem in the West but not in India." At the G-20 meeting in May 2009, the IMF placed before the leaders a grim assessment (for first the first time in 60 years) that the world was experiencing economic contraction in the last quarter of 2008; global GDP had fallen by 5% and the crisis had "battered global economic activity beyond what was anticipated"; globally, the IMF report reminded G-20 countries that fiscal policy was still falling short of the 2% of GDP stimulus the IMF thought was needed to tackle the situation; it also warned of "the rising spectre of trade and financial protectionism."

According to Prof. Paul Krugman, Nobel Laureate in Economics, 2008, the prospects for fundamental financial reform in USA were fading. The USA banking crisis is not over. The period of economic weakness is likely to continue and real recovery of the economy be postponed. In such a situation, if economy stays depressed for a long time, banker will face much bigger trouble than the stress tests. If the economy has to incur bigger losses in future, it is evidence of government unwillingness either to own banks or let them fail—a situation of heads, profits they (banks) win, tails (losses) we (people or economy) lose (bear). If the bankers win, it is fine and if the current strategy fails, tax payers will be forced to bear (pay for) another bail out. Prof. P. Krugman feels that the prospects for fundamental financial reform are fading. Mildness of bank policy followed so far, though Federal Reserve and Obama administration are committed to higher financial regulation and greater oversight, show that bankers will be able to resort to playing the same old game earlier done.

Studying July 2, 2009 jobs report, Paul Krugman pointed to the severe real impact of the crises on US economy. It revealed the need for a bigger stimulus President Barack Obama will have to implement. He observes that since the recession began, the USA economy has lost 6.5 million jobs—the grim employment report confirmed the US continues to lose jobs at a rapid pace—a distressing situation indeed. The economy has to create 1,00,000 plus new jobs each month to keep pace with the growing population and job-seekers entering the job market; US requires about 8.5 million jobs on the whole. Moreover, the deeper the hole gets, the harder it will be to bring the unemployed out of the hole. The other bad picture the report revealed was of wages stalling and were on the border of outright decline. Added to this is another bad news in the report—the fiscal crisis of the states. Major portion of stimulus of the Federal Government will be undone by budget retrenchment at the state and local level. Hence President Obama and his officials need to push up their efforts, with a programme and a plan to make the stimulus bigger. Despite the possibility of opposition to his new stimulus plan from Republicans and few reputed economists, Prof. Paul Krugman advised President Obama, to convince his economic team and his political leaders to work on additional stimulus now, otherwise he may face his own personal 1937 (the year Franklin Roosevelt gave in to the deficit and inflation hawks with disastrous consequences both for the economy and his political agenda).

Another clear indicator of impact of the crises is galloping deficit. The US federal deficit has reached top level of $ 1 trillion for the first time (in the nine months this fiscal) even as president

Barack Obama ramped up spending to counter the recession and is definitely to reach upto $ 2 trillion by this fall, with the fears of higher interest rates, inflation and the strength of the dollar. In June, the deficit according to US Treasury Department, totaled $ 94.3 billion, pushing the figure, since budget started in October, to $ 1.09 trillion (June 2009) and may reach to $ 1.84 trillion in October. Government spending is on the increasing spree to meet the worst financial crisis (since great depression) and an unemployment rate that reached 9.5%. American parliament (called Congress) already approved a $ 700 billion financial bail out for banks, automakers and other sectors and a $ 787 billion economic stimulus package to jump start a recovery. (Outlays in the first nine months of this budget year would total $ 2.67 trillion up by 20.5% from the same period a year ago). Obama administration is contemplating about the necessity of a second round of stimulus. It means higher burden on the US economy, with debt standing at $ 11.5 trillion. The interest payment on the debt costed $ 452 billion last year, the largest spending amount after medicare, medicard, social security and defense.

Section III

GLOBAL ECONOMIC MELTDOWN : IMPACT ON INDIA

Global economic crisis had its impact on India since it has close integration with global economy. This fact has been clearly mentioned by our Finance Minister in budget speech of 2009-10. A single budget speech cannot solve all our problems. However he budgeted for a larger fiscal deficit (6.8%). He put emphasis on using government spending to sustain growth. This is a logical growth process in 2008-09 when the global crisis hit the economy. The economic survey 2008-09 mentioned that the usual large contribution of private consumption to growth collapsed last year, 2007-08, but the economy grew by 6.7% manually because government consumption made good this fall, with longer than usual contribution to growth. As the crisis is not yet fully overcome, it is natural that the budget provides for increased government outlay, mostly on investment, to boost demand. However, this may not be sufficient. The gross budgetary support for central plan would increase by Rs. 35,000 crores in 2009-10, compared to 2008-09 (RE). The deceleration of

Indian economy is to be seen even in the period preceding the crisis mainly due to declining trend in capital formation (Mihir Rakshit and R. Nagaraj, 2009). The very important demand reducing factor in operation (even in pre-crisis period) was severe decline in exports; export growth fell down to 7.5% in 2007-08 from 18.9% in 2006-07 (C.S.O data). The deceleration phase of the Indian economy started even before US mortgage market fell down, but no doubt, global crisis speeded up the Indian economys meltdown, making the task of containing and reversing the situation more difficult. Some of the broad characteristics of the India economy helped understand the real nature of the economy. The fall in GDP and industrial growth started in the first quarter of 2007-08, nearly six months before the US financial crisis, more prominent since the fourth quarter of 2007-08 and first quarter of 2008-09 (Aug.-Sept.) respectively, i.e. more than three to six months after the appearance of the sub-prime crisis. The related cause was the sharper slowdown in private consumption as well as aggregate investment from early January/May 2008. During March/August 2008, both export, and import growth was higher than in the previous crisis period, a peculiar rise up that cannot continue later. India's trade flows got their adverse impact since September 2008 from the global economic crisis. The rare combination of shaper fall in domestic demand and rise of exports and imports is a clear riddle seen in the Indian economy during this period. Another riddle to be seen is in NRI remittances which accelerated in growth of more than 38% between second quarters of 2007-08 and 2008-09, a clear case of no impact of the crisis on NRI remittances. However, it is in the third quarter of 2008-09, having experienced heavier deceleration of investment and private consumption as well as deep fall in export growth, the economy got sucked into greater whirlpool of the global crisis.

After a year or more, the crisis raged and engulfed the financial sectors of developed economies leading to heavy losses and substantial bankruptcies, etc., Indian banks were not seriously affected by such development. But through other routes the crisis cast its full shadow on financial markets and on the real sector of the economy. The first impact was an the country's capital flows, particularly external commercial borrowings (ECBs) and foreign institutional investment (FII).

Soon after the crisis started, net ECBs and FII fell sharply between October and November 2007, from $ 3.6 billion and $ 5.7 billion to $ 2.2 billion and minus $ 1.6 billion respectively, not because of better prospects in US compared to India, but because of shoring up the balance sheets of developed country financial firms in the times of heavy loses suffered by them. This led to gradual fall in the value of rupee inspite of heavy running down of foreign currency assets by RBI between October 2007 and November 2008. The drying up of foreign flows into the Indian economy led to the bursting of the Indians stock market bubble. Though Indian banks are free from economic crises, the global financial meltdown has had some adverse consequences for credit financial activities; the credit crunch was serious for traders; exporters found difficult to secure credit from foreign banks. The crisis through credit crunch, had a greater impact on Indian exports than imports.

India as an emerging market suffered heavily than was thought of earlier. The impact has been quite heavy, after Lehman crises and according to R.B.I. Governor D. Subba Rao, it occurs through three channels—trade channel, the financial channel and confidence channel. Through trade channel, it was found to be bearable as it would affect growth only by 1 to 1.5% (because merchandise exports may form about less than 15% of GDP). But through financial channel the situation is different; it is seen by financial integration which would be the total external transactions (gross current account flow plus gross capital flows); this has more than doubled from 46.8% in 1997-98 to 117.4% in 2008. When such integration takes place, impact occurs in three related ways: reducing Indian companies access to overseas finance, lowering domestic liquidity and causing stock prices to fall.

Due to adverse global conditions Indian firms access to global fianance was very much limited in various forms. Fresh ECGS—external commercial borrowings—have become difficult and existing ones are not easily paid to firms, long-term finance for foreign acquisitions is not easily available, buyers credit became scarce for international transactions; Indian banks overseas branches and subsidiaries were not able to access funds in the wholesale market and had to be made available with dollar funds by their parent banks from India.

One can see higher impact on the Indian economy from foreign flows—FDIs and FIIs. The gap between domestic investment and savings (called current account deficit) of nearly 1.5% of GDP reveals the potential impact on the Indian economy of foreign inflows. If the current account deficit is of the order of 1.5% of GDP, the economic growth should not decline by more than 0.5 to 1%, but projections for economic growth for 2008-09 at around 6.5% and even lower for 2009-10 (6%), means that financial integration has taken higher price in adverse conditions. In 2009 the adverse balance of payments position reduced the reserves to $ 2.5 billion (April-Sept. 2009) from $ 40.4 billion (April-Sept. 2008) which affected domestic liquidity.

The fall in domestic stock prices is another adverse impact of the crisis through financial integration and fall in foreign flows for this purpose. (FII inflows of $ 6.6 billion in April-September 2008-09 compared to $15.5 billion in the same period in 2007-08). When share prices are low, firms may not get access to capital market. If bank finance fail to substitute fully capital markets, investment plans of firms may not succeed.

Indian banks were less affected by the global financial crisis compared to the banking system in US and Europe. In the latter countries, banks were the main source of crisis; they precipitated it and hence suffered from heavy losses, credit crunch, loss of confidence and fall down of the real economy. However in India, banks were restrained and constrained by RBI and its severe monitoring eyes and hands; but the real economy suffered through different channels and banks got affected from the slowing down of the economy. Indian economy is affected by global financial crisis is an accepted reality viewed from any angle of judgment or based on any analytical study of each sector of the economy. As our country is less impacted compared to USA, Europe, Japan and other developed countries, some economists argued for decoupling of the Indian economy from the global economy. But the responses form the top person of the country's Apex Bank (RBI Governor Dr. D. Subba Rao) and top political administrative leader (Prime Minister Dr. Man Mohan Singh) have shown the correct policy decision of the government of India. Their stance is that the notion that Indian economy could be decoupled from the global economy is discredited now and impossible for government to implement in real terms. The decouple idea is flawed on the contention that the Indian Banking sector was less exposed to "tainted assets" and that "exports constituted only 15% of the countries GDP", is not wholly correct. No doubt Chairman UN committee on Global Financial Crisis, Nobel Laureate Joseph Stiglitz stated that the economy of USA would not have been in such a mess if America had a Central Bank Chief like Y.V. Reddy who adopted monetary policies which resulted in the country's economy remaining unaffected by the global financial meltdown and for steering the monetary policy in a time of international turbulence that adversely affected the entire world, but he steered Indian Banking out of this adverse effects. However, the world is much more globalised today, not only because of trade flows, but also because of greater financial integration. Further, Indian exports, imports and invisibles formed about $1/4^{th}$ of GDP ten years ago; they now share a little over two-thirds of GDP. The Indian economy is linked, therefore, to the recovery of the global economy as India is a supply constrained economy, not a demand constrained economy.

Higher and severe the impact of global financial crisis, larger the stimulus package for revival of the economy. This has been amply proved by the huge government spending plan proposed to be implemented by the latest budget of union government for 2009-10. It has followed Keynesian path of stimulating the demand by spending-led path to growth. It has made experts across the country nervous about its success. But the Finance Minister (Sri Pranab Mukherjee) boldly initiated spending binge so as to put more money into the hands of people to create cascading effect to spur demand. He announced a spending programme in excess of Rs. 10 lakh crores for 2009-10, up from Rs. 7.55 lakh crores of 2008-09 budget that he justified in the present situation of economic slowdown. He emphasized on the politically rewarding inclusive growth formula and justifiably increased the outlay (for 2009-10) for its NREGS and other similar programmes. Continuing inclusive growth agenda, the budget proposed schemes to please even the income tax paying community; the removal of fringe benefit tax also pleased corporate India, but it may shift the onus on employees. He also daringly deviated fiscal responsibility path by increasing the fiscal deficit to 6.8% of GDP (or Rs. 4 lakh crores) up from 2008-09 budget estimates Rs. 1.3 lakh crores or 2.5% of GDP. Even the revenue deficit will increase from 1% (Rs. 55184 crores in 2008-09 budget estimate) to Rs. 2.83 lakh crores or 4.8% of GDP in 2009-10. This heavy revenue deficit is a cause for concern as it does not result in the creation of assets (due to money spent for normal running of government departments and different services, interest payments on debt and subsidies). To meet such huge deficit government has to resort to market borrowing which is placed at Rs. 4.52 lakh crores in 2009-10 which means nearly 60% of the borrowing will only be used for funding the revenue deficit. It is like borrowing to eat and is major concern to the economy. The fiscal deficit if viewed in the context of slowdown of GDP growth rate to 6% (2008-09), a fall from 9% in the previous three years, and which affected job creation and investment in some sectors, will help one understand the reasonableness of high fiscal deficit. He no doubt preferred huge risk in moving in this direction for the sake of energizing the falling Indian economy and to put the economy back on higher growth track. Dr. Montek Singh Ahluwalia, Deputy Chairman, Planning Commission, endorsed the high fiscal deficit (6.8%) as higher government spending which will stimulate economy because the global economic situation is very difficult. He said that government expenditure is oriented towards inclusiveness and it is trying to maintain a stimulus in the economy with higher deficit (in 2009-10 budget) and the same would be brought down in coming years, once the economy is on high growth path. The gross budgetary support is proposed to increase by Rs. 40,000 crores to Rs. 3.25 lakh crores for the current fiscal (2009-10) as the government made provision of Rs. 2.85 lakh crores for this purpose in the interim budget. Government of India in 2009-10 budget attempted integration of agriculture activities and rural development schemes, mostly because they helped to prevent the global meltdown from adversely affecting the rural economy and also with the belief that the two sectors could lift the country out of the crisis rut. For example, Rs. 70,000 crore bailout package for indebted farmers and jobs for rural workers below the poverty line under NREGA are the strong measures to be implemented during 2009-10. The job measure intends to bring marginal and small farmers eligible for NREGA works to make them earn more income and improve land productivity and therefore raised the allocation to the programme from Rs. 30,000 crores in 2008-09 to Rs. 40,000 crores in 2009-10.

Delivering J.R.D. Tata Memorial Lecture in New Delhi on Friday 31, July 2009, RBI Governor Dr. D. Subbarao cautioned against another round of inflationary pressure going forward unless a balance is maintained "between short-term compulsions and medium-term rationality with care and good judgment." He therefore, emphasized for a roll back of the fiscal stance and expansionary monetary policy now in place to counter the impact of global financial crisis. He said creation of high power money in the face of large fiscal deficits, even if there is no direct financing, is not costless; it can sow the seeds of the next inflationary cycle. No doubt, counter cyclical public spending was necessary in the short-term, but the main focus in that situation was to spend that money quickly, effectively and to create durable assets. On the monetary side, the increased fiscal deficit will pose more than a proportionate challenge. RBI at present is trying to maintain a comfortable liquidity position while at the same time controlling inflation expectations. RBI had made available a liquidity of Rs. 5.60 lakh crore-9% of GDP to help overcome liquidity crisis following the global meltdown started by the collapse of US investment banker Lehman Brothers in mid-September 2008. Government borrowing has resulted in increasing yields, inspite of the substantial excess liquidity, militating against the low interest rate regime that India wants. During 2009-10, RBI has managed delicate balance between government borrowing and maintaining ample liquidity to meet the demand for private credit that may increase in the coming months as growth moves up.

Economic survey 2008-2009 provided a clean picture of the Indian economy due to the impact of global economic crisis. The first effect on India was the slowdown in the macro-growth rate and its ramification on the sectoral growth rates, external trade, foreign investment flows into economy as well as fall in infrastructure growth, etc. All there facts are presented below.

Economic growth decelerated in 2008-09 to 6.7%, a fall of 2.1% from average growth rate of 8.8% in the previous five years (2003-04 to 2007-08). It means a definite slowdown from the average growth of 7.3% per year during the previous five years as well as deceleration from high growth of 9% and 9.7% in 2007-08 and 2006-07 respectively. The global financial meltdown and economic recession in developed countries is the major factor for India's economic slowdown. The present global crisis is considered as the worst since great depression in the developed counties, naturally developing country like India suffered as it is too difficult for it to remain immune to the global economic shock in the highly interlinked and integrated system of global economy.

India cannot insulate itself from the adverse developments in international financial markets which are now closely interrelated with an economy. In the beginning of global crisis due to sub-prime crisis, India benefited through increased FII flows (during September 2007 and January 2008). As global crisis intensified, net portsfolio flows to India declined seeking foreign lands. The current account was affected after September 2008 with fall in exports. The economy experienced fluctuations in stock market prices, exchange rates, inflation levels, etc.

The deceleration of growth in 2008-09 spread across all sectors (except mining and quarrying and community, social and personal services). The growth in agriculture and allied activities fell from 4.9% in 2007-08 to 1.6% in 2008-09. The manufacturing, electricity and construction sectors declined to 2.4%, 3.4%, and 7.2% respectively during 2008-09 from 8.2%, 5.3%, and 10-11% respectively in 2007-08.

The latest round of survey of professional forecasters conducted by RBI in June estimated the overall median GDP growth rate higher at 6.5% for 2009-10 against 5.7% results of earlier survey conducted in March 2009. The survey also indicated the average inflation in the fourth quarter of 2008-09 to be about 5.4% (W.P1) but as per CP1, inflation is at higher levels of 8.6% to 11.5% for different consumer price indices in May/ June 2009. But Reserve Bank of India Governor (Dr. D. Subba Rao) placed the growth production for GDP for 2009-10 at 6% with an upward bias, based on current assessment, a slight improvement over the figure of 6% shown in annul policy statement. The uptrend in growth has to wait until the middle of 2009-10.

The future growth depends on the emphasis of the

government on "inclusive growth", but it is not likely to increase the incomes of the poor along with the growth of productivity. In other words, it follows the mantra of rising growth, sans increase in employment and income of the poor so as to accelerate effective demand which only, as per Keynesian prescription, will make Indian economy overcome the present recessionary crisis. This policy of inclusive growth may not succeed. In the present context of fall in growth rate, rise in current account deficit of balance of payments and decrease in capital account surplus, achieving the goals of government is highly difficult. When India attracted huge flows of foreign capital, the country succeeded in growth target following debt financed private consumption and investment-led growth. In the financial crisis period, this policy may not give viable result. Hence the present strategy of Indian growth process may not be viable if the financial crisis and severe economic downturn (especially in US) persist for medium-term of three to four years.

Section IV

SUGGESTED SOLUTIONS

Global financial crisis resulted in global economic meltdown. Hence solutions have to be found both at international, national and local levels.

International

International credit control instituted on the lines of Nuclear Control Commission have to be created with effective control mechanism. One should think constructively about the global economic crisis and how to deal with it. Hence the point that immediately comes to mind is about the discussion the members of UNO should have and decide on how to implement the recommendations of UNO appointed Stiglitz Committee on the global financial crisis. IMF, world Bank, WTO, Asian Development Bank, etc. also have to be invited for this discussion for evolving an effective UNO Institution with full powers to eliminate situations and conditions for the recurrence of global economic crisis and also to implement measures for immediate action to rejuvenate the affected economies through global financial packages and bail out schemes, programmes, etc.

National

The present financial crisis has originated from USA due to failure of regulated mechanism at the Federal level. The causes are found to be top political authorities' flawed decisions and the effect is financial crisis on account of the soft attitude of apex bank, the Federal Reserve, towards wrong mechanisms and non-bankable policies followed by large banks in that country. The top persons with supreme powers had small and low ideas, took wrong decisions and left them to be implemented without proper control and strong punishment for allowing implementation of wrong policies. Hence, Federal Reserve should possess strong controlling powers approved by the Congress (top law-making body in USA) and the President of America. Similar salutary and effective steps have to be taken by all countries in Europe, North America, Asia, Africa, etc. for non-occurrence of such avoidable economic crisis through wrong political decisions.

Local

The local refers to Indian situation. In the early period of global financial meltdown (March-September 2008) the government and encomiasts were of the view that the global crisis will have least effect on the India economy. No doubt the RBI and its top brass headed by wise-headed persons (in particular Dr. Y.V. Reddy) followed viable banking policies with strong regulated and cautions mechanism and reduced the vulnerable impact of global crisis. However as Indian economy is more globalized now than five years earlier, any happenings or crisis in any country will definitely spread to India. With necessary provisioning and correct policy measures, the impact can be subsided, reduced and possibly avoided. Inclusiveness is the order of the day.

The bailout packages have been implemented by government of India following Keynesian interventionism to accelerate effective demand. Nearly Rs. 18,600 crores have been allocated for this purpose by government of India in 2009-10 budget, besides increasing substantially the allocation on NREGS, National Sadak Yojana, education and health, so as spur effective demand.

Naturally the fiscal deficit has shot up to 6.8% of G.D.P. in

2009-10, from 2.5% of G.D.P. in 2008-09. Increased deficit is unavoidable, but care has to be taken to utilise increased deficit amount productively to create assets that would earn higher income for the economy. In other words, deficit should promote higher growth latter than raise up deficit further upwards. It should lead to more savings and higher investments in the economy.

From this point of view, larger allocation of Rs. one lakh crores for infrastructure projects by government of India is justifiable. In other words, it must enable higher connectivity of rural economy with urban economy, promoting assimilation between two parts of the national economy. India is experiencing neglect of rural economy at the cost of urban economy which is to be avoided in the present crisis, because higher growth of agriculture to the level of 5% in 2009-10 from the present level of 1.5% 2008-09 will definitely throw up demand for industrial goods and IT services, once information technology is effectively utilised for agricultural growth as in developed countries like USA, UK, Germany, France, Italy, Japan, etc. and China in the present period.

Production for export through liberal support to export-led development is essential. For ninth month in a row in June 2009, exports have fallen by 25% for lack of demand of Indian goods in foreign countries due to continued economic slowdown and recession in the US and European Union, the biggest markets for India. Export promotion measures have to be given higher emphases in 2009-10 budget and in future to see that the export growth is steadily increased. The textiles export, for example, declined by 1.71% in 2008-09 at $ 21.75 billions and resulted in loss of million jobs in the last few months. The government has to make exports tax free during the slowdown period. To help textile sector under Technology Upgradation Fund Scheme (JUFX), the government provided in 2009-10 Rs. 3140 crores for subsidy, out of which Rs. 2546 crores have been paid by 31 July 2009. (*The Hindu*, Friday, August 7, 2009, p. 14). As favoured by our Prime Minister Dr. Manmohan Singh and supported by Prof. Ch. Hanumantha Rao (2009), India has to follow "inclusive growth" policy in respect of all sectors and all regions in India by both the Central and State Governments for meeting effectively the present economic and financial crisis that originated in USA in Sept. 2007 and slowly spread to India with adverse effect in 2009. RBI is following liberal monetary policy- and cautious fiscal policy-making available sufficient liquidity for best utilization by banks, entrepreneurs, industrialists, farmers, administrators, etc. avoiding political aberrations, for achieving higher growth rate of more than 10% per year from the present low level of 6% to meet the economic crisis on sound lines for the benefit of all sections in India.

The Central Government has to create a more invest-friendly atmosphere for investors; the investors be provided with loans at low interest rates. Government intends to borrow Rs. 4.52 lakh cores to meet very high fiscal deficit (6.8% of GDP) which may crowd out private sector and make it suffer from insufficient loans. Hence the government has to encourage banks to provide sufficient loans with low interest rates for meeting the private sector investment needs during the period of crisis.

The tensions between monetary and fiscal policies have to be eliminated by following the coordinated strategic crisis management efforts by government and RBI to cushion the economy. The large borrowings by government will impede monetary transmission and may militate against the objective of ensuring low interest rates. Hence the government and RBI to achieve the goal (of low interest rates) and accelerate economic growth will have to strike a balance between short-term compulsions and medium-term sustainability with great care and judgment to boost up the economy in the crisis period to reach a growth rate of 10% along with increase in employment to people.

SUM UP

Global financial crisis is considered to be the severest crisis of the century as it originated first in USA, spread to Europe and slowly swept fit the whole world including Asia. As the globe is more inclusive now with trade, commerce and communication technology, the crisis also enveloped India. The causes are many for the present global crisis, but the prime reason is the game played in US that pushed that country into 'Sub-prime crisis' and the globe into a great financial and economic meltdown. 'Sub-prime' means simply irresponsible lending to borrowers who do not fulfil any conventional or standard credit criteria. It is not the collapse of the market economy and failure of capitalism; it is, however the market that was exposed the unethical and unsustainable operations of the market players. The market also exposed the pitfalls in capitalism which can be misutilised by the greedy leaders for meeting their selfish end—become rich easily through unethical means at the cost of the economy and people. The global financial crisis is a reality and being faced by all regions and sectors in almost all countries. The search of crisis revealed the part played by six main characters in USA—Alan Greenspan, Bill Clinton, George Bush, the banks, the system of fair value accounting and the credit rating agencies.

The crisis hit the US, European economies very adversely and to meet it the governments have released heavy bailouts in millions and trillions to push their economies on to the accelerated growth path and reverse the fall of jobs. In other words, they revisited Keynesian intervention policy for raising effective demand and at the same time imposing regulatory polices on the credit distributors, i.e. banks and encouraging production activity of auto majors and industries to provide more jobs and arrest the fall of employment. It may take two to three years to regain the lost growth path in USA and make it a leading nation in the world. Europe and other countries are also implementing bailout packages for making their countries regain old development path.

India is also affected by global financial crisis but its severity was realized only by the end of 2008 and in the early period of 2009. All the sectors were affected in the economy with fall in production, trade, exports, job loses. To meet such a situation, government of India announced heavy bailout packages amounting to Rs. 10 lakh crores in 2009-10. This resulted in very high fiscal deficit of 6.8% of GDP and government entering into higher borrowing targets. RBI also made its Monetary and Fiscal policies very liberal and made available huge liquidity of Rs. 5,61,700 crores. (*The Hindu*, Aug. 3, 2009, p. 14) to the economy and advised banks to provide liberal credit at reduced interest rate for productive activities in the economy. Government and RBI are also following export friendly and investment promoting policies to promote higher infrastructure investment in the economy to accelerate effective demand and to promote more exports to foreign countries. The higher deficit has to be utilized for productive activities and to create income generating assets as well as providing more income into the hands of job losers by creating more jobs which will also promote higher economic growth of 10% in the future. The tensions between Monetary and Fiscal policies have to be eliminated by following the coordinated strategic crisis management efforts by government and RBI to galvanize the economy to achieve higher growth rate with more job creation methods. Hence there is greater need to strike a balance between short-term compulsions and medium-term sustainability with prudence and practical judgment to speed up the economy and employment levels in the crisis period.

References

Arun Kumar (2009), "Tackling the Current Global Economic and Financial Crisis: Beyond Demand Management" in the *Economic and Political Weekly*, March 28, pp. 151-52.

Guilhem Fabre (2009), "The Twligh of 'CHIMERICA'?, China and the Collapse of the American Model" in the *Economic and Political Weekly*, June 27, pp. 299-300.

Mihir Rakshit (2009), "India Amidst the Global Crisis" in *Economic and Political Weekly*, March 28, pp. 94-10.

Pulin, B. Nayak (2009), "Anatomy of the Financial crisis: Between Keynes and Schumpeter" in *Economic and Political Weekly*, March 28, April 3, p 158.

T.T. Ram Mohan (2009), "The Impact of the Crisis on the Indian Economy" in the *Economic and Political Weekly*, March 28, p. 111.

Tapan Babu, Economist based in New York, U.S.A. (2008), "Six Characters in Search of a Crisis" in *Economic and Political Weekly*, November 2008, pp. 32-36.

14

Global Economic Crisis and the Indian Economy

Purna Chandra Mishra*

INTRODUCTION

These are exceptional times. Exceptional for what has happened to financial markets—it can only be described as a meltdown. And exceptional for what has not happened, at least not yet, to the broader economy—the onset of a severe recession.

As 2009 wounddown, 'Financial Meltdown' and 'Economic Recession' became amongst the most frequently used words in the business journals and business meetings. In India, the US and elsewhere, business leaders who until 2009 had tried to get government out of business are now urging governments to vigorously save business.

The current global financial crisis is attributed to significant mis pricing of risks in the financial system. The impact was compounded by relatively easy monetary policies at major financial centers and globalization of liquidity flows without adequate safeguards. Complex and structured derivatives and inadequacy of majority of stakeholders in understanding these innovations also played their part.

The collapse of Citigroup, Bear Stearns, Merrill Lynch, Goldman Sachs, AIG, Lehman Brothers, Freddie Mae, Fannie Mae, RBS, ING Fortis and other Wall Street Icons led to global down which affected the US, the European Union and Japan and engulfed creeping recession and worsened the situation.

This all pervasive crisis did not allow India to stay insulated from it. The contagion is truly global in a globalised world. The financial crunch is having its impact on foreign institutional investors (FII), foreign direct investments (FDI), exchange rate, remittances, balance of payments, forex reserves and all the macroeconomic variables in India. The immediate impact on the stock market on 10th of October, i.e. a crash of 1000 points before recovering some 200 points, an intra-day drop of some 800 points paved the way for slowdown of growth. No economy was escaped from this worldwide recession.

A redeeming feature of the current crisis is that its magnitude is much lesser than that of the great depression of the 1930's when unemployment rate in the United States exceeded 25 per cent. Currently, it stands at 6.5 per cent and is predicted to remain around eight per cent by the end of 2009.

ROOT CAUSE OF THE CRISIS

For at least the last year and a half, as banks took successive write downs related to deteriorating mortgage backed securities, the conventional wisdom was that we are facing a crisis of bank solvency triggered by falling housing prices and magnified by leverage. However, falling housing prices and high leverage alone would not necessarily have created the situation we are right now in. The basic cause of the crisis was largely an unregulated environment, mortgage lending to sub-prime borrowers. It occurs because of the large proliferation of conduits and SIVs created by them off-balance sheets, in order to avoid regulatory capital consumption, to invest in long-term assets, financing them by issuing commercial paper backed by these assets. Nevertheless, the main problem with the banks in the United States and Europe is not only that their conduits were invested in sub-prime and other low quality credit structured products, but that, when their assets-backed commercial paper market financing dried up, the borrow-short-lend-long wheel stopped. The conduits have to pay-off their short borrowing positions, but have problems selling off their long lending positions.

This left the banks with two options: take them into their balance sheets, provoking a credit crunch, or get enough temporary liquidity from the central bank to refinance them to keep the wheel turning, as it were. It led the situation to become worst in the US and Euro area.

THE ACUTE STAGE OF THE CRISIS

The evolution of the current financial crisis seems remarkably similar to the emerging markets crisis a decade ago.

Americas crisis started with creditors fleeing from sub-prime debt in summer 2007. As default rate rose, investment tgrade debt—often collateralized debt obligations (CDOs) built out of sub-prime debt—faced large losses. The exodus of creditors caused mortgage finance and home building to collapse.

The second stage began with the Bear Sterns in March 2008 and extended through the bail out of Fannie Mae and Freddie Mae. As investment Banks evolved into proprietary trading houses with large blocks of liquid securities on their books, they became dependent on their ability to roll over their short-term loans, regardless of the quality of their assets. And in a matter of days, despite no major news, Bear Sterns was dead. However while the Federal Reserve and treasury made sure that Bear Stearns equity holders were penalized, they also made sure that creditors were made whole—a pattern they would follow with Fannie and Freddie. As a result, creditors learned that they could safely continue lending to large financial institutions.

This changed in September 15 and 16 with the failure of Lehman and the rescue of AIG, which saw a dramatic and damaging reversal of policy. So Lehman's ability to borrow money was evaporated and the Fed let Lehman go bankrupt. Overnight, however without any fundamental changes, the market decided that AIG might be at risk and the fear became self-fulfilling.

As a result, creditors and uninsured depositors at all risky institutions pulled their funds-shifting deposits to treasuries, moving prime brokerage accounts to the safest institutions and cashing out of securities arranged with any risky institutions. LIBOR shot up and short-term US Treasury yields fell as banks stopped lending to each other and lent to the US government instead. The collapse of one money market fund and the pending collapse of more, sent the US Treasury into crisis mode.

In each case, creditors lost confidence that they could get their principal back and rushed to get out at the same time and policy-makers around the world seemed incapable of stopping these waves and at the same time, the credit market shock waves spread quickly throughout the world.

IMPACT ON INDIAN ECONOMY

India too is foreced to weather the negative impact of the crisis. As the impact on India unfolds, there are two frequently asked questions : First, how is that India is affected when it came out of the Asian crisis relatively unscathed? Second, why is India affected even when its exports account for only 15 per cent of its GDP? The answer to both the question lies in globalization. We are certainly more integrated to the world today than ten years ago at the time of Asian Crisis. Integration into the world implies more than just exports. Going by the common measures of globalization, India's two-way trade (merchandise export plus import), as a proportion of GDP, grew from 21.2 per cent in 1997-98, the year of the Asian crisis, to 34.7 per cent in 2007-08. If we take an expended measure of globalization, that is, the ratio of total external transactions (gross current account flows plus gross capital flows) to GDP, this ratio has increased from 46.08 per cent in 1997-98 to 114.7 per cent in 2007-08. These numbers are clear evidence of India's increasing integration into the world economy over the last ten years.

There is an important difference between the crisis in the advanced countries and the developments in India. While in the advanced countries the contagion spread from the financial to the real sector, in India, the slowdown in the real sector is affecting the financial sector, which in turn has a second order impact on the real sector.

The global slowdown has its implications on the domestic economy. During the last three years Indian Economy grew at an average annual rate of 8.6 per cent. For the first time the economy has shown signs of deceleration and grew at 7.8 per cent in the first half year of 2008-09 (April-September). The service sector, which contributes more than 50% share in the GDP and is the prime growth engine, reported to be slowing down, mainly in the transport, communication, trade, and hotels and restaurants sub-sectors. The industrial growth has decelerated sharply during April-November 2008 encompassing all the constituent sectors. In manufacturing sector, the growth has come down to 4.0 per cent in April-November 2008 as compared to 9.8 per cent in the corresponding period of last year. The slowdown occurred in all the use-based categories, except consumer goods where it has accelerated.

The industries most affected by weakening demand were airlines, hotels and real estate. Besides this, Indian exports suffered a setback and there was a setback in the production of export-oriented sectors. The government advised the sectors of weakening demand to reduce prices. It provided some relief by cutting down excise duties, but such simplistic solutions were doomed to failure. Weakening demand led to producers cutting production. To reduce the impact of the crisis, firms reduced their workforce, to reduce costs. This led to increase in unemployment but the total impact on the economy was not very large. Industrial production and manufacturing output declined to five per cent in the last quarter of 2008-09. Consequently, a vicious cycle of weak demand and falling output developed in the Indian economy.

A weakening of demand in the US affected our IT and Business Process Outsourcing (BPO) sector and the loss of opportunities for young persons seeking employment at lucrative salaries abroad. Indis's famous IT sector, which earned about $50 billion as annual revenue, is expected to fall by 50 per cent of its total revenues. This would reduce the cushion to set off the deficit in balance of trade and thus enlarge our balance of payments deficit. It has now been estimated that sluggish demand for exports would result in a loss of 10 million jobs in the export sector alone.

SUB-PRIME CRISIS : THE BURGEONING PROBLEM OF THE GLOBAL ECONOMIC CRISIS

The global economy is under severe pressure on account of the liquidity issues affecting the banking system following the outburst of the "sub-prime crisis" (SPC), whose widespread effect covered the global financial market, owing to the close knit relationship shared by the capital markets world over.

Concept and Meaning

Sub-prime mortgage (SPM) means "offering loans to borrowers who do not qualify for them at market rates due to their deficient or poor credit history".

Sub-prime borrowers normally comprise of financially troubled people like those who lost jobs, those with a history of previous debts, people with marital problems or those with unexpected medical conditions. Hence sub-prime lenders assume a higher degree of risk and to offset the same resort to a generous hike in the interest rates. It manifests in the form of SPMs for home loans, car loans, credit cards/plastic money, personal loans, etc.

Sub-Prime Crisis : Scenario in India

When the investment in developing large economies started pushing up stock prices as well as land prices beyond comfort levels, the need to invest in USA arose. The Indian Banking sector does not boast of structured finance instruments like in the US, and hence the quantum of securities held by them is meager. But owing to the depreciation in the value of securities bought by them in the international market, the impact of SPC cannot be dismissed. The tendency in India was investment made in CDOs from oil surpluses and pension funds and presently the losses are notional. With the inflow of foreign funds in the form of FDIs and FIIs, Indian banks resort to better risk management, instead of financial profits to alleviate monetary crisis.

The Indian Capital markets are handicapped to an extent, as foreign Institutional Investors have sold off their investments in Indian Companies to cover huge losses. With the capital inflow being affected following the SPC in USA, the Indian capital market is exposed to more risks. A paradigm shift to domestic issues like corporate earnings, local issues and political uncertainties have become the cynosure of the capital markets, following the liberalization of current and capital accounts by RBI and the government. The re-pricing of the credit risk is dependent on RBI, which has changed the rules of securitization of banks.

Initiatives Adopted by the Indian Government to Combat SPC

- A government circular introduced for taxing investment gains prompted foreign funds to book profits.
- As the reason for SPC is identified as loans to low income borrowers, commercial banks have been warned against dangerous lending and asked to exercise due caution.
- In the event of dangerous loans being extended to vulnerable people, the precautionary measures are adopted to take the form of "risk mitigating instruments" for the benefit of the weaker sections.
- As a measure to ascertain the creditworthiness of the borrower, savings becomes a precondition, when one desires to avail a savings linked banking product.
- A proposition has been made to include insurance cover on delayed payments, because of crop failure or unemployment.
- Following the SPC in India, the World Bank has initiated funding development of new financial instruments for home finance to the unorganized sector in India.
- Extension of a "guarantee fund" would be contributed by the government permitting flexibility in the payment schedule so that lesser payments are also allowed to prevent amortization.
- Banks are encouraged to use the services of credit information Bureau (CIB) where the membership to it is made mandatory for financial institutions for allowing credit information to individual borrowers.
- Credit Rating Agencies to tackle the potential risks

due to innovation and adequate factor using their rating mechanism.

- Using a continuous monitoring system, the risk management framework is to be accordingly strengthened.
- Based on the recommendations of the Basel II Committee, RBI insists on commercial banks to raise additional capital, when there is a sharp increase in lending.
- Capital markets to strictly adhere to internationally accepted norms in accounting, capital adequacy, income recognition, asset classification, provisions, etc.
- To maintain *status quo* with respect to short-term interest rates.
- To focus on domestic issues for national economic growth rather than global issues, which affect credit and financial flows.
- To achieve the targeted growth of 9%-10% by the Indian Economy according to the 11th Five Year Plan, inclusive growth has to be stressed upon.

Effect of Economic Slowdown on Employment

With a view to assess the impact of the economic slowdown on employment and wages of labour force in the country during the quarter October-December 2008, the Ministry of Labour and Employment asked Labour Bureau in the third week of December 2008 to carry out a quick Survey in the industries/sectors supposed to be badly affected by the slowdown and submit the report by the fourth week of January 2009.

It may be observed from Table 1 that the total estimated employment in all the sectors covered by the survey went down from 16.2 million during September 2008 to 15.7 million during December 2008 resulting in job loss of about half a million. It is seen that the employment declined every month during this period. It has also been observed that the employment in all the sectors/industries studied went up significantly over the period from March 2008 to September 2008. Beyond September 2008, it has however, decelerated at all industries/sectors level at an average rate of 1.01 per cent per month.

TABLE 1

Trends in Average Employment

Period	Average Employment in (Millions)	Percentage Change
September 2008	16.2	
October 2008	16.0	-1.21
November 2008	15.9	-0.74
December 2008	15.7	-1.12
Average Monthly Change		-1.01

Source: Ministry of Labour and Employment, Labour Bureau, Govt. of India, January 2009.

Sector/industry level analysis of the data (Table 2) reveals that the decrease in employment has been experienced in all the sectors, except the IT/BPO sectors, wherein it has gone up marginally during the October-December 2008 period. Average monthly decline in employment was highest (8.58 per cent) in Gems and Jewellery followed by Transport (4.03 per cent), Automobiles (2.42 per cent), Metals (1.91 per cent), Textiles (0.91 per cent) and Mining (0.33 per cent).

TABLE 2

Industry-wise Change in Employment of Export and Non-Export Units

Industries	Exporting Units	Non-Exporting Units	Overall
Mining	-0.32	-0.33	-0.33
Textiles	-1.29	0.32	-0.91
Metal	-2.6	-1.24	-1.91
Gems & Jewellery	-8.43	-11.9	-8.58
Automobiles	-1.26	-4.79	-2.42
Transport	0.0	-4.03	-4.03
IT/BPO	-0.33	1.08	0.55
Overall	-1.13	-0.81	-1.01

Source: Ministry of Labour and Employment, Labour Bureau, Govt. of India, January 2009.

In the export sector, maximum decline in employment has been experienced by Gems and Jewellery sector (8.43 per cent) followed by Metals (2.6 per cent), Textiles (1.29 per cent),

Automobile (1.26 per cent) and Mining (0.32 per cent). Employment has not been adversely affected in the remaining sectors studied.

In the domestic sector units, decline in employment was maximum in Gems and Jewellery (11.9 per cent) followed by Automobiles (4.79 per cent), Transport (4.03), Metals (1.24 per cent) and Mining (0.33 per cent).

TABLE 3

Industry-wise Change in Employment of Manual and Non-Manual Workers

Industries	*Manual Workers*			*Non-Manual Workers*		
	Direct	*Contract*	*Total*	*Direct*	*Contract*	*Total*
Mining	0.41	-1.41	-0.57	-0.35	1.71	-0.05
Textiles	-0.92	-1.63	-0.95	-2.4	67.81	-0.64
Metal	-1.33	-5.22	-2.54	-0.33	8.58	0.15
Gems & Jewellery	-9.97	-4.51	-9.27	-6.17	-0.76	-5.52
Automobiles	-0.33	-12.45	-2.53	-1.95	-9.77	-2.08
Transport	4.39	-10.18	-5.58	-0.08	1.13	-0.03
IT/BPO	1.96	-0.05	0.22	0.51	1.89	0.56
Overall	-1.07	-5.83	-1.88	-0.13	6.46	0.16

Source: Ministry of Labour and Employment, Labour Bureau, Govt. of India, January 2009.

It may be observed that in the manual contract category of workers, the employment has declined in all the sectors/ industries covered in the Table 3. The most prominent decrease in the manual contract category has been in the Automobiles and Transport sector where employment has declined by 12.45 per cent and 10.18 per cent respectively. The overall decline in the manual contract category works out to be 5.83 per cent. In the direct category of manual workers, the major employment loss is reported in the Gems and Jewellery (9.97 per cent) followed by 1.33 per cent in Metals. However, in case of non-manual contract workers, the estimated employment has increased by 6.46 per cent during the period Oct.-Dec. 2008, which probably indicates increased level of contractualisation.

Global recession may not immediately show its full impact on the employment due to existing labour laws preventing factory sector to lay-off its regular workers in the short-run. This may however, result in lower capacity utilization, thus resulting in disguised unemployment. Keeping this in view, information on capacity utilization on monthly average change basis of the manufacturing and mining sector is presented in Table 4.

TABLE 4

Per centage Change in Capacity Utilization

Industries	*Average Monthly Change*
Mining	-0.32
Textiles	-0.09
Metals	-5.68
Gems & Jewellary	-1.03
Automobiles	-7.05
Overall	-1.32

Source: Ministry of Labour and Employment, Labour Bureau, Govt. of India, January 2009.

The table shows that the utilization of production capacity has gone down but not very significantly over the period of the study. It appears that the capacity utilization estimated is on the lower side. The most affected sector is the Automobile where, on an average, the capacity utilization has declined by 7.05 per cent per month, followed by 5.68 per cent in the Metal sector. At overall level capacity utilization has decreased at the rate of 1.32 per cent per month during the period of study.

POLICY STAND OF THE GOVERNMENT

To lift the economy out of the recession the government announced a package of Rs. 35,000 crores in the 1st instance on December 7, 2008. The main areas to benefit were the following:

(a) Housing

A refinance facility of Rs. 4000 crores was provided to the National Housing Bank and all the public sector banks announced to provide small home loan seekers loans at reduced rates to step up demand in retail housing sector:

(i) Loans up to Rs. 5 lakhs—maximum interest fixed at 8.5%,
(ii) Loans from Rs. 5-20 lakhs—maximum interest rate at 9.25%,
(iii) No processing charges to be levied on borrowers,
(iv) No penalty to be charged in case of pre-payment,
(v) Free life insurance cover for the entire outstanding amount, and
(vi) The borrower can get a loan upto 90% of the value of the house.

(b) Textiles

An allocation of Rs. 1400 crores has been made to clear the entire backlog in the technology upgradation fund (TUF) scheme. However it is described as disappointing package by the AEPC Chairman.

(c) Infrastructure

To boost the infrastructure: The India Infrastructure Finance Company Ltd. (IIFCL) has been authorized to raise Rs. 14,000 crores through tax-free bonds which will be used to finance infrastructure, especially highways and ports.

(d) Exports

Exports which accounted for 22 per cent of the GDP are expected to fall by 12 per cent. The government's fiscal package provides an interest subsidy of two per cent on exports for the labour-intensive sectors such as textiles, handicrafts, leather, gems and jewellary. The Federation of Indian Export Organization felt the measures are not enough to cover the loss of 1.5 million jobs in the export sector during 2008-09 on account of the $15 billion decline in the expected exports.

(e) Small and Medium Enterprises (SMEs)

The government has announced a guarantee cover of 50 per cent for loans between Rs. 50 lakhs to Rs. 1 crore for SMEs. The lockin period for loans covered under existing schemes will be reduced from 24 months to 18 months to encourage banks to cover more loans under the scheme.

Just within one month, the government announced another package to bail out the Indian Economy. The purpose of the new package announced on January 1, 2009 was to minimize the pain which includes the following measures:

1. To boost investment and spending to revive growth, the RBI cut the Repo rate from 6.5% to 5.5% and the Cash Reserve Ratio (CRR) from 5.5 to 5 per cent.
2. To revive exports which has resulted in a contraction of industrial output, drawback benefits have been enhanced for some exporters. Export-Import Bank also got Rs. 5000 crores as credit from the RBI.
3. To help the realty sector, realty companies have been allowed to borrow from overseas to develop "integrated townships".
4. To boost infrastructure: The India Infrastructure Finance Company Ltd. (IIFCL) has been allowed to raise Rs. 30,000 crores from tax-free bonds.
5. To make more funds available, ceiling on foreign institutional investments (FIIs) in corporate bonds has been increased to $15 billion from $6 billion with a purpose to seek much bigger FII investment.
6. To stimulate the Commercial Vehicles (CVs) sector, depreciation benefit on commercial vehicles has been increased from 15 to 50 per cent on purchases.

Again on February 24, 2009, the government announced a slashing down of excise duty from 10 per cent to eight per cent. Since 90 per cent of the manufactured items attract 10 per cent excise duty, this measure is designed to reduce the prices of colour TV sets, washing machines, refrigerators, soap, detergents, colas, cars and commercial vehicles. Cement prices are likely to drop Rs. 4-5 per bag of 50 kg while steel prices may cost Rs. 500-600 per tonne less. In addition to this, the government decided to cut service tax from 12 per cent to 10 per cent. A two per cent reduction in service tax will directly touch the lives of over 500 million persons by reducing monthly expenses. The entire stimulus package of Rs. 30,000 crores was announced to boost demand in the economy and thus reduce the impact of recession. Again, Commerce and Industry Minister announced a small relief package of Rs. 325 crores for leather, textiles, gems and jewellary on February 26, 2009.

Summary of the Select Monetary Measures Taken by the Government of India and the RBI—

Sept. 2008 to Jan. 2009

A. Rupee Liquidity

* Repo rate under LAF (liquidity adjustment facility) reduced from 9.0 per cent to 5.5 per cent.
* Reverse Repo rate under LAF reduced from 6.0 per cent to 4.0 per cent.
* Cash Reserve Ratio reduced from 9.0 per cent to 5.0 per cent.
* Statutory Liquidity Ratio reduced from 25 per cent to 24 per cent, with exceptional reductions for specified conditions.
* Repo facility for Rs. 60,000 crore under LAF to banks for lending to Mutual Funds and NBFC's.
* Scheme to advance Rs. 25,000 crore to financial institutions under Agricultural Debt Waiver and Debt Relief Scheme.

B. Forex Liquidity

* Interest rate ceiling on FCNR(B) and NR(E)RA term deposits increased.
* ECB up to $500 million permitted for rupee/foreign currency expenditure for permissible end use under automatic route.
* Systemically important non deposit taking NBFC's and Housing Finance Companies registered with NHB permitted to raise short-term currency borrowing under the approval route.
* Buy back/Pre-payment of Foreign Currency Convertible Bonds permitted.
* Swap faciiity with Indian banks for foreign currency

C. Credit Delivery

* Extension of the period of pre-shipment rupee export credit (at concessional rates) from 180 days to 270 days.
* Eligible limit of the ECR facility for banks enhanced to 50 per cent of the outstanding export credit eligible for refinance.
* Advance allocation of Rs. 3,000 crores to SIDBI and NHB against estimated shortfall in priority sector lending by banks.
* Provisioning requirement for all types of standard assets reduced to 0.4 per cent
* SPV for providing liquidity support to NBFC's to the tune of Rs. 25,000 crore
* Government to seek authorization of additional plan expenditure up to Rs. 20,000 crore in the current year. Total spending programme in the balance four months of 2008-09 expected to be Rs. 300,000 crore.
* Across the board cut of 4 per centage points in the *ad valorem* CenVat rate (except for petroleum products).
* Measures to support exports like interest subvention of 2 per cent for pre/post-shipment export credit, additional allocation of Rs. 350 crore for export incentive scheme, service tax refund on foreign agent commission and government back up guarantee to ECGC.
* Refinance facility of Rs. 4,000 crore to National Housing Bank and of Rs. 7,000 crore to SIDBI for lending to MSME sector.
* Additional allocation of Rs. 1,400 crore to clear the entire backlog under the TUF scheme (for textile sector).
* Higher quantum of road projects announced.
* Authorize IIFCL to raise Rs. 10,000 crore through tax free bonds by 31 March 2009.
* Reprioritizing of budgeted expenditure by key government departments.
* Government departments allowed to replace vehicles.

* Export duty on iron ore fines eliminated and that on lumps reduced to 5 per cent.
* Guarantee cover under Credit Guarantee scheme increased from 50 per cent to 85 per cent for credit up to Rs. 5 lakh.
* State governments permitted to raise additional market borrowing of 0.5 per cent of their GSDP, i.e. Rs. 30,000 crore for capital expenditure.
* IFCL being enabled to access Rs. 30,000 crore through tax free bonds (to fund highway and port projects).
* To support exporters, DEPB rates restored to pre-Nov 2008 levels.
* EXIM bank receives a Rs. 500 crore line of credit from RBI for lending to exporters.
* Exemptions from CVD and basic customs duty being withdrawn.
* One time assistance under JNNURM, to states for purchase of buses for urban transport system.

Assessment of the Impact of the Measures taken to bail out the Indian Economy

The success of the package depends on the quality and speed of implementation so that delays in implementation may not aggravate the economic recession to move into the dangerous zone of depression.

One of the major stumbling blocks which may neutralize the positive effects of large expenditure on infrastructure is corruption. If it is not curbed to reasonably low level, it may delay and reduce the much desired effect in enlarging infrastructure. It may result in the Indian infrastructure network being geared into a temporary employment generation with much smaller impact on the economy as against the intended objectives. Two things that need to be ensured for reducing corruption are transparency and avoidance of arbitrariness.

Secondly, there is a need to orient the fiscal package towards inclusive growth so that the weaker sections benefit which requires special emphasis on rural infrastructure and much larger expenditure on primary and secondary education, health and sanitation.

Thirdly, the chances of our exports increasing are very limited unless the G-3 economies, namely, the US, EU and Japan, are able to bring about a positive shift in their growth in the near future for which the predictions at present are not very optimistic. So, the Indian economy should concentrate on developing the domestic market. Thus inward looking policies should be preferred as against the outward looking approach of integrating the Indian economy to the world economy.

Fourthly, it may be mentioned that the quasi fiscal deficit (the deficit left out of the Budget) is presently estimated as six per cent of GDP. A comprehensive view of the fiscal deficit(as shown in the Budget and kept outside the Budget) would be in the range of nine 9 to 9.5 per cent of GDP, though it may now be lower due to a very sharp decline in international crude oil prices from $140 per barrel to about $40 per barrel at present. This is a welcome relief. If the government is also able to push the fertilizer prices to lower levels which is possible in the changed circumstances, eventually the total fiscal deficit (shown as well as kept outside the Budget) may come down to 6.5 to 7 per cent of the GDP.

The package has also provided finances to the non-banking finance companies (NBFCs), but there is a serious lack of skill with the NBFCs on project appraisals and to ascertain the credit worthiness of the borrowers and the accompanying project risks. There is a need to organize a national campaign for training the NBFCs in the project appraisals.

Similarly, the State governments must improve the share of their implementation and co-operate with the Central Government to improve various infrastructure projects in their domain or in collaboration with the Center.

CONCLUSION

We need to build economic models and financial markets through a calibrated reform process that takes into account the glaring disparities in our society. Definitely far away from the socialistic model but equally distant from the "free for all the market". India needs a modified free market economy model—shepherded, however by a body of independent regulators. A model that is prey neither to the machinations of the left or the right nor self-serving interests.

References

Agarwal, Yogesh. "The Present Economic Crisis and its impact on India", A Speech at the Haryana Institute of Public Administration, Dec. 20, 2008.

Bhattacharya, Abhijit. " Strategic Meltdown", *Economic Times*, 19 December 2008.

Brunnermeir, M.K. (2009). "Deciphering the 2007-08 Liquidity and Credit Crunch", *Journal of Economics Perspectives*, Vol. 23(1), Winter 2009, pp. 77-100.

Datta, Ruddar. "Global Meltdown and its Impact on the Indian Economy", *Mainstream*, Vol. XLVII, No. 15, March 28, 2009.

Dominique Strauss-Kahn. "Systematic Solutions for Systematic Crisis", *Economic Times*, 30 September, 2008.

EAC (Economic Advisory Council to the Prime Minister). Review of the Economy, 2008-09, January 2009.

Karthikeyan, G.B. and Malathishri, K.P. "Sub-Prime Crisis: The Burgeoning Problem of the Global Economy and its impact on India", *Economic Challenger*, January-March 2009, p, 42.

Mussa, Michael. "World Recession and Recovery : AV or an L", Paper Presented at the Fifteenth Semi annual Meeting on Global Economic Prospects, April 2009.

Parigi, A.P. "Lessons from Global Financial Crisis", *Economic Times*, 20 September 2008.

Rao, Govinda, M. (3rd March 2009), "The 3rd Stimulus Package and Fiscal Conundrum", *Business Standard.*

Report on Effect of Economic Slowdown on Employment in India (October-December 2008), Ministry of Labour and Employment, Govt. of India.

Subbarao, Duvvuri. "The Global Financial Turmoil and Challenges for the Indian Economy", Speech at the Bankers' Club, Kolkata, 10 December 2008.

15

Global Financial Crisis and Its Impact on the Indian Economy

SWAMI PRAKASH SRIVASTAVA

The effect of the global financial crisis has been more severe than initially forecasted. The turning point was the decision in September 2008 to let Lehman Brothers fail, an event that had a series of ruinous cascading effects. Given the depth of the crisis in the US and Europe, it was only to be expected that India too would be affected. But India's well regulated banking system and adequate policy responses should ensure that the fallout, at least on the banking sector, will be contained. Many have termed it the "worst financial crisis of the last century."

INTRODUCTION

The global financial crisis of 2008 is the worst of its kind since the Great Depression, beginning with failures of large financial institutions in the US rapidly evolving into a global crisis resulting in a number of European bank failures. The US budget deficit in 2009 is set to triple to $1.75 trillion, the largest ever, from last year's figure of $ 450 billion. The bank of England has fixed the lowest interest rates since it came into being in

1634. Toyota has announced its first ever losses. The largest housing mortage companies, Freddie Mae and Fannie Mae, the largest insurance company, AIG and banks like Citibank exist because they have been rescued with hundreds of billions of dollars pumped in by the US government. Major world economies are in recessioı or their rates of growth have plunged. In the last quarter of 2008, the US economy declined by more than 6% a year, the Euro Zone contracted by 1.5%. "The world economy is expected to shrink by 2.6% in 2009, according to the pessimistic scenario of the forecast presented in January," the World body said in a mid-year report by UN Department of Economic and Social Affairs (DESA). With its increasing impact both in scope and depth worldwide, the global financial crisis poses a significant threat to world economic and social development, including the fulfilment of the Millennium Development Goals and other internationally agreed development goals, according to DESA.

The report predicted that with a coordinated, development-oriented policy scenario, the world economy would recover to an annual growth of 4.5% in 2010-15, led by a robust growth of 7% a year in developing nations. "This is a contrast to the uncoordinated scenario in which developing countries would recover at only half that rate," DESA said. Although the crisis originated in developed countries, "it is now evident that developing countries are being hit disproportionately hard through capital reversals, rising borrowing costs, collapsing world trade and commodity prices, and subsiding remittances flows," it stated. During the first quarter of 2009, world trade dwindled at a "dramatic" annual rate of more than 40%, with the deepest impact being felt by the exporting countries of Asia. Growth in Africa's gross domestic products is expected to slow to 0.9%, down from 4.9% in 2008. South American economies may shrink by almost 1% on an average in 2009, while Mexico and the Central America are projected to fall by more than 4%. The report estimated that 73-105 million more people will remain poor or fall into poverty in comparison with a situation in which pre-crisis growth would have continued. "Most of this setback will be felt in East and South Asia, with between 56 and 80 million people likely to be affected, of whom about half are in India." The report added, "at present the stimulus is unbalanced. 80% of the stimulus is concentrated in developed countries, while most developing countries lack the fiscal space to provide social protection and counteract the consequences of the crisis. In a more balanced global response, about $ 500 billion in additional development finance would be made available for countercyclical responses by developing countries."

The world economy is expected to contract in 2009 by up to 1%, the first such contraction since the second world war; open unemployment is expected to touch an accelerating manner and is projected to fall by as much as 9% this year, again the sharpest fall since the numbers began to be tracked six decades ago. This paper explores some facets of the crisis, including its impact on the Indian economy and Indian banking.

The paper is divided into 17 sections including the introductory section. Section II presents Review of Literature followed by Section III that gives Causes of Global Financial Crisis, Section IVth explains the Severity of the Present Crisis, Section V explains Global Meltdown and its effect on Developing countries. Section VIth discusses about lessons from Great Depression, Section VIIth presents Impact of stimulus package. Section VIIIth explains Impact on the Indian Banking systems. Section IXth shall focus on Strategies of India to Stabilize its economy. Section Xth discusses about Impact of Global Recession on FDI. Section XIth shall focus on Recession in Services Sector. Section XIIth examines the impact of slowdown on Poverty. Section XIIIth examines the Global Crisis and Financial Sector Reforms in India. Section XIVth shall focus on Opportunities in the Slowdown. In Section XVth we examine the Mitigating of Global Financial Crisis. In Section XVIth we shall focus on IMF predictions regarding Banking, Currency and Debt Crisis Since 1970. In section XVIIth we shall asses the Conclusion, Suggestions and Recommendations.

SECTION II

REVIEW OF LITERATURE

A recent study on the impact of financial crisis by Reinhart and Rogoff (2008) seems to clear out this gloomy view. The author's note, "Broadly speaking, financial crisis are protracted affairs." However, they quickly make it clear that they are talking of "severe" financial crisis. In their later paper Reinhart and Rogoff (2008) focus on 18 major post-war banking crisis in the developed world and three in emerging markets.

The IMF (2008) study found that "episodes of financial turmoil characterized by banking distress are more often associated with severe and protracted downturns than episodes of stress centered mainly in securities or foreign exchange markets." Of the 58 episodes that were followed either by a slowdown or a recession, 35 (or 60%) were banking related.

The crisis provide opportunities for advancing a social democratic vision of a moral society, with more of a balance between economic democracy and political democracy, especially in finance; one in which states regain confidence to surveil markets, as in the Keynesian era (Lakoff, 2002, Vestergaard, 2009, Shonfield, 1969, Dore, 2000).

SECTION III

CAUSES OF GLOBAL FINANCIAL CRISIS

The financial sector in the US offered excessive credit to the housing sector, financed with excessive short-term leverage. The combination was explosive—as real estate prices dropped, credit losses mounted, financial institutions looked increasingly unstable, and it become harder for them to roll over their borrowing. Excessive credit and excessive leverage led to funding difficulties, problems that are now spilling over to the rest of the economy as credit is tightened. What lessons can we draw from all this and what implications does it have for India? First, excessive credit growth can emerge anywhere in the system and impinge on the entire system. In the US, the finger is being pointed at unregulated mortgage brokers. India too has unregulated areas: for instance, non-bank finance companies are lightly regulated because they do not take deposits. But they too could impinge on the system because they borrow from banks. By ignoring these links and by overburdening the regulated banking system, we risk drives more and more activity into the lightly regulated areas.

Other Reasons

1. Globally, companies and individuals have an ever increasing demand for capital for both personal and corporate investments.
2. Traditionally, banks have been very conservative and stringent in their requirements. This makes access to finance difficult for the majority of the people.
3. Banks and other financial institutions in the US have gone through a long period of inappropriate lending.
4. Relaxation of lending terms for mortgages was as a result of the boom in the housing sector.
5. Millions of Americans with poor credit history who might not have bought their homes were granted sub-prime mortgages.

SECTION IV

SEVERITY OF THE PRESENT CRISIS

Financial crisis can have a severe effect on economies. This is well known.

A recent study on the impact of financial crisis by Reinhart and Rogoff (2008) suggested a possible variety of indicators like asset price inflation, level of leverage, size of the current account deficit and the slowing down of economic growth. Going by these indicators, the authors suggest that the present financial crisis qualifies as "severe." In their later paper Reinhart and Rogoff (2008b) focus on 18 major post-war banking crisis in the developed world and three in emerging markets. They arrive at the following conclusions:

1. Real housing prices declined by an average of 36% over five years and equity prices by 56% over three and half years.
2. The unemployment rate rose by 7 per centage points on the average over a period of four years while output felt from peak to trough by 9% over a shorter period, two years.

3. The real value of government debt tended to have explode, rising by an average of 86% in the major post-second world war episodes.

The encouraging thing, as the authors point out in their paper, is that such crises do end and that output declines last only two years on the average. The implication seems to be that when hit by a financial crisis, we must chin up and bear it.

"Financial crisis" is a very broad term that covers a whole range of events, including crashes in the housing market, stock market, foreign exchange market, current accounts of nations and of course, problems affecting the banking sector. There is evidence that the really severe financial crisis are those in which the banking sector is affected. In the present crisis, the banking sector is clearly affected. Reinhart and Rogoff contend that, going by several indicators, the crisis is severe. This means that output decline should stretch over about two years. Since the crisis started in August 2007, a positive spin would imply that we should be nearing its end around August, 2009. Even if we were to take a pessimistic view, December 2009 should mark the beginning of the end. This view is shared by several commentators. It is worth-mentioning that the IMF had a different view on the severity of the present crisis until a few month ago. The IMF (2008) noted that "financial stress episodes are more likely to be followed by severe economic downturn when they occur in the context of a rapid build up in credit and house prices and a heavier reliance on credit by firms and household." In other words the greater the imbalance and excesses, the greater the fall. The IMF compares data for the current crisis against data for six major episodes in the past. It notes, "The current imbalances and adjustments appear generally much smaller than those for the six episodes examined here, except for US residential real estate investment and the US current account." The IMF report came out in October 2008 and presumably the conclusions were arrested a month or two before that—or before the collapse of Lehman Brothers in September 2008. The point is that the IMF at the time did not believe the financial crisis in the US was of the same severity as some of the bigger crisis in the past—contrary to the conclusion that Reinhart and Rogoff have drawn in their later paper, the draft of which was published in December 2008.

SECTION V

GLOBAL MELTDOWN AND ITS EFFECT ON DEVELOPING COUNTRIES

The global meltdown has affected the developing countries adversely. The developing countries, as a group, had been growing at a rate of about 7 per cent for the last several years, but they have ceased to do so. In 2008, the growth rate declined to 5.9 per cent according to tentative estimates. If the forecasts of the UN report are to be believed, the growth in the developing countries may come down to 2.7 per cent during 2009. The UN forecasts say that Africa is going to have a bleak future. For the developing countries, the global financial crisis is a great setback for poverty reduction and achieving the Millennium Development Goals. The tightening access to credit and weaker growth will cut into public revenues to meet the necessary investments into education, health and other development goals.

Impact on Emerging Markets

Views on how far the convulsions in the US economy will affect emerging markets, including India, have evolved with the unfolding of the crisis. In the initial stages, there was a fairly high degree of optimism about the capacity of at least some of the emerging markets, particularly leading lights such as China and India, to insulate themselves substantially from the crisis. Such optimism has since worn thin and, of late, one finds more doomsayers. Successive issues of the IMF's WEO report over the crisis period reflect this evolution. In the initial stage of the crisis, several reasons were put forward as to why the emerging markets might hope to get "decoupled" from the US and other advanced economies:

1. The US slowdown was related to factors specific to the US economy, especially corrections in the housing sector, rather than to more generalised factors such as an oil shock or adverse equity market developments.
2. Trade linkages of the emerging economies with the US had diminished and trade among emerging

markets had become more important than in the past.

3. Growth in some of the leading emerging markets was driven overwhelmingly by domestic demand.
4. The emerging markets were new savers in the world economy, not borrowers.
5. Over the past decades, the emerging markets had effected several economic reforms, as a result of which they had become more stable and efficient.

A better way of judging the impact on an emerging market of a slowdown in the US economy, therefore, would be to take into account trade flows as well as financial flows. As the IMF (2007) puts it.

While export exposure to the US appears to be an important determinant of the severity of the response to US recessions, "openness" in general seems to be more of a factor for emerging market economies. More open emerging market economies, in terms of both trade and financial openness... consistently show larger declines in output gaps during US recessions.

SECTION VI

LESSONS FROM THE GREAT DEPRESSION

The current crisis is different from the Great Depression of 1929-33. Economies then were less integrated than they are today. Mobility was less and agriculture and primary goods production were the mainstays of most economies in the world. A large part of the workforce was employed in agriculture. Finance was important but to a lesser extent than at present because a substantial amount of production was in the local economies in small or family units. In the Great Depression, the stock market, output and employment all collapsed as business confidence declined and investments froze. Banks failed in large numbers when businesses collapsed. That was due to a shortage of demand. The problem was compounded by the conservative monetarist stance of the policy-makers. MNCs were growing but had not become the behemoths with global reach that they have become today. Stock market were important but their reach was much more limited and only a tiny per centage of the population was involved in them.

In 2008, the growth rates of the world economy and of the US were positive till almost the middle of the year and the fall was not as sharp as in 1929. The decline in the stock markets was gradual to begin with and picked up speed later. Unemployment had risen but not so precipitously. Policy-makers and analysts have been surprised because they were in a denial mode. This time around, fiscal deficit everywhere had been allowed to soar to unprecedented levels. This may have temporarily slowed down the downturn but the decline is continuing. This is the other surprise. It may be argued that the stimulus is inadequate or that there is a lag effect and that matters will improve. But the signs are that the collapse is deepening. That there is a difference from the earlier downturns and from the Great Depression of 1929-33 needs to be understood. For this a better understanding of the current crisis is needed.

To meet the challenge, it was considered appropriate that the budget be balanced. So, as the crisis deepened and revenue fell, government expenditure was curtailed rather than raised to counter the fall in demand. As a consequence, demand fell even further and the depression became deeper. Further, investment was considered inadequate because of the lack of profitability and wage cuts were propounded as a measure to boost profitability. This only resulted in a further fall in demand of investment, which always comes with a time lag. Thus, employment and the wage rate both fell, leading to a further decline in demand. It was only the New Deal and the rapid rise in the public expenditure irrespective of the budget deficit that pulled the economy out of the depression.

Section VII

IMPACT OF STIMULUS PACKAGE ON EXPORTS

Stimulus packages and steps announced in the current Budget are having a positive impact on industry. The signs of stimulus packages can be seen in steel and cement. Consumer durables in particular would also grow and we may see similar trend in IIP (index of industrial production). However, that growth in the core sector does not mean that India has fully recovered from the impact of the global economic crisis. The six core sectors—coal, crude oil, electricity, finished steel and petroleum refinery products—grew by 5.1% a year ago in June 2008. Besides coal and cement, power generation increased by 7% and crude oil 4% in June 2009. Petroleum refinery output, however, declined by 3.7% in the same month. The core sectors account for 26.7% in the IIP. Industrial growth in May was 2.7%, more than double that of April, when growth turned positive after being in negative territory almost each month since October 2008.

SECTION VIII

IMPACT OF SLOWDOWN ON THE INDIAN ECONOMY AND THE POLICY RESPONSE

India, like other emerging markets, has suffered a more severe impact than supposed earlier. The impact has been pronounced after the Lehman crisis and as, RBI Governer D Subbarao (2009) has pointed out, it arises from three channels: the trade channel, the financial channel and the confidence channel.

It was assumed that the impact on India would be primarily through the trade channel. Since merchandise exports account for less than 15% of gross domestic product (GDP), the trade channel impact was assumed to be bearable—it would set back growth only by more than 1.15%. In a time of global economic crisis, a higher level of financial integration impacts the economy in three related ways: reducing Indian companies' access to overseas finance, lowering domestic liquidity and causing stock prices to fall. Adverse global conditions have limited Indian firms' access to global finance in various forms: fresh international borrowings, external commercial borrowings have become difficult and existing ones are not easily being rolled over; long-term finance for international acquisitions made earlier through bridge finance is not available; buyers' credit has become scarce for international transactions; Indian banks 'overseas branches and subsidiaries find they are unable to access funds in the wholesale market and have had to be provided with dollar funds by their parents from out of India; and so on. There is much broader impact on the Indian economy arising from foreign inflows in forms such as FDI and FII. These inflows had contributed to accretion of foreign exchange reserves. Any accretion to reserves enhances domestic liquidity; any decline in reserves constitutes a reduction in liquidity.

The gap between domestic investment and savings or the current account deficit—of around 1.5% of GDP—in recent years understates the potential impact on the Indian economy of foreign inflows. As Subbarao (2009) points out, capital flows in 2007-08 amounted to 9% of GDP, vastly in excess of the current account deficit. In the period 2003-08, the share of investment in India's GDP rose by 11 per centage points. Of this, roughly half was financed by corporate savings but a significant portion of the balance came from external sources.

The Monetary Response to the Financial Crisis

The monetary response to the financial crisis has been activated primarily since September 2008 following the Lehman collapse. Prior to that, the RBI had focused on fighting inflation and had adopted measures that contributed to tightening rather than relaxation. The flight of capital from India as well as the drying up of dollar credit abroad meant that both rupee and dollar liquidity were tightly squeezed. The sharp depreciation of the rupee with respect to the dollar required the RBI to intervene with dollar sales and this also impacted negatively on rupee liquidity. The principal monetary response since October 2008 include:

1. Reduction in the repo rate from 9% to 5.5% and in the reverse repo rate from 6% to 4%.
2. Reduction in the cash reserve ratio from 9% to 5%.
3. Reduction in the statutory liquidity ratio from 25% to 24%.

This was supplemented by a wide variety of measures to support liquidity, including to distressed segments of the financial system such as non banking financial companies (NBFCS) and mutual funds. The RBI estimates that its initiatives have helped augment liquidity to the extent of Rs. 3,88,000 crore or nearly 75% of additional commercial credit growth over the year up to 2 January 2009 (RBI, 2009).

SECTION IX

IMPACT ON THE INDIA'S BANKING SYSTEM

India's banking system has been considerably less affected by the ongoing crisis than banking system in the US and Europe. This is because the causes of the crisis in India are quite different from those elsewhere. In the advanced economies, the banking system suffered huge losses, this led to a collapse in the flow of credit and in confidence and dragged down the real economy. In India, it is the real economy that has been affected through various channels and banks are feeling the effects of a slowing down of the economy. India's banking sector is in far better shape than its counterparts in the western economies. There is heightened appreciation today-even among long standing detractors of the RBI—that the bias towards caution in matters of regulation has stood India in good stead. Important features of regulation in recent years have been: a gradualist approach towards capital account convertibility; prudence in opening up the sector to private and foreign banks; stringent norms on exposure to sensitive sectors; pre-emptive action in respect of housing, real estate and consumer credit;stricter norms for securitization; prudential limits on inter-bank borrowing; and tighter regulation of NBFCS. It is unlikely that there will any major departure from these in near future and we can expect additional regulation based on the lessons drawn from the sub-prime crisis.

There are two key issues with respect to the banking system, the volume of credit; and the cost. We shall address each of these in turn.

(i) Volume of Credit

Commercial credit had grown by 24% year on year up to 2 January 2000. In the corresponding period last year, it grew by 22%. Even after adjusting for credit extended to cash strapped oil and fertilizers companies, commercial credit growth has been 22%. This year's credit growth has happened in the face of a deceleration in economic growth in the second half of FY 2008-09. Industry contends that bank credit growth has not been adequate in light of the drying up of credit from a variety of sources. The RBI has put out data on total flow of funds to the commercial sector (Table 1). This indicates that total resources have been lower than last year by Rs. 15,000 crore or by about 3%. This is not a shortfall that should warrant an outcry about lack of funds of the sort we have been hearing.

TABLE 1

Flow of Financial Resources to the Commercial Sector

Item	2007-08 *(Up to 4 January 2008)*	2008-09 *(Up to 2 January 2009)*
From Banks	2,24,921	2,93,243
From other sources	2,74,563	1,91,470

Source: Microeconomic Review, January 2009, RBI.

However, trends in non-food credit growth as well as in forex reserves during the year present something of a puzzle. Table 2 presents trends in growth of non food credit in 2007-09 and 2008-09. In the period of April-October 2009, credit grew by a staggering Rs. 1,40,700 crore over growth in the previous year. In one month, October, growth in non-food credit was Rs. 76,725 crore more than in previous October. By January 2009, the trend mysteriously reverses-credit expansion in the year to date is Rs. 11,153.

TABLE 2

Growth in Non-Food Credit (Rs Crore)

	2007-08	*2008-09*	*Difference*
April-26 Sept	115,802	1,79,777	63,975
April-31 October	141,837	2,82,537	1,40,700
31 October-26 Sept	26,035	102,760	76,725
April-Jan 30	2,84,456	273,303	-11,153

Source: Statistical Supplement RBI.

The trends in forex reserves (Table 3) are also a puzzle. In just one month, October 2008, forex reserves fell by $ 33 billion or nearly 12% of the total. Between March and September 2008, the decline had been just $ 24 billion. In one month, October 2008, which was the month consequent to the Lehman failure, the forex reserve fell substantially.

TABLE 3

Forex Reserves

($ billion)

September 2008	286
October 2008	253
Difference	33

Source: Microeconomic Review, January 2009, RBI.

(ii) Cost of Credit

There is also a clamour for a steep reduction in policy rates to facilitate a sharper decline in lending rates. Policy rates have been falling steeply since October 2008, but lending rates have not followed suit. While the repo rate has declined by 350 basis points, the prime lending rate at public sector banks(PSBS) has declined only by a maximum of 150 points and that at private banks by 50 basis points. Private banks are said to be market savvy while PSBS lending decisions are said to be subject to political direction.

Impact on NPA of Commercial Banks

The downturn in the economy in the first financial year (2008-9) is also reflected in the large scale loan defaults that resulted in huge non performing assets (NPAs) which rose by more than Rs. 11,000 crore in 2008-09 alone. The NPAs of commercial banks increased from Rs. 55,800 crore in March 31, 2008 to Rs. 66,900 crore in March 2009, according to Finance Ministry data. The increase in NPAs has been largely in the small scale industry and other priority sectors. On the contrary, NPAs in the agriculture sector have decreased Increase in NPAs may be attributed to the consolidated impact of the cyclical nature of business, delay in the implementation of projects and credit growth.

SECTION X

STRATEGIES OF INDIA TO STABILISE ITS ECONOMY *VIS-À-VIS* THE GLOBAL MELTDOWN

India's high fiscal deficit of 6.7% of GDP is not a serious issue, but a large part of the government's borrowings can be invested in infrastructure, as part of a stimulus package, to revive the economy. And the government's slackness on the public sector reforms is a worrying issue as this is an opportune time for it. If the government use the present slowdown as an opportunity to develop infrastructure, it will not only enable it to achieve 7% growth in 2009-10, but would also help enter sustained high growth trajectory of 9%. As India's savings is high around 35% of GDP, it can generate resources to build infrastructure.

Government's huge borrowing programme of around Rs. 4,00,000 crore need not be inflationary. If the crude prices remain less than $ 80 per barrel, inflation will remain well within tolerable limits. At the same time, the chances of oil to remain below $ 80 per barrel is high, as the demand from developed world would be low for quite some time and the production capacity of crude is likely to be higher than the consumption. Investment in infrastructure will improve the efficiency of the companies, which will lead to higher growth. This will make India an attractive investment destination. At a time, when the global economy is not likely to return to high growth path in the near future, growth centers like India and China will attract foreign investments, provided they could maintain the momentum.

SECTION XI

IMPACT OF GLOBAL RECESSION ON FDI

The global financial crisis has added new risks to the world economy, and the country is set to miss the $ 35 billion target for global foreign direct investment (FDI) inflows in the current year. India would receive $ 30 billion FDI inflows, falling short of the target by about 14%. We will be able to go to $ 30 billion. India registered 17 per cent increase in FDI inflows last year on the back of robust growth, improved investment environment and further opening up of several sectors. The liquidity crunch will pull down worldwide FDI flows by 10 per cent this year, although flows to the developing world would remain fairly stable.

The government had announced major changes in the FDI policy simplifying the calculation of indirect and direct foreign investment. This would give more elbow room for Indian promoted companies to raise more foreign funds. The policy review has been on the works for the last few months amidst hopes of attracting FDI to $ 35 billion in the current financial year, much higher than last year's $ 16 billion. India is however still expected to remain a hotspot for global investors. United Nations Conference on Trade and Development (UNCTAD) report said India is the second only to China as preferred destination for FDI, ahead of US, UK and Germany.

Section XII

RECESSION IN SERVICES SECTOR

India is a larger among prominent developing countries. The services /GDP share is 66% in South Africa, 64% in Brazil and 57% in Russia. Even Kenya, which remains highly agricultural, has 58% ratio. Some backward African economies have a lower share of services than India. But, by global standards, India's services share is actually low, not high. That makes India more vulnerable than others to a global downswing, not less. IT services have made India world famous for computer software, business process outsourcing and knowledge process outsourcing. IT services exports have grown from almost nothing to $ 40 billion last year, a fantastic achievement.

Section XIII

IMPACT OF SLOWDOWN ON POVERTY

The World Bank said new research showed more people were being pushed into poverty in developing countries due to the global financial crisis. It said new 2009 estimates compiled by the Bank show that weaker economic growth will push 46 million more people below the poverty line of $ 1.25 a day than was expected before the crisis emerged in 2007. An additional 53 million people will stay trapped on less than $2 a day. This is on top of the 130 million-155 million people pushed into poverty in 2008 because of soaring food and fuel prices. The Washington-based development lender, whose mission is to fight global poverty, said the new forecasts highlight the risk that the world will fail to meet a universally agreed target to have global poverty by 2015 under the UN Millennium Development Goals. While much of the world is focused on bank rescues and stimulus packages, we should not forget that poor people in developing countries are far more exposed if their economies falter.

SECTION XIV

THE GLOBAL CRISIS AND FINANCIAL SECTOR REFORMS IN INDIA

The IMF in 2008 surveyed 113 episodes of financial stress in 17 countries. Of these, 43 episodes were driven mainly by stress in the banking sector. In 17 episodes, stress arising elsewhere in the financial system had a significant impact on the banking sector. Thus, a total of 60 episodes—or a little over half of all the episodes of financial stress—were banking related. Of the 113 episodes studied, 29 were followed by slowdowns and 29 by recessions. The remaining 55 episodes—or nearly half the episodes of financial stress—were not followed by an economic downturn. There is no reason, therefore, why every financial crisis should inspire pessimism. The Indian financial system, in many ways, is modern, innovative, and growing fast—be it the state of the art trading and settlement systems at the National Stock Exchange, or ATMs catering to the illiterate, or cell phone banking, which aims to enhance the reach of the banking system. The financial needs of the Indian economy, whether for infrastructure estimated at $ 500 billion over the next plan or for foreign acquisitions, will be enormous in the coming years and it is time to plug the remaining gaps.

SECTION XV

OPPORTUNITIES IN THE SLOWDOWN

There are opportunities in the slowdown. As the world's 'youngest' country, as a land of entrepreneurship with the large number of the self employed, India has an unmatched talent for creativity in the face of adversity. It offers space for ingenuity across diverse and large markets, the diversity allowing room for a range of products and services. In the context of the global financial and economic turmoil, these traits hold the promise that India can successfully emerge from this crisis.

India enjoys in-built protection against the global meltdown to a greater degree than most economies, thanks to its domestic market, conservative banking system, savings rate and young workforce. Indian businesses have focused more on the domestic than the export market, stepping up marketing beyond the metro cities in recent years. In the IT industry, for example, fiscal 2007-08 saw the domestic market for products and services grow by 34 per cent, faster than the 27 per cent growth in the export market. The market for the white goods has been growing at 20 per cent per annum; the four-wheeler market has doubled in the last five years; and the telecom subscriber base is adding 100 million every year. A 2008 study by Planet Retail put consumer spending in India at over $ 700 billion a year. Some cutbacks in spending may be seen in the short-term, but given that per capita use of consumer products and services—from telecom connectivity to automobile ownership, shampoos to refrigerators—is still low, especially in rural areas, the untapped market potential is enormous and among the largest in the world. 2008 saw rural markets grow at rates of 20 to 25 per cent. Fast moving consumer goods' manufacturers report that 60 per cent of their sales are in rural areas, while India's biggest automobile company announced that rural India accounts for a third of its sales.

Rural India is seeing a new revolution in infrastructure building, from an expanding road network to more agriculture produce collection centers. But telecom connectivity has probably been the single most revolutionary infrastructure development after the railways network set up almost a century ago. Mobile services have brought technology to farmers' doorsteps, providing information on market prices, transport and marketing opportunities. Connectivity has helped improve governance, empowering rural households to access education, healthcare, civic and other facilities.

Manufacturing

India's basic potential as a market and manufacturing hub remains but there are caveat. The attraction of its large workforce is affected by the fact of low skill levels. Low cost manufacturing is offset by poor, unreliable infrastructure facilities. India's large market potential is tampered as much by poor transport infrastructure as by poverty and unemployment levels that restrain qualitative growth. Finally, the manufacturing sector still faces infrastructure and cost deficiencies.

India's Vision 2020

India's vision 2020—with its physical and social infrastructure development goals—presents the way out of the conundrum. Education for all, increased employment, financial inclusion are some key goals. But implementation of the vision is itself a challenge, primarily in terms of capital investment at a time when credit availability worldwide has shrunk. Several infrastructure projects have already fallen behind schedule because of paucity of credit and 2008 saw a net outflow of capital by foreign institutional investors. But India has vast requisite capital. It has one of the highest rate of savings at more than 34 per cent. Funds from corporate sources are also available but lie unutilized. In the telecom sector, for example, infrastructure growth—especially in rural areas—is lagging, partly for lack of funds. Significant amounts remain unused with the Universal Service Obligation Fund, funds contributed by industry for telecom infrastructure development.

India needs to release its wealth of entrepreneurial talent. Around 52% of Indians are self employed, about 55% in rural communities and 41% in urban areas. Many of these (about 20%, according to the ILO) are at the bottom of the pyramid, alternating between wage labour and self-employment by selling skills and engaging in minor business such as vegetable vending. About 15% of self-employed are believed to be entirely dependent on such activities. Boosting such entrepreneurship would grow employment, lift income levels, strengthen the domestic market and reduce dependence on exports. It would encourage innovation and productive services. India expects a growth rate of between 7 and 8 per cent in the next 10 years, far outpacing the expected global growth of between 1 and 2 per cent. Given that, it would experience a slowdown only in comparison to the dynamic 8% average growth of the previous five financial years ending March 2008, not in the context of current global economic reality. Bringing together India's creativity in entrepreneurship and youthful dynamism would ultimately allow for sustained inclusive growth in the process of tiding over the slowdown. Converting this slowdown into an opportunity would enhance India's position within the global economy and attract much higher domestic and international investment for multiplier growth.

Section XVI

MITIGATING THE GLOBAL FINANCIAL CRISIS

It is now clear that global financial and economic crisis, originating in the western world, has affected the western world very badly. It is threatening to set back the gains made over the past decades in terms of poverty alleviation and achievement of the millennium development goals by developing countries. Millions of peoples have lost their jobs and have been pushed back into poverty.

The impact is particularly severe in developing countries because of very large concentration of poor, unorganized and vulnerable people combined with a general lack of social security system and limited capabilities of the governments to take care of the affected sections. While the so-called 'green shoots' of recovery are beginning to be spotted, the western economies are unlikely to regain their status of being the engines of growth for the world economy in the near future. A global crises of such proportions obviously needed a global response even though the national governments across the world have been adopting fiscal stimulated packages to revive demand depending upon capacity. To be fair, the international community has responded to it in a spirit of cooperation and to contain further deepening. The G-20 leaders met in Washington DC in November 2008 and in London in April 2009 to chart out a global plan for recovery and reform. The UN Conference on the World Financial and Economic Crisis and its impact on development was held on 24-26 June 2009 with leaders and ministers of many countries adopting an outcome document containing some proposals for addressing the concerns of developing countries. The two initiatives need to be seen in a complementary manner. The G-20 process addressed the most immediate task of restoring confidence and assisting recovery by providing a package of 1,100 billion at the disposal of international finance institutions and multilateral development banks to restore lending.

The UN Conference being able to bring together nearly all of the humanity came up with a more inclusive and comprehensive agenda for action in the medium and longer term. It was able to highlight the challenges faced by developing, especially the poorer countries underlining, for instance, the plight of developing countries with the sudden reversal of private capital flows, large and volatile movements in exchange rates, falling revenues and reduced fiscal space for taking corrective measures. It called for a coordinated and comprehensive global response focusing on restoration of the flow of development finance without unwarranted conditional ties and debt relief to developing countries for 'fostering an inclusive, green and sustainable recovery', among many other measures. It also emphasized on the importance of South-South cooperation and triangular cooperation for assisting the developing countries in recovery. More importantly, it emphasized the importance of the long pending reform of international financial architecture to enhance the voice and participation of emerging markets and developing countries and acknowledged the importance of examining the calls for reform of current global reserve currency system. It recognized the importance of regional financial cooperation and its potential to complement global initiatives.

It is now time to act on these important proposals. In particular, the Asian regions have some real opportunities for financial cooperation to speed up their recovery and restoration of rapid growth path. Asian +3 countries have recently created a multilateral pool of foreign exchange reserves amounting to $ 120 billion. There is a need to build on this initiative in terms of scope and coverage.

With over four trillion dollars in forex reserves, the Asian region now has the resources to foster a major programme of regional Keynesianism, building regional infrastructure and other public goods through catalyzing private public partnership while facilitating mutual trade by creating a unit of account such as Asian currency unit and providing balance of payment support. The generation of additional demand in Asia will not only assist the recovery in the region but also of the global economy, given the economic interdependence.

Section XVII

IMF'S PREDICTION REGARDING BANKING, CURRENCY AND DEBT CRISIS SINCE 1970

The economic turmoil sweeping across the world has created a bunch of myths. Among the more popular ones is that capitalism is dead, or its flipside, that because governments are intervening, they have turned socialist. This arises from another myth that the current crisis is a rare occurrence, an aberration in an otherwise smooth path of progress. This is far from the truth, since 1970, that is, in the past 38 years, there have been 395 events of banking, currency or debt crisis in 161 countries. Of these, 124 have been banking crisis, 208 have been currency crisis and 63 have been debt defaults. Many countries have suffered from some form of crisis several times, while others have seen all three types in quick succession. This startling data has been revealed in a working paper. According to the study released recently, a banking crisis is one in which there is a run on the banks. Worried depositors start withdrawing their money so fast that the bank is unable to honour its commitments. A currency crisis is one in which the value of a currency drastically falls. Debt defaults are those in which a country is unable to repay its debt. All three types of crisis are countrywide or may occur in several countries at a time. There were 42 cases of a twin crisis—banking and currency occurring and 10 cases of a triple crisis when all three types happened together. Banking crisis have been increasingly common in the 1990s, with 1995 being the high point with 13 such events. Currency crisis were common in the first halves of the 1980s and 1990s. Sovereign debt defaults were most common in the 1980s. There are some features that distinguish the currently unfolding crisis from past ones. It is much bigger, mainly because it is spreading out from the global economic nerve centre the US.

Most of the earlier crisis took place in third world countries, with the western countries (or the IMF) moving in to tackle the aftermath. This time round, it is the richest countries that are starting into an abyss. The financial system too has become much more complex and integrated in the past decade and a half, as can be seen from the fact that US mortgage defaults are bringing down giant banks in Europe and elsewhere. Because of this, scale and depth, the banking crisis is bringing in its wake a recession, which will cast a shadow over the whole world. While the earlier crisis hit mostly third world countries in Africa, Latin America and Asia, the present crisis has moved to the centre of metropolitan finance in North America and Europe.

The IMF study put 42 of these crisis, affecting 37 countries under the scanner, to find out what kind of rescue efforts are usually taken. The results dispose off the other myth that government intervention is something new or unusual. Injection of cash into the financial system and guaranteeing bank deposits were the two most common measures adopted by governments to limit the crisis. In over 71% of cases, government infused liquidity into the financial system, and in 30% of cases it also undertook to protect bank deposits, by standing guarantee. In some cases, bank holidays and deposits freezes were undertaken. In 86% of cases, there was large scale intervention by the governments in the banking sector through nationalization, closures or assisted mergers. Another important intervention was recapitalization of banks through various means. This occurred in 76% of the cases. On an average, the study found that total costs for fighting the crisis are as high as about 13% of GDP, although in some extreme cases these have gone up to 55%. So, far from being a rare event, the current economic turmoil appears to be a fairly standard occurrence.

Section XVII

CONCLUSION

To conclude, therefore, time has come to take the proposals of international and regional cooperation in the area of finance to the next level. As the emerging centre of gravity of the world economy, Asia should take the lead in exploiting the potential of regional cooperation for generating additional demand for expediting the recovery of the world economy from the worst crisis since the great depression while pursuing an agenda for inclusive and sustainable growth.

The world is in the midst of a severe financial crisis, meaning a crisis that will have a huge cost in terms of lost economic growth. It is not true, however, that all financial crisis are severe. There is a high probability of a financial crisis having an impact on the real economy when there is disruption of the banking sector. Second, the severity of the crisis is not independent of the policy response. An appropriate policy response does help contain the depth and period of an economic downturn.

India will not escape unscathed in the present crisis because its economy has become more integrated with the rest of the world over the past decade and a half. Overseas finance has become increasingly important for Indian corporates and the drying up of such finance is bound to tell on their fortunes. There is also a broader impact arising from tighter liquidity conditions and a decline in stock prices. India's authorities have responded to the crisis with both fiscal and monetary stimuli although the scope for the former appears somewhat limited given India's fiscal position. The Indian banking sector is well placed to weather the storm because it is not directly exposed to the financial crisis. It faces secondary effects arising from the slowdown of the economy.

It is in India's interest that it should not view China's emergence and the US's economic decline with equanimity. India should have a long-term interest in the stability and health of the US economy. As ours is a liberal democracy, it will be good for us if the US re-emerges as an economic power. It is a fact that as far as global economy is concerned we do not have rather can not have any control. But we must follow a pragmatic policy so that we may become a strong and vibrant economy. When we talk of industrialization of the country, we must say that we did not pay any heed to the western suggestion regarding trade liberalization like China. We followed phase-wise industrial and trade strategies. It helped us achieve great success in expediting industrial development and growth. It is a proven fact that while export expansion can help in expediting economic growth, the same is not the case with import liberalization. Besides, the experience of the developing countries during the last three decades makes a compelling case for the relevance of infant industry protection and other policy interventions for industrialization and development.

References

Business Today, Feb 8, 2009.

Business Today, March 8, 2009.

Economic and Political Weekly, March 28, 2009, pp. 107-14.

Floyd Noorij (2008), New Analysis: Another Crisis, Another Guarantee, *The New York Times*, Sept. 17, 2008.

George Soros (2008), The Worst Market Crisis in 60 years, London, *The Financial Times*, Jan. 22, 2008.

Kumar Naresh, Mitigating global financial crisis, *The Economic Times*, July 2009, p. 10.

Ram Mohan, T T(2008), "From the Sub-prime to the Ridiculous ", *Economic and Political Weekly*, November 8.

RBI (2009), "Third Quarter Review, January 2009", Reserve Bank of India.

Soros, George (2009), "The Game Changer", *Financial Times*, January 28.

Subbarao, D. (2009), "Impact of the Global Financial Crisis on India :Collateral Damage and Response", Speech Delivered in Tokyo, Feb 18.

Subodh Varma, 'Financial Crisis not new phenomenon', *The Times of India*, June 28, 2009, p. 6.

Global Economic Crisis and the Indian Economy

CHANDRA KANT SINGH AND RAJESH KUMAR

INTRODUCTION

The National Bureau of Economic Research (NBER), a body of economists responsible for tracking the business cycles in the United States, has pronounced that the country's economy has been in recession since December 2007. In doing so, it has only formally recognized the ground reality, the impact of which has been felt across the world. The economic downturn, which has already exceeded the average duration of all recessions since the Second World War, may well set a new record. It may also end up inflicting more pain than any other recession since 1980-81. Significantly, the NBER has not taken into reckoning the fact that the economy actually grew, albeit marginally, during the first two quarters of 2008. Most other factors, notably employment and personal income, continued to be on the decline. The methodology is relevant for India too, in that the growth story, if judged by the quarterly GDP data alone, can mask, for instance, declines in specific sectors. With the NBER's announcement, the world's largest economy officially joins the

15 Euro Zone countries as well as the United Kingdom and Japan that are in recession. Its assessment seems to affirm the prognosis of The World Bank and the IMF that the economies of the developed countries would contract during 2009. In contrast to the developed countries, the developing ones, such as India and China, are expected to perform better. Their economies, although witnessing a disturbing slowdown, would end up with relatively higher growth rates. The theory that developing economies are "decoupled" from the developed ones seems quite misleading in this context. The sharp slowdown in the U.S. economy has had several deleterious consequences especially for trade and investment. In November, the WTO scaled down its forecast of global trade growth from 5.5 per cent to 4.4 per cent. For the first time in seven years, India's merchandise exports, expressed in dollars, fell during October. The flight of foreign institutional investors from Indian stock markets is largely attributed to the financial sector crisis, the precursor to the global economic slowdown. The official acknowledgment of the U.S. being in recession has had its biggest impact on investor sentiment. Led by the Dow Jones index, which dropped by about 680 points, stock market indices around the world, including in India, closed sharply lower on the day the news broke. Even at the global level, stock market sentiment has been weak for a long time.

DILEMMA ON THE FISCAL FRONT

Finance Minister Pranab Mukherjee has stated that his government is unambiguously committed to restoring growth and employment but it would also strive for fiscal consolidation over the next two to three years. These two macroeconomic goals are not antithetical to each other. The government needs to spend more to stimulate the economy, for which it will have to borrow additional money. A higher GDP growth rate will arrest the decline seen recently in tax revenue, both direct and indirect. As RBI Governor D. Subbarao has pointed out, economic recovery can be sustained only by practicing financial rectitude. The forthcoming budget for 2009-10 should provide the lead by drawing up a time-table for fiscal consolidation, while simultaneously laying out large sums for infrastructure development and social welfare programmes. Managing the trade-off between short-term compulsions and long-term sustainability will be one of the important challenges before the government. According to the Finance Minister, additional stimulus measures will be decided after the government completes its assessment of the impact the three stimulus packages and the interim budget have had.

The stimulus packages have largely been in the nature of monetary intervention. Although since September last year, the RBI has signaled lower interest rates, there is considerable scope for banks to lower the cost of credit and lend more. Monetary and fiscal policies will necessarily have to go hand in hand. The interim budget had clearly pointed to a deterioration in the health of public finance. For 2008-09, the revenue and fiscal deficits estimated at 4.4 per cent and 6 per cent of the GDP are sharply higher than the budgeted one per cent and 2.5 per cent respectively. The consolidated fiscal deficit of the Centre and the States including the off-budget items is estimated at over 11 per cent of the GDP. While the presence of excess capacities in many sectors would help in containing inflationary pressures, the growing fiscal deficit will increase the already large government borrowing and militate against the softening of interest rates. The government will have to fine-tune its machinery for evaluating public expenditure programmes. That would include, among others, specific steps to ensure greater accountability, efficient targeting, weeding out of wasteful expenditure, and constant monitoring. These are not new goals but they assume a special significance at a time when the public policy goals for the short-term vary sharply from those for the medium-term.

THE PRESENT CRISIS AND THE WAY FORWARD

John Maynard Keynes, writing during the Great Depression, had suggested an alternative stimulus, namely, a comprehensive "socialization" of investment, whereby the state acting on behalf of society always ensured a level of investment in the economy, and hence a level of aggregate demand, that was adequate for full employment. This entailed not only a jettisoning of the free market system in favour of state intervention but also restraints on the free global mobility of finance, since meaningful state intervention could not be undertaken if the nation-state faced internationally mobile capital. "Let finance be primarily national," he had said.

The Keynesian stimulus was adopted in the post-war period, during what has been called the "Golden Age of Capitalism." But the process of globalization, involving above all the globalization of finance, which began during the period of Keynesian demand management itself, put an end to that stimulus, and removed a host of regulatory measures that characterised the Keynesian regime. Boosts to aggregate demand now come increasingly from the stimulation of private expenditure, associated with the creation of bubbles in asset prices, rather than from an adjustment of public expenditure within the context of reasonably stable asset prices. Not surprisingly, the frequency of financial crises, associated with the bursting of these bubbles, has increased greatly after 1973. The current crisis underscores the need for a new stimulus. Till now, governments have only injected liquidity into the system for stemming the crisis. They initially planned to do so by purchasing "toxic" securities, but eventually had to inject liquidity against equity, through part-nationalization of financial institutions.

But such injection is not enough. Credit does not start flowing simply because banks can access more liquidity; there has to be adequate demand for credit for viable projects by solvent borrowers. This is absent. Since the injection of liquidity does not improve the solvency of firms saddled with "toxic" securities, the risk associated with lending to them remains prohibitively high. Besides, the anticipation of a recession makes borrowers chary of borrowing and lenders chary of lending.

This anticipation derives from several factors. The bursting of one bubble is not necessarily succeeded by the immediate formation of another. Moreover, the very scale of the current financial crisis gives rise to an anticipation of a prolonged recession. Finally, since the recession has already started, the prospects of crisis prevention now through the usual monetary instruments (including liquidity injection) appear distinctly dim. The mutually reinforcing tendencies, of increased liquidity preference on the part of private individuals and institutions, and of the real economy sliding downwards, have already started, and will continue unless governments now act to inject demand into the economy directly.

The third world countries will not escape the effects of this crisis. Many of them whose financial systems are still not sufficiently "opened up" will escape the direct impact of the world financial crisis, but they certainly will have to face the impact of the recession of the real economy. Their export earnings, both merchandise and invisibles, will be hit, causing unemployment and output contraction on the one hand, and foreign exchange crisis, exchange rate depreciation and accentuated inflation on the other. (The latter will be aggravated by the outflow of speculative capital that had come in earlier to the "newly emerging markets" under the aegis of Foreign Institutional Investors).

Two areas are of special concern here. One is the inevitable decline in the terms of trade for primary commodities that will occur in a recession, which will push cash crop growing peasants into even greater distress. The other is the loss of food security over much of the third world that will inevitably occur.

The loss of food security will occur for several reasons: First, the loss of foreign exchange earnings owing to the decline in exports and in the terms of trader will cause a decline in foodgrain availability in food importing countries. Secondly, even if food availability is somehow maintained, the decline in the incomes of exporting peasants, small producers and the unemployed will mean inadequate purchasing power in their hands to buy necessary food. And thirdly, if the terms of trade of non-food primary commodities decline relative to food, as has been happening, then both the above problems will be greatly aggravated.

There is a tragic irony here. The booms fed by asset price bubbles not only did not benefit the large mass of peasants, petty producers, agricultural labourers, craftsmen, and industrial workers in the third world, but were actually accompanied by an absolute deterioration in their living standards. This happened not despite the boom but because of it. With the interlinking of global financial markets, asset price booms in the U.S. tended to produce stock market booms, and more generally financial sector booms, even in third world countries, where banks and other financial intuitions withdrew from productive sector lending to speculative lending from rural lending to urban lending, and from agriculture and small-scale sector lending to consumer credit to the affluent, and loans against securities. This damaged the productive base of the peasant and small-scale sector. Secondly, the changed role of the state in the new dispensation where it was more concerned with supporting the financial sector boom than with sustaining peasant and petty production, entailed a withdrawal of state support from the latter sector; input subsidies, the price support system, essential public investment, and state spending on rural infrastructure and on social sectors were all drastically curtailed, to the detriment of the entire small producer economy. Between 1980-85 and 2000-05 the per capita cereal output in the world declined absolutely by 8 per cent, which also meant an absolute decline in per capita world cereal consumption. But since, taking both direct and indirect consumption into account, the advanced countries witnessed an increase, the decline was particularly sharp in the third world. Even China and India which experienced remarkably high GDP growth rates, did not escape this trend.

Paradoxically, this decline was not accompanied by any rise in relative cereal prices. In fact between these two years the terms of trade of cereals *vis-a-vis* manufacturing in the world economy declined by nearly 40 per cent, which suggests that the squeeze on the purchasing power of the masses in the third world was even greater. The other side of the speculative boom therefore was a drastic squeeze on the living standards of the masses, especially in the third world (which is why describing the U.S. as the "locomotive" of the world economy is so inapposite: this locomotive while pulling some coaches, pushed back some others). But even though the third world masses suffered from the effects of the speculative boom, they would also suffer additionally from the effects of its collapse.

The need of the hour is the injection of demand through direct fiscal action by governments across the world. For activating governments for this, two conditions have to be satisfied. The first is control over cross border financial flows, for otherwise governments will continue to remain prisoners to the caprices of globally-mobile speculative finance capital. The second is the setting up of an international financial facility, operated on principles different from the Bretton Woods Institutions, which not only makes concessional finance available to developing economies, but also enables them to substitute long-term loans for their current short-term borrowing.

The general objective of larger government spending must be the reversal of the squeeze on the living standards of the people everywhere. In India, China and other third world countries, however, in addition to welfare state measures, larger government expenditure has to be oriented towards a substantial increase in agricultural, especially food grains, output.

In short, the new paradigm must entail inter alia a foodgrain-led growth strategy (on the basis of peasant, not corporate, agriculture), sustained through larger government spending, which simultaneously rids the world of both depression and financial and food crises. The trade and financial arrangements of the world economy have to be oriented towards achieving this end.

References

Ben, S. Bernanke, "Financial Markets, the Economic Outlook, and Monetary Policy", Washington, D.C. (2008-01-10). Retrieved on 2008-06-05.

Ben, Steverman and David Bogoslaw (October 18, 2008, 12:01 AM EST), "The Financial Crisis Blame Game, Business Week", Businessweek.com. Retrieved on 2008-10-24.

Bernanke, Ben, S., "Mortgage Delinquencies and Foreclosures", Columbia Business School's 32nd Annual Dinner, New York, New York (2008-05-05). Retrieved on 2008-05-19.

"How severe is subprime mess?" msnbc.com, Associated Press (2007-03-13). Retrieved on 13 July 2008.

Lasch, Christopher, "The Culture of Consumerism", Consumerism 1, Smithsonian Center for Education and Museum Studies. Retrieved on 2008-09-15.

Lognathan, Dr. P. and Sakthivel, A. (2009), "Impact of Financial Speculation on Global Food Crisis". Third concept, New Delhi, February, pp. 21-26.

Menon, Meena (2009), "Of a Crisis and an opportunity" *The Hindu*, 6 January.

Patnaik, Prabhat (2008), "The Present Crisis and the Way Forward", *The Hindu*, 14 November.

Ramchandran, B. (2009), "Global Financial Crisis", Third concept, New Delhi, January, pp. 50-51.

Reference Annual published by the Ministry of Information and Broadcasting, New Delhi, 2008, pp. 340-45.

Report of the Indian State Hunger Index (ISHI), 2008.

Report of the International Food Policy Research Institute, 2008.

Sainath, P. (2009), "The Meltdown: Whose crisis is it, Anyway?, *The Hindu*, 9 February.

Singh, Dr. Chandra Kant (2009), "Economic Meltdown, 2008: Global Perspectives", R.K. Publishers and Distributors, Delhi, pp. 48-91.

World Bank Policy Research Working Paper, 2008.

Global Financial Crisis and its Impact on the Nepalese Economy

R.K. Shah

BACKGROUND

Beginning with the bankruptcy of Lehman Brothers on September 14, 2008 the financial crisis entered into an acute phase marked by failures of prominent American and European banks and efforts by the American and European governments to rescue distressed banks and financial institutions (BFIs). Actually, the current financial crisis began in August 2007, when investors lost confidence in the value of securitized mortgages in the USA. This gradually resulted in a liquidity crisis, which prompted a substantial liquidity injection into financial markets by the various central banks including Federal Reserve Bank of USA, Bank of England and the European Central Bank. In many countries the government intervened in the financial system as well. Large stimulus package had been announced in several countries including USA, Europe, Australia, China, India, etc. The current global financial crisis is rooted to the sub-prime crisis. Around the world, stock markets have fallen, large financial institutions have collapsed or been bought out. Many people are concerned that a global financial crisis will affect the livelihoods of almost everyone in an increasingly inter-connected world. Hence, the situation evolved into a global financial crisis verging on a systemic crisis that did not affect only banking and credit. It spread also to financial markets like stock exchanges and derivative markets, where it developed into a market crash. There was a great pressure on public finance due to the bailout actions and increased exchange rate volatility. However, the direct and immediate impact of the global financial crisis in the Nepalese economy seems to be small at the moment. But, it could be expected that the crisis would have multiplier impact on the Nepalese economy as some of the East Asian and gulf countries have initiated controlled policy on foreign labour due to the recession in their economies. This will cause reduction in remittance flow in the country and it can also be envisaged that the export and tourism sector would also be affected by the worldwide recession.

WHAT IS A FINANCIAL CRISIS?

The term financial crisis is applied broadly to a variety of situations in which some financial institutions or assets suddenly lose a large part of their value. Many financial crises were associated with banking panics and many recessions coincided with these panics. Other situations that are often called financial crisis include stock market crashes, currency crisis and sovereign defaults. A greater understanding of the causes and nature of financial crisis is essential for their better management as well as for designing policies to reduce their likelihood. The common features of financial instability could be enumerated as below:

- They have typically been preceded by financial deregulation and by liberalization of capital transactions.
- Banking crisis have been associated with excessive lending on certain categories of assets such as real estate, housing and stocks and with speculative bubbles. Such lending has taken place in the context of weak financial regulation and supervision.
- Currency crisis have typically been preceded by

periods of sharply increased capital inflows attracted by a combination of an interest rate differential and relatively stable exchange rates, which motivated to borrow abroad by increasing exposure to currency risk.

- The level of borrowing to finance investments is frequently cited as a contributor to financial crisis. When a financial institution or an individual invests its own money, it can lose its own money. But when it borrows in order to invest more, it can potentially earn more from its investment, but it can also lose more than all it has. Therefore, leverage magnifies the potential returns from investment, but also creates a risk of bankruptcy.
- The asset-liability mismatch between the BFIs' deposits and loans could be seen as one of the reason BFIs runs occur.
- The increase in liquidity in the banking sector resulting from capital inflows generates tendencies to currency appreciation and deterioration of the balance on the current account.
- Reversals of capital flows are often associated with a deterioration of macroeconomic conditions resulting from the effects of the inflows. But almost all major episodes of capital outflows and debt crisis in developing countries have been associated with rising international interest rates.
- Excessive regulation has also been cited as a possible cause of financial crisis. In particular, the Basel II Accord has been criticized for requiring banks to increase their capital when risks rise, which might cause them to decrease lending precisely when capital is scarce, potentially aggravating a financial crisis.
- Fraud in mortgage financing has also been cited as one possible cause of the 2008 sub-prime mortgage crisis.
- Contagion effects of financial crisis may spread from an institution to another, as when a BFIs run spreads from a few BFIs to many others, or from one country

to another, as when currency crisis, sovereign defaults or stock market crashes spread across countries. The failure of one particular BFI threatens the stability of many other institutions.

THE SUB-PRIME LOAN

In any financial market where ratings are available, all people do not have same credit ratings. Some may have high, some moderate and some low ratings, depending upon their respective credit histories. All lenders would like to lend to those people who have good credit ratings or histories, and set this objective as their prime goal. They even offer low interest rate to these borrowers retaining the thinnest margin for them. However, a large segment of the market remained financially deprived as lenders would hesitate to provide loans to people with poor credit ratings and histories since this would be nothing other than to loose. However, due to lack of the first choice prime borrowers and also to tap the opportunity to bring this non-prime segment of the market into their folds, the lenders around the globe, especially U.S.A. and U.K. entered into the market full of high default-rated borrowers remodeling their products with revised terms and conditions, like higher interest rate, longer repayment period, etc. Lenders look on the risks of lending to the people with poor credit ratings but made higher return through higher interest rates than they would otherwise make from prime borrowers. Such a practice of making loans is called the sub-prime lending.

Hence, the term sub-prime loan refers to the loan made for those who do not qualify for low or competitive market interest rates set for prime borrowers due to various risk factors like income level, size of margin/down payment, credit history, and employment status. It is the loan provided to the people with high default risk or those who do not qualify as per the underwriting guidelines. It is also meant as near-prime or non-prime or the second chance loan.

Although there is no specific definition of sub-prime loans, in US all the borrowers are given a FICO score to indicate the rate of default, and those scoring below 680 are called non-prime borrowers. However, if a non-prime borrower has sufficient income, then he or she may qualify for sub-prime loan. These sub-prime loans can be for any purpose like for credit card, purchase of an automobile or purchase of a new house.

Straightforwardly, making sub-prime loans looks like hitting one's own knee with an axe as it absorbs higher risks, which put public money in unsafe hands, but some banks may bring sub-prime loans as separate product in the name of meeting the need of low-income people. It can be said that this practice is the result of the complexity and sophistication of today's financial institutions and instruments. In U.S., many banks are involved in making sub-prime mortgage loans. According to a research, a loan out of every 5 has come from sub-prime in the U.S. today.

THE MORTGAGED BACKED SECURITIES

In order to ensure that the mortgage market remains buoyant, lenders require constant access to sufficient funds. Traditionally, mortgage lenders rely on public deposits and mortgage covered bonds as a source of funding. However, those lenders with weak and unreliable deposit base and needing high credit rating to access money market credit may think of alternatives. They may turn their loans into marketable securities through a process known as securitization and then sell off the loans to the issuers of the Mortgage Backed Securities (MBS). The buying company repackages the mortgages in the form of marketable securities and sells them in the market.

In U.S. the ability to create mortgage-backed securities was authorized by 1968 Charter Act, which created Fannie Mae, a government sponsored enterprise. The purpose was to allow banks to sell off their mortgages so that the funds could be freed up to lend to more homeowners. Other companies issuing MBS are Freddie Mae and Ginnie Mae.

THE SUB-PRIME CRISIS

Sub-prime mortgages crisis is the financial crisis caused by sudden rise in the failures in mortgage loan payment and resulting foreclosures in the U.S. financial market. The crisis was rooted during the closing years of 20th century but it became popular through the media in 2007 only.

The first sub-prime loan was believed to have made in 1993. But, the details are not common. In 1999, the U.S. government took the policy of making American, including minority and low-income buyers, able to afford houses, under pressure from the then Clinton Administration. The nation's largest government-sponsored home mortgage underwriters, Fannie Mae and Freddie Mae, relaxed their credit requirements on the loans which they would purchase from other banks and lenders. The government was putting pressure on these enterprises including the Department of Housing and Urban Development, to increase their sub-prime portfolios. As the default rate was high, the lenders charged higher interest rates so that this could offset the anticipated higher operating costs. Failures of these institutions were not thought as they were backed by government guarantee.

In 2001, after the 9/11 attack, American government feared slowdown in the economy. It then took the policy to decrease the market interest rate attracting even poor people to afford expensive purchases. Money became cheaper. The market liquidity was also higher. In search of market, financial institutions also entered into the sub-prime market for granting loans. Debt-financed consumption of the Americans soared up, resulting in housing market boom. The house ownership rate also increased in U.S. from 64 per cent in 1994 to 69.2 per cent in 2004, accordingly to a research data. The growth in demand for house ownership increased the house price up from 100 per cent in 1997 to 124 per cent in 2006. Some homeowners were also able to refinance their mortgaged houses at lower interest or at the appreciated value and financed their consumption spending with the additional finance. As a result of all these, the U.S. household income in 1990 lose to 127 per cent in 2007, and 134 per cent in mid-2008, this overflow of credit and rising housing price reached the boom in mid-2006.

The pressure then appeared on the reverse side. The market had turned so lucrative for home borrowers that anyone could finance homes with bank loan starting with low interest rate for few years, and then with the market interest rate, called adjustable-mortgages. One would think to finance first at lower interest rate and pay till the grace period ends. Then the market interest rate starts, he would think to refinance it from another bank with lower interest rate together with higher value loan covered by appreciated value of the house. In this way, the repayment of the loans was defaulted in a legal manner. In another words, the accounts were regularized before the defaults could happen.

Similarly, financial institutions also issued securities backed by their home loan, also called mortgage-backed securities, in order to meet their rising need of liquidity. Many investment institutions invested their money into these securities as it was returning beneficially in the initial period.

When U.S. house prices began to decline in 2006-07, the poor borrowers could not refinance their properties and then, they failed to repay. Re-failure soared up, and widely held financial firms, lost most of their values. The result was a large decline in the worth of many banks and enterprises, as the loss was charged on the capital. It not only decayed the capital of the banks and institutions but also tightened the credit flow in the U.S. economy. In lack of credit in the credit-driven U.S. economy, many business firms downsized their transactions and reduced their employees. The financial crisis/depression emerged.

The Case of Lynch and Lehman, and the Global Crisis

During the housing boom, Merrill Lynch was increasingly involved in packaging and selling pools of securities tied to sub-prime mortgages. This increased its exposure to these collateralized debt obligations, abbreviated as CDOs. It was involved in the packaging and selling of a particular type of CDO called Norma that bet heavily on a rise in defaults of sub-prime mortgage loans. While this increased returns, it also increased the chances that losses for investors would be magnified in the future. In underwriting risky Norma, Lynch earned fees as higher as 1.5 per cent of the value of a Norma. From 2004-07 the company became the top underwriter of CDOs and generated hundreds of millions of dollars in profits, however as the housing bubble burst, home prices began to fall and defaults on mortgages rose. The value of sub-prime backed securities and CDOs such as Norma began to fall quickly. Financial instruments such as Norma became responsible for the tens of billions in write-downs at some of the world's largest banks, including Lynch. In the face of large losses, the company approached Wachovia Corp. with a merger offer. In the end, the merger did not go through. Ultimately, Bank of America acquired the company.

Lehman Brothers was formed after the names of the three brothers, namely Henry Lehman, Emanuel Lehman and Mayer Lehman in 1850. These brothers had emigrated to U.S. from Bavaria. Initially, Lehman was a dry-goods store. Finding cotton as an important crop in Southern U.S., it started accepting cotton as payment for merchandise. It then began its business in cotton. In 1899, it started underwriting business. Hence, it changed into house of issue from commodities house. Acquiring Abraham & Co. in 1975 and merging with Kuhn, Loef & Co., Lehman became the country's fourth largest investment bank.

Lehman had excessively invested in high-yielding mortgaged backed securities, i.e., securities backed by sub-prime mortgages. As the crisis in sub-prime market emerged, its assets value deteriorated resulting into huge losses. Having large positions in sub-prime sector, Lehman suffered huge loss in 2008. In its second fiscal quarter, it reported losses of $ 2.8 billions. Its stock lost 73 per cent of its value. The U.S. government did not announce any plans to assist the possible financial crisis with Lehman. Lehman, then, had talks with Bank of America and Barclays for its sale. However, both Barclays and Bank of America ultimately declined to purchase the company. Following this failure, Lehman Brothers filed for Chapter 11 Bankruptcy Protection on 15 September 2008, citing bank debt of $ 613 billion, $ 155 billion in bond debt, and assets worth $ 639 billion.

Had the home prices in the U.S. housing market not fallen, Lehman Brothers could not have failed as the sub-prime failure could not happen. The causes of Lehman's failures are said to be the following:

(a) Very High Leverage

Between 2004 and 2007, Lehman's balance sheet increased by almost $ 300 billion by purchase of MBS. However, in the same period the firm added only $ 6 million in equity.

(b) More and More Risky Products

Lehman invested in ever more toxic mortgage-backed securities. This kept its profits ever increasing. The risk loss was hidden.

(c) Short-term Debts

Lehman did not have stable retail deposits. So, it had to rely on short-term debts for buying securities. It needed those short-term debts to be constantly refinanced (either renewed or swapped). The refinance was possible until the mortgages and other securities held were stable or rising in value. The real trouble started when the real estate slump started as refinance was not possible and to meet current obligations, Lehman could not sell the securities in its portfolio at a reasonable value.

(d) Long-term Structural Factors behind the Crisis

The following six factors have received considerable attention in the literature:

- Great Moderation
- Global Savings Glut
- Loose Fed Policy under Greenspan
- Home Price Bubble
- Sub-prime Lending Growth
- MBS (Mortgage Based Securitization)

Triggering of the Crisis

What really triggered off the crisis was the steep downturn in housing prices from mid-2005, as a result of which sub-prime mortgage defaults rose sharply in 2006 leading to extensive foreclosures.

IMPACT ON THE GLOBAL ECONOMY

Housing plays an important role in the economy. It accounts for a considerable part of a country's GDP. Hence, the then U.S. policy-makers targeted to make housing affordable through making easy accessibility to sub-prime borrowers. However, the poor credit rated borrowers ended up with defaults. The sub-prime crisis could not confine itself within U.S.

sub-prime mortgage market only and it caused the worldwide financial crisis.

Over the last few decades, housing markets were undergoing remarkable changes in U.S.A., U.K. and some Asian countries. Homeownership rates were surging up reportedly. Prices in the housing market were increasing, appreciating the home equities of the borrowers. In order to free up more funds to make more and more investment, the lenders then started using mortgaged backed securities. Individual mortgage loans were pooled and used as collaterals. They were sold to investors, who could be from all around the world. Home financing then became international phenomenon. It is through this increased use of securitization that U.S. sub-prime housing market was linked with the worldwide financial market, which put the spill over effect from U.S. economy to other global capital markets. The housing market may seem too small a share of GDP to cause a recession by itself. But the spill-over effects can cause severe problems for the broader macro-economy. The impact of the crisis like in U.S. housing market on any country's national economy can cause the following losses:

(a) Investment Loss

The global financial markets today have been interconnected. Development of different capital market securities like mortgage-backed securities have created attractive investment opportunities. The loss from the investment made in one country's market can be felt in another country's market.

(b) Liquidity Loss

In order to operate international monetary transactions, banking institutions around the world maintain their accounts with each other, and clear off their international payments through these accounts. However, the liquidity crisis in one of these institutions obstructs international payments causing liquidity crisis at another institution.

(c) Transaction Loss

Financial institutions worldwide deal with each other for financial transactions like financial guarantee, Letter of credit, etc. However, any default from one side in the past may deteriorate its credibility causing its business transactions to reduce in the future.

Table 1 shows the output growth, inflation and interest rates of the selected countries:

TABLE I

Output Growth, Inflation and Interest Rates in Selected Countries

Region/Country	*Real GDP**				*Consumer Price Inflation*		*Short-term Interest*
	2007	*2008*	*2009*	*2010*	*2007*	*2008*	
1	2	3	4	5	6	7	8
World	5.2	3.4	0.5	3.0	--	--	--
Advanced Economies	2.7	1.0	(-2.0)	1.1	2.1	3.5	--
United States	2.0	1.1	(-1.6)	1.6	4.1	3.8	0.36
Euro Area	2.6	1.0	(-2.0)	0.2	3.2	3.1	2.05
Japan	2.4	(-0.3)	(-2.6)	0.6	0.7	1.4	0.61
Emerging Economies	8.3	6.3	3.3	5.0	6.4	9.2	--
Developing Asia	10.6	7.8	5.5	6.9	5.4	7.8	--
China	13.0	9.0	6.7	8.0	6.5	5.9	1.34
India**	9.3	7.3	5.1	6.5	5.5	8.2	4.78
South Korea	5.0	4.1	-2.8	--	3.9	4.9	2.93
Singapore	7.7	1.9	-2.9	--	4.4	6.6	0.56
Thailand	4.8	3.4	-1.0	--	4.3	5.5	2.22
Argentina	8.7	5.5	-1.8	--	8.5	8.6	15.13
Brazil	5.7	5.8	1.8	3.5	4.5	5.7	12.66
Mexico	3.2	1.8	-0.3	2.1	3.8	5.1	7.16
Central and Eastern Europe	5.4	3.2	-0.4	2.5	--	--	--
Russia	8.1	6.2	-0.7	1.3	12.6	14.1	13.0
Turkey	4.6	2.3	0.4	--	8.2	10.5	14.02

Updated from World Economic Outlook, January 28, 2009 and 'The Economist' – February 7, 2009

* Average annual change, in per cent;

* For India, Wholesale prices.

Note: Interest rate per cent per annum.

Source: IMF World Economic Outlook and the Economist And Reserve Bank of India, India's Financial Sector—An Assessment, Volume III, Table 1.1, 2009.

FACTORS AFFECTING THE HOUSING MARKET

The financial crisis that appeared in the developed economies was primarily from the housing market. Specifically, the financial institutions invested their funds in the sub-prime mortgage sector either as loans or investment in securities backed by such loans. The rise of the sub-prime lending was contributing to the housing market boom. More sub-prime borrowers were taking out the easy loans and those who had already financed were going for the second or refinancing the first with another financier so that they could escape from the harder payment dates. As the housing market started going down and housing prices fell, the entire sub-prime sector was shocked badly.

There could be some specific forces causing the housing market in the U.S. to fall, or specific causes of an investment company like Lehman and Lynch for failure, but in general, economists take these forces both from the demand side and supply side. The demand side forces are responsible for manipulating the demand for houses due to which the price in the housing market, if the supply is unchanged, is affected. Similarly, supply side forces help increase the supply of houses in the housing market, and consequently, price can be adjusted.

(A) Demand-Side Factors

(a) Economic Growth/Real Income

Together with the growth of the economy, the real income of the people also increases. Rising incomes enable people to go for expensive house purchases. With the rise in incomes, the people are enabled to put more margin while financing the house. And the bank is also enabled to increase the loan amount within its standard financing ratio. Hence, the rising income enables people to look for high value houses, which causes house prices to rise. If the economy goes into recession, unemployment rises and real income decreases. This causes the demand for buying houses to fall significantly, resulting in fall in housing prices.

(b) Interest Rates

Interest rates affect the cost of paying for a mortgage. Rate of interest affects loan repayments, as the latter will rise together with the former. Depending on the interest rate and loan tenure, the monthly repayment is structured. If the interest rates and mortgage repayment rise, people are more deterred to buy houses. Similarly, if the central bank cuts its bank rate, market interest rate goes down increasing the demand in the housing market.

It is the interest rate, which determines the size of buy to let market. A buy to let investment is the one where a house or a property is bought to let out to get rental income, which can cover all costs associated with managing such investment or the mortgage. The size of buy to let market is estimated to be higher in developed countries like U.S.A., and U.K. These investments were considered superb a decade earlier in these countries.

So far as the market interest rate on a mere saving deposit remains lower than the yield from holding a housing investment (rental income plus capital gain net of all operating costs), the demand for houses is likely to remain higher. Due to sharp rise in the housing prices in the initial stage, the yield rate drops at the later stage, which can reduce the demand for houses and fall in their prices at the later stage. People hold houses until the rental income offsets the capital losses and operating costs. If housing price falls further below the break-even, there remains no incentive to retain a property or buy a new one as this could lead to negative equity. Investors then rush to sell what they can get presently as a reasonable value. Falling housing prices puts more houses on sale, as people would like to lock in the appreciated value of their houses and escape from capital loss or reduce capital loss from further increasing. Hence, a falling yield of housing investment increases the supply of houses in the market, and decreases the demand of the other side.

(c) Financial Market

The financial factors related to housing market, such as availability of mortgage finance, credit crunch period, are also considered important demand side factors.

(i) Availability of Mortgage Finance

If the market is deregulated and number of financial institutions increases competition increases. And banks and financial institutions bring, in the market a number of mortgage products, easing people to afford house purchase.

(ii) Credit Crunch

When more banks are faced with mortgage defaults and bad debts, the credit requirements may be tightened increasing the price of credit (including inter-bank lending rate) and decreasing the supply of loans. The rising interest rate and lower rate of loan sanction put a break on the housing market by reducing the affordability.

(d) Demographic Factors

Factors related with the family size, higher aged homeowners and age of first time buyers are important demographic factors putting impact on demand side of housing market.

(i) Average Family Size

The number of households can rise faster than the population if the average family size declines and there are more people living alone. Demand for houses can increase for other various reasons such as increase in divorce rates, net immigration, life expectancy, children leaving home early, etc.

(ii) Homeowners Downsizing

Some economists believe that the homeowners with higher ages say over 50 years of age, more likely to look into capitalizing on the huge gains in the property market by selling up their large houses and downsizing to smaller retirement homes. This hits the supply side resulting in a decline in the housing market and puts more pressure on public to act hastily to sell their properties.

(iii) Age of First Time Buyers

The age of first time homebuyers is also an important force to affect housing market. If the age of first time homebuyers increases, the demand for houses also increases leading to housing market rise. Falling market price is really good news for first time buyers. However, they are exposed to huge risk of going into negative equity, which may lead to increased risk of mortgage default. Lack of first time buyers entering the housing market creates problem to the homeowners who are already unable to sell and move to larger properties due to lack of demand and poor house sales

(e) Speculation

Not everyone buys a house to live in. An increasing number of property investors buy houses for both capital gains and rental income. These investors are called buy-to-let investors. They buy when housing prices are rising and sell before reaching saturation. Other than price appreciation, it is the rental income, which allures investors to invest in houses. Some houses earn rental income enough to service the repayment obligation and nothing goes out of the investor's pocket.

(f) Inherited Wealth

Many people use inherited wealth or parental wealth to buy houses. Some parents also provide their children a deposit as margin to help them get their houses. Though house prices are rising, people find ways around it and the demand ever increases.

(g) Unemployment

Level of employment has a relationship with the demand for houses. In countries where there is higher level of unemployment, people live in common houses, and hence, the demand for houses is at lower side. When unemployment improves, demand for houses increases.

(h) Remittance

When people of a country work abroad and send their incomes to their family back home, these incomes help improve the spending capacity of unemployed nationals at home receiving the remittances. Those who had no houses or were in common house would now demand a new one to live in separately. Also, together with increase in inward remittance, the liquidity in the banking channel increases and home finance becomes more available and cheaper.

(B) Supply-side Factors

To meet the increasing demand for houses in the short-run, the supply of houses cannot be increased; as to erect a new house overnight or within a month is not so feasible, except the few. It takes time to construct houses. Hence, the degree of elasticity of short-run supply of houses is low, and, therefore, demand affects price more than supply. However, if the supply of houses is inelastic in the short-run, then an increase in demand will lead to a big increase in house price. Only if the government reduces capital gain tax on property investment, those whose property's value was rising at a higher rate in initial stage may take this as an opportunity to sell the property to lock in profits which they had from appreciation in the value of their property. This worsens the housing market with more second-hand houses put on sale

In the long-run, all factors on the supply side are manageable, and hence, can be increased to meet higher demand. Price can be at an equilibrium point.

IMPACT OF THE GLOBAL FINANCIAL CRISIS ON THE NEPALESE ECONOMY

Though Nepal does not have any direct link with current global financial crisis, some indirect negative affects on macro-economic indicators could be envisaged. For example, export, tourism, overseas employment or remittance, debt servicing, foreign direct investment and foreign assistance are likely to be affected. The global financial crisis is hitting gradually in many developing and least developed countries like Nepal. The countries have responded by partially adjusting domestic fuel prices, cutting development spending and tightening monetary policy. The adverse effects have been substantially noticed in the South-East Asian and South Asian countries, deflected in a slowdown of growth, worsening of macroeconomic balances and huge inflationary pressures. It seems that the global financial crisis is also likely to worsen these trends further, particularly on the growth and balance of payments front. The crisis in the global economy is adversely affecting exports and could also upset remittance income. Lower foreign capital flows will reduce domestic investment. Both the situations will make lower economic growth of the country.

The current global financial crisis affects developing countries like Nepal in several ways:

Slowdown in Nepal's Stock Exchange Market

There could be financial contagion and spillovers of the stock market. Stock markets across the world have all dropped substantially since May 2008. As the psychological effect, the Nepal Stock Exchange (NEPSE) index has been gradually coming down since September 2008 and crashed to 609 on 22 January 2009 (from 1178 points in August 2008). The monetary policy announcement by the Nepal Rastra Bank (NRB) and the recent policies of the government of Nepal (GoN) on taxes have also played indirect role for crashing the NEPSE Index. It is felt by most of the regulators and investors that NEPSE was not moving with the market fundamentals for several years and now it is assumed that the NEPSE is currently moving in the direction of correction phase.

Decline in Remittances

The present global financial crisis could displace foreign workers around the world and cause major changes to the dynamics of international migration. The rise in social tensions could lead to discrimination and racism in the international labour market. The remittances to developing countries like Nepal will decline in the long-run as the Malaysia and UAE already announced ban on foreign workers.

More Debt Service Liability

As Nepal is heavily dependant on foreign aid, it might have to pay a heavy price due to the current global financial crisis. There has been a sharp appreciation of the US dollar due to the present global financial crisis, which has already increased the government's debt service liability for the current fiscal year 2008/09 by approximately Rs. 1 billion. The effect of the exchange rate has already shown some negative effects on the balance of payments front. There has been vulnerable impact on industries based on plastic, artificial fibers, iron, copper, steel and aluminum, vegetable ghee and edible oils.

Poor Financial Indicators

The financial sector of Nepal is very weak in terms of financial indicators with poor governance, tax licensing policy, inadequate regulation and supervision, lack of risk management system, connected lending, speculative lending, large non-performing loans and low capital adequacy. The global financial crisis is already causing psychological anxiety in Nepalese financial system. The BFIs should be cautious and even discouraged by the global gloom. However, the small size of Nepalese economy will reduce impact and will be affected in indirect ways only.

Decreasing Foreign Direct Investment

Due to the global financial crisis, the foreign direct investment (FDI) and equity investment in Nepal will also come under pressure. The global liquidity crisis may also affect big budget projects and FDI in Nepal. Hence, the risks to the macro-economy come from a potential expansionary budget in an environment of a deteriorating global economy.

Decline in Tourism Industry

Indirect effects of the global financial crisis will soon be felt through a possible decline in tourism. As most of the tourists coming to Nepal are from the USA, Europe, Japan, China, India and other countries, their numbers will be reduced due to the recession in their economies. The economic downturn in the developed countries may also have significant impact on the developing countries. The impact could be on trade. The growth in China and India is likely to slowdown in future, which will affect vulnerably the least developing and neighbouring countries like Nepal.

Less Foreign Grants and Assistance

Similarly, present level of liquidity may help the Nepalese BFIs from a global financial crisis. However, the analysis of global financial crisis has indicated that Nepalese banking and financial sector may not be fully safe. If the global financial crisis continues for longer period, Nepal might get less foreign grants and assistance, which would affect the development projects; especially the mega projects like hydropower projects and ultimately effect the employment and gross domestic product.

Heavy Lending in the Real Estate and Housing

Nepalese financial sector has to learn the lesson from the

recent global financial crisis. The recent data shows that the number of BFIs are growing up rapidly. However, their lending portfolio indicates that the bigger chunk of the fund of most BFIs is being invested in the hire purchase of motorcycles, cars, real estate, housing and margin lending. The consumer financing and personal loans do not create positive multiplier effect in the economy. It only increases import, which will ultimately reduces foreign currency reserves and creates imbalances in the balance of payment situation. Besides, due to the heavy lending in the real estate and housing, the land and housing prices in capital city Kathmandu and urban areas of the country has been soaring up. It is revealed from the informal sources that most of the buyers of the land are real estate developers, land brokers and individual land speculators funded by the BFIs and co-operatives.

High Inflation

In the beginning of 2008, the possibility of an economic crisis was suggested by several important indicators of economic downturn worldwide. These included high oil prices, which led to both high food prices and global inflation. The substantial credit crisis leading to the bankruptcy of several large and well established investment banks has increased unemployment and the possibility of a global recession. The prices of many commodities, notably oil and food, rose so high as to cause genuine economic damage, threatening stagflation and a reversal of globalization. If the liquidity crisis continues, there could be an extended recession or worse. The continuing development of the crisis prompted fears of a global economic collapse. The financial crisis is likely to yield the biggest banking shakeout since the savings and loan meltdown. In 2009, the world would see a clear global recession, with recovery unlikely for at least two years. As such, the Nepalese economy may also have to face the contagion effect of the global recession even with little late recovery.

Negative Impact on Housing Market

The crisis in U.S. housing market did not remain in that economy only, but over the periods, the crisis swept over to Europe and to Asia and Japan. It transmitted around the global financial markets through increased global network. This has made the financial market in Nepal more cautious than before. Initially, it is estimated that the crisis will put less impact on the financial system of Nepal.

Crisis in Liquidity

Liquidity has played an important role to give birth to the current crisis. Money markets were in a tight situation. International funding markets experienced considerable pressure. Banks became more restrictive in providing liquidity to other banks. They wanted to protect themselves against potential additional liquidity needs coming out from further breakdown in their outstanding loans and furthermore they were uncertain about their counterparts' risk exposure to sub-prime securities. Monetary authorities in the economies affected by the crisis injected liquidity into the market through different programs. Some were directly involved in rescue operations. Against the background of the worldwide linkages of the institutions, the dimension of the international problems is tremendous. The crisis has shown that the regulation of the housing market around the globe needs to be better written including ours.

SUGGESTED POLICY ACTIONS

The Asian financial crisis had four main causes, namely, weaknesses in the macroeconomic management leading up to bubbles, lax supervision, excessive risk taking of both the financial sector and the private sector in general and the inadequate legal and information infrastructure. At the moment, emerging markets look less vulnerable to financial disturbances. The least developed countries like Nepal are learning to live with heightened uncertainty in the world to benefit from the financial globalization in promoting growth, development and financial stability. Thus, the regulators need to ensure its soundness and stability as the Nepalese financial market is expanding and getting modernized. In an economy like Nepal when the market opens up, private investors get attracted, as we have witnessed in the financial sector with the number of BFIs increasing rapidly. The step to address this situation is consolidation, which ensures a safe exit of troubled BFIs without affecting the economy much. The government as well as other regulatory bodies should move this process forward. The financial crisis occurs if there are loopholes in the regulation. Insufficient and inefficient regulation is one of the major reasons for the recent turmoil in the global market.

The current global financial crisis is among the greatest challenges to the world economy since the end of Second World War. Unlike past financial crises, which were confined to particular regions, the current financial contagion is quickly spreading across continents. Unless appropriate action is taken to restore confidence in the global economy, the world will face a deep and prolonged recession. In view of these, it is obligatory to understand the nature of the financial linkages, root causes of crisis and its contagion effect. The government, regulatory bodies, policy-makers and the economists should sit together for the formulation of proper policy actions to address and check the probable effect of global financial crisis in the Nepalese economy. Thus, the Nepalese economic policy must vigorously address the substantial risks to financial stability and economic growth. The GoN and the Nepal Rastra Bank (NRB) should focus on the appropriate interest rate policy, liquidity policy and policies to stabilize the banking and financial system. Moreover, the Government of Nepal (GoN), the NRB and other stakeholders must take all necessary steps in a coordinated way to minimize systemic risk. As a good gesture, the GoN should come up with the stimulus financial package and the NRB should revisit the monetary policy stance. The coordinated effort of the GoN and NRB should promptly formulate appropriate policy actions, on the following matters, to check the probable effects of global financial crisis in the Nepalese economy:

- Appropriate interest rate structure.
- Adjustment in cash reserve requirement (CRR) for emergency liquidity assistance.
- Coordination of fiscal and monetary policy for active liquidity management.
- Appropriate regulations in support of market trading activities.
- Strengthen inspection and supervision capacity of the regulating authorities.

- Revise licensing and branching policies for BFIs.
- Resource mobilization for investment in infra-structure, e.g. hydropower, roads, irrigations, etc.
- Reduce level of taxes.
- Integrated policies for proper development of housing and real estate.
- Stabilize fuel prices.
- Provide support to farmers by micro-credit facilities.

If the GoN and NRB work together, there is no need to panic. However, the people have to be careful and diversify their investments. Similarly, for the small BFIs, it will be much better to go for consolidation and merger. There is greater investment demand in hydropower, tourism, manufacturing, infrastructure and technology. Hence, there is a need to ensure a steady credit flow to the real sector of the economy in order to sustain demand even while maintaining credit quality. It is also noteworthy that it is always better to identify the drawbacks in the present regulatory system and indicate possible solutions.

CONCLUSION

The recent global financial crisis has caused considerable economic slowdown in developed countries. The USA and UK face the greatest financial crisis since the 1930s. While there are reasons for optimism, many developing countries are likely to face challenges in the near future. The only cause of the current financial crisis was the massive housing loan provided by many banks in the USA and Europe. The current financial crisis was triggered by increasing defaults on sub-prime mortgages and the turn of the housing cycle in the USA.

The BFIs failure occurs due to the poor governance and bad management, which is frequently evidenced by poor lending practices, bad concentrations of credit, connected lending, poor internal control, insider abuse and fraudulent activities. When BFIs are insolvent, executives have nothing else to loose. They "bet" the BFIs by taking huge risks for personal benefit. They hide losses cosmetically with the techniques of creative accounting. As the result, BFIs are exposed to failure.

In order to put aside the potential BFI failure, the central bank has a variety of different enforcement actions at their disposal. These actions vary substantially in their severity and impact and can be used by the regulators and supervisors very effectively to address concerns they may have relating to risks to which the BFIs may be exposed. In both industrial and emerging market economies, BFI rescues and mergers are far more common than outright closure of the BFIs. Hence, if the Nepalese BFIs are not to be allowed to fail, it is essential that corrective action be taken in time when the BFI still has adequate cushion of capital. This would minimize the cost to the public exchequer in the event of a forced liquidation of the BFI.

To protect the BFIs from failure and attain financial stability is the main responsibility of the central bank. Despite massive bank bailouts in Europe and America, fears of global recession are keeping stock markets down worldwide. But, relatively low level of global integration and the underdevelopment stages have so far protected Nepal from the current global financial crisis. Even so indirect effects of the worldwide economic stagnation will soon be felt through a possible downturn in overseas employment, tourism, exports, foreign aid and investment and the after-effect of slower growth in India and China. It is also noticed in the Nepalese economy that global financial crisis is already causing psychological anxiety in Nepalese BFIs. The Nepalese investors are cautious and even discouraged by the global gloom.

The Nepalese financial sector has benefited from being a relatively isolated economy. Nepalese BFIs have also diversified investments by reducing concentration. However, most BFIs' lending in these days is more or less concentrated on margin lending and real state business. It is worth-mentioning that to attain financial stability in the country, the Nepalese BFIs should be regulated and supervised effectively and efficiently on regular basis. While supervising BFIs, NRB supervisors should focus on non-compliance of rules, regulation and directives, inadequate governance and management capacity of BFIs, connected lending and poor loan quality, weak risk management systems, weak accounting and auditing, inability to promptly force exit and resolve BFI failures.

It is accepted that intervention should be guided by rules

rather than left to the discretion of supervisors. Last but not the least, the NRB should review the present BFI licensing and branching policies and conduct fit and proper test very stringently, so as to provide banking services all over the nation with the fair and transparent banking practices. This will ultimately help to build up resilient banking and financial system, which will reduce regulatory and supervisory burden and keep the Nepalese financial distant from the current and future global financial crisis.

REFERENCES

Brunnermeir, M.K. (2009); Deciphering the 2007/08 Liquidity and Credit Crunch, *Journal of Economics Perspectives*, Vol. 23(1), Winter 2009, pp. 77-100.

Buiter, W. (2008); Lessons from the North Atlantic Financial Crisis in Felton, A.&C. Reinhard (ed.): The First Global Financial Crisis of the 21st Century, (www. Voxeu, org/index. Php?=node/1352)

EAC (2009); Review of the Economy 2008/09, EAC (Economic Advisory Council to the Prime Minster), January 2009.

Felton, A.&C. Reinhard (ed.) (2008); The first Global Financial Crisis of the 21st Century.

Fisher, I. (1933);The Debt-Deflation Theory of Great Depressions, *Econometrica*, Vol. 1(3), pp. 337-57.

Giovanni, A.&L. Spaventa (2008); Filling the Information Gap in Felton, A.&C. Reinhard (ed.): The First Global Financial Crisis of the 21st Century. (www. Voxeu, org/index.php?=node/1352.

Jeseph, Stiglitz (2008); A Crisis of Confidence, *The Guardian*, October 22, 2008.

John, Bird (2008); Sub-prime Crisis, February 14, 2008.

Joseph, Stiglitz (2008); Bail Out Wall Street Now, Change Terms Later, Democracy Now, *The Guardian*, October 2, 2008.

Nachane, D.M. (2007); Liberalisation of the Capital Account : Perils and Possible, Safeguards, *Economic and Political Weekly*, Vol. XLII, No. 36, Sept. 8-14, pp. 3633-43.

National Commission for Enterprises in the Unorganized Sector (NCEUS) (2007); Financing of Enterprises in the Unorganized Sector and Creation of a National Fund for the Unorganised Sector (NAFUS), Govt. of India, Nov. 2007.

National Commission for Enterprises in the Unorganized Sector (NCEUS) (2008); The Global Economic Crisis and the Informal Economy in India, Govt. of India, Nov. 2008.

Nocera, J. (2008); How India avoided a Crisis, *New York Times*, 20 December, 2008.

Portes, R. (2008); Ratings Agency Reform in Felton, A.&C. Reinhard (ed.): The First Global Financial Crisis of the 21st century.

Rao, Govinda, M. (2009); The 3rd Stimulus Package and Fiscal Conundrum, *Business Standard*, 3 March, 2009.

The Economist (2008); The Decoupling Debate, 6 March, 2008.

Index

Acute Stage of the Crisis, 238
Ahluwalia, Montek Singh, 227
Arunachalam, R., 28
Augmented Dickey Fuller Test, 146

Badhani, K.N., 151
Bad Loan, 218
Bandyopadhyay Dhiraj Kumar, 94
Banerjee, Amalesh, 48
Banking System, 70
Bhattacharyya, Saikat, 78
Bhatt, Rajiv Kumar, 201
Busht, L.S., 151
BOP, 71
BSF Sensex Variation, 154

Capital Flows, 6
Concept of Volatility, 151
Cost of Credit, 267
Crisis and the World, 125
Crisis in Liquidity, 306
Crisis;
    Root Causes, 237

Dealing with the Crisis, 15
Debreu, Gerald, 17
Decline in Tourism Industry, 304
Decoupling Theory, 72
Decreasing Foreign Direct Investment, 304
Dilemma on the Fiscal Front, 280

East Asian Crisis, 28
Economic Growth Rate, 68
Effectively Tackle the Crisis;
    Policy Paradigm, 72
Effect of;
    Slowdown, 157
    Crisis and Counter Measures, 9
Emergence of Keynes;
    Great Depression, 13
Employment, 72
    Effect of Economic Slowdown, 243
Exchange Rate, 70

FDI (Foreign Direct Investment), 6
Financial Crisis, 127
    Impact on the World Economy, 125
    Impact on the Indian Economy, 127
    Impact, 37
Financial Sector, 68
Fiscal Stimulus Packages, 20
Forex Liquidity, 249

Genesis of;
    Global Financial Crisis, 57
    Depression, 49
    Global Financial Meltdown, 80
Ghosal, Ratan Kumar, 78
Global Economic Crisis, 1, 94, 236, 279
    Ideas of Keynes Reinstated, 13
    India's Revival Agenda, 48
    Macroeconomic Explanation of Structural Causes, 96
    Indian Economy, 84
Global Economic Meltdown, 222
Global Economic Rebalancing, 11
Global Economy;
    Impact of Recession, 175

Global Financial Crisis, 56, 215, 254
Causes, 257
Global Economic Meltdown;
Origin, 174
Global Impact on Western Developed Countries, 218
Globalization and Global Meltdown, 78
Global Slowdown;
Impact on Emerging Economies, 37
Great Depression;
Lessons, 261
Greenspan, Alan, 216

Homeowners Downsizing, 300
Housing Market, 297
How has RBI Responded?, 211

Impact of Global Financial Crisis, 201
IMF, 97
Debate on the Role, 31
Impact on;
Capital Market, 179
Fiscal Sector, 183
Foreign Trade, 180
India;
Current Global Crisis, 50
Global Financial Crisis, 21
Indian Economy;
Impact of Global Financial Crisis, 68
Impact of Crisis, 4
Global Financial Crisis, 28
Global Financial Meltdown, 173
Impact of Global Recession, 177
Indian Growth Process Prior to the Crisis, 3
Indian Insurance Sector;
Impact on the Crisis, 94
Indian Policy Response, 7
India's Revival Agenda, 53
India's Vision 2020, 272
Interrelation between London and Indian Stock Market, 148
Investment Loss, 296
IOSC (International Organisation of Securities Commissions), 75

Johansen, 189
Joseph, Stiglitz, 215
Juselius, 189
Kalecki, M., 108
Krugman, Paul, 220
Kumar, Abhishek, 173
Kumar, Rajesh, 279

Liquidity Loss, 296
London Market;
Stock Price Variation, 155
Lynch, Merrill, 59

Macroeconomic Explanations, 60
Manjushree, P.V., 215
Marx, Karl, 96
Minsky, Hyman, 15
Mishra, Purna Chandra, 236
Mishra, S.B., 56
Mitigating the Global Financial Crisis, 273
Monetary Response;
Financial Crisis, 264
Mortaged Backed Securities, 291

Naidu, K. Mahesh, 215
Nauriyal, D.K., 127
Nepalese Economy;
Global Financial Crisis and its Impact, 287
NREGS (National Rural Employment Guarantee Scheme), 53

Occurrence of;
Global Financial Crisis, 216
Opportunities in the Slowdown, 270

Panda, Manoj, 1
Panigrahi, Ritisnigdha, 148
Plaza Agreement, 2
Policy Options, 89
Policy Stand of the Government;
Housing, 246
Textile, 247
Infrastructure, 247
Exports, 247
Poor Financial Indicators, 303

Poverty;
Impact of Slowdown, 269
Prakash, Shri, 148
Pre-Global Economic Crisis Developments, 108
Present Crisis and the Way Forward, 281
Prices of BSE and FTSE 100, 155
Inter-relation, 155

Ranawat, Mahendra, 187
Rao, L.K. Mohan, 215
Real Economy, 182
Recession in Services Sector, 269
Reddy, Y.V., 18
Reforming the Regulatory System, 18
Regression of BSE SENSEX, 156
Revisiting Keynes' Theory of Depression Economies of the World, 101

Sahoo, Bimal, 127
Shah, R.K., 287
Short-term Debts, 295
Singh, Archna, 13
Singh, Chandra Kant, 279
Singh, Man Mohan, 225
Slowdown in Nepal's Stock Exchange Market, 303
Stock Market in India;
Contagian Effect of Global Financial Crisis, 187
Sub-prime Crisis, 241
Sub-prime Loan, 290
Sub-prime Mortgage Crisis, 59

Trade Flows, 5
Transaction Loss, 296
Trends in India's Foreign Trade, 181
Triggering of the Crisis, 295

Understanding the Present Crisis, 14
U.S. Financial Crisis, 32

Volume of Credit, 265

What is a Financial Crisis?, 288

Yadav, Veenu, 187

Zedong, Mao, 96

Economic